Choking in Fear
a memoir of the Hollandsburg murders

by Mike McCarty

Mike McCarty

This is not a work of journalism; the only claim I make regarding interchanges with the people portrayed here is that they are a recreation of my own emotions and memory. Some of the names of people in this story have been changed to protect their privacy.

Choking in Fear
a memoir of the Hollandsburg murders

Copyright © 2014 Mike McCarty

All rights reserved.

No part of this book may be reproduced or transmitted in any form or by any means, electronic or mechanical, including photocopying, recording, or by any information storage and retrieval system, without permission in writing from the publisher.

ISBN-13: 978-1497522848

ISBN-10: 1497522846

Cover design by Kelly O Stanley

Mike McCarty

DEDICATION

To Trish, Logan, Evan, DeLaney, Zack and Olivia and the memory of Lori, Greg, Ralph, Raymond, Reeve and Betty Jane.

ACKNOWLEDGMENTS

Thanks to Betty Jane Spencer for opening up her life and personal journals so that I could learn more about Ralph, Reeve, Raymond, and Greg. And thanks to Dan Stonebraker for agreeing to participate so that what I learned might be used to help other children avoid his mistakes. Thanks to retired Indiana State Police Officers Dave Blue, who has unfortunately passed away since the book was first published, Loyd Heck (especially for taking time out of his vacation in 1995 to answer all of my questions), Stan Kenny, and my dad, Tom McCarty. And a special thanks to Donna Ferrato for inspiring me to continue with the book and to Stephanie Rodriguez who pushed me to find my voice and write this as a memoir. I also want to thank Scott Flood for reading the manuscript and providing technical feedback. And a real special thanks to Kelly Stanley, author, and friend since high school who has provided encouragement, editing and graphic design. And I have to thank my wife Trish for reading and re-reading the manuscript and allowing me to skip cooking dinner or forgiving me for waking her as I got up at the crack of dawn to work through the manuscript when I could find peace and quiet in a house with five kids.

Mike McCarty

FORWARD

Placing blame and knowing why: these two things are important to us when something wrong or tragic occurs that we do not understand. Blame is an easy target in this story. It belongs squarely on the four men who participated in pulling the triggers against the Spencer family. I am one of these men.

Knowing why is a little more difficult, even for me. This was a brutal and tragic case which wounded the soul of our society, especially in the Midwest. There have been many multiple homicides, but this one was so senseless. With no motive, such as robbery, revenge, or drug debts (as so many people incorrectly speculated), it is hard to understand why.

My participation with the police, in granting several interviews, and in assisting with this book, is largely due to the debt I feel I owe society.

Mike McCarty has written an accurate and detailed account of the events that are the most shameful of my life. I have participated in this endeavor in hopes that the society I have offended may know the facts, come to their own conclusions, place the blame, and maybe answer the most elusive question, "Why?"

A wise man once said that we can be sure that our sins will find us out. I have found relief in exposing my own evil deeds. I find it comforting to know that good still triumphs over evil. Even in prison that truth makes me sleep a little better.

To all of those whom my crimes have terrified and deeply offended, my sincerest apologies.

Daniel Stonebraker
Inmate # 11818

PROLOGUE

FEBRUARY 14, 1977

The young man sat quietly outside the courtroom. His long hair was freshly washed and parted down the middle. The prescription glasses were tinted, hiding his eyes and a thick goatee circled his mouth and masked the smirk. The smirk was his way of pissing on authority, the police and anybody who had ever tried to hold him responsible for anything.

Even though it had been a short night, not much sleep, he looked fresh, alert and excited. Oddly, he was not a bit nervous considering he would be facing a huge battle today after spending most of last Friday telling his story, and what a story it was becoming. There was a lot on the line, years of freedom, but he felt good. He had used the weekend break to take care of some unfinished business.

People were pouring into the courtroom next to him, looking for any remaining seats. He was in no hurry. He had a reservation on the front row.

David was already seated in the courtroom although today he had decided it was best not to have him armed with the .38 revolver. Too much risk after last night.

Pockets of police officers were gathered in the hallway, talking, killing a little time before court was called to order. Normally, these conversations were light, filled with gallows humor. But there was an abnormal charge to the quiet discussions. Something horrific had happened. That was obvious. The officers' faces were filled with concern.

He smiled to himself, checked his watch and stood to make his way into the courtroom. He worked his way through the crowded courtroom and took his seat. He took a deep breath, exhaled slowly, satisfied. A sense of accomplishment.

The judge entered the courtroom. "All rise."

He stood slowly, a calculated move, then sat back down quickly.

You cannot give the judge too much respect.

"Mr. Drollinger, you want to re-take the witness stand, please?" Judge Dowd said as he brought the courtroom to order.

Roger Drollinger stood from behind the defense table and causally strutted to the witness chair and sat down. He seemed very calm for a man facing the next forty years in prison.

Deputy Prosecutor Donald Hopper stood and said, "Mr. Drollinger, I assume you're aware that you're still under the same obligation to tell the truth that you were last Friday?"

"Yes, sir," replied Drollinger. His voice a bit soft but calm and confident.

"I believe last Friday, Mr. Drollinger, you testified that you knew Reginald Shireman, is that correct?" asked Hopper.

"Yeah, I recognize him. Yes," replied Drollinger.

"How did you meet Mr. Shireman, do you recall the first time you met him?"

"The first time I met him personally was at the Clark Oil Station," replied Drollinger.

"Do you recall how you came about meeting him there? What the circumstances were?" asked Hopper.

"Well, I suppose someone brought him in and introduced him to me," Drollinger said with a shrug.

Drollinger seemed focused. More so than last Friday when he spent the day in the witness seat.

"And I believe your testimony Friday was that at some point in time, you found out he was an undercover agent working for the DEA, isn't that what you said?"

"Yes," replied Drollinger. A bit annoyed by the process.

Hopper continued. "Why did you go ahead and sell drugs to him when you knew that he was an undercover police officer?"

"Well," replied Drollinger. "Simply because that was my orders."

"You were to sell to whom?" asked Hopper. "What were your orders in regard to selling?"

"Anybody that wanted to buy large quantities," replied Drollinger. "To sell the Strativex D or speed to."

"Didn't you think it a little risky to be selling to an undercover officer?" pressed Hopper.

"Well, when you've been shown that if you don't do what you're told, that you would be sent to prison," replied Drollinger.

"Mr. Drollinger, how did you expect to be sent to prison?" Hopper's tone laced with disbelief. "Did the officers, in your testimony, did any officers or anyone tell you as to how you were going to prison?"

"Probably just like before," said Drollinger. "Just ... they'd just sentence me to something that didn't make no sense and give me the papers and send me up there."

"In other words, the judge or a jury then would convict you for no reason at all, is that what you are saying?"

"Probably," Drollinger replied. "Maybe some judge or something would sentence me to something like finding me guilty of the '35 Firearms Act or for marrying or divorcing who I well pleased. I thought that was sort of hilarious."

"Weren't you convicted by the court on that occasion?" Hopper snapped.

"Well, we went to the courthouse and went through a farce of a trial," responded Drollinger.

"Now, in what relation in time did that occur to your conviction on this statutory rape charge?" asked Hopper.

"Yes, I was supposed to get off on probation, but they wouldn't let me off on probation," replied Drollinger. He was cool under pressure. On game. Nothing rattling him.

"Wasn't it a fact that your probation was revoked on that statutory rape charge because of that '35 Firearms violation?" Hopper was not backing down.

"It was revoked because I was marrying and divorcing who I well pleased and contrary to whether I broke the law."

"Are you certain of that Mr. Drollinger?" asked Hopper, his voice raising.

"That's what.." started Drollinger.

"Or was your probation revoked-"

"That's why I was found guilty of the '35 Firearms Act," shot Drollinger.

"No," Hopper snapped. "My question is, was it because you were convicted of the '35 Firearms violation which was in turn a violation of your terms of probation on the statutory rape that you went to prison on, isn't that a fact?"

"Yeah, because of Louis Swenke," said Drollinger.

"No, because of the conviction on the '35 Firearms, isn't that a fact?"

Drollinger paused to gather his thoughts. His mind wandered to earlier in the morning. It was Valentine's Day but it was not the day for lovers that had him excited.

Mike McCarty

PART ONE

MURDER IN THE AIR

CHAPTER ONE

Vance's Café was buzzing with the regular Saturday morning breakfast eaters and coffee drinkers. Families with children commanded the booths that hugged the walls while all the farmers and jack-of-all-trades filled the large circular tables in the center. This was gossip central for Waveland. If anything happened, you were sure to hear about it over breakfast, lunch or dinner.

My dad stopped at one of the larger tables to swap some gossip with his buddies. I slid into a booth halfway between the door and the kitchen and peeled off my winter coat and layers of clothing. I really didn't care who won the high school basketball games last night, what the weather forecast was or who was getting divorced. Don't get me wrong, I enjoyed the small talk at the center tables when it involved things my mom said I should not be hearing. But this was Saturday morning and the men would have it toned down for all the moms sprinkled around the cafe.

And it was early and I was hungry. In the war of gossip versus hunger, hunger won every time.

"Hi, hon. Pancake and a large chocolate milk?" Marge asked as she slowed to a trot, arms full of dirty dishes.

I nodded my head. Only an outsider or an idiot would order more than one pancake. They were the size of a hubcap. I was always curious how Kenny flipped them. Truthfully, some things were just better left unknown. Like a question my dad always asked about the gay baker in a neighboring town, "How does he get those holes in the doughnuts?" The question was always timed perfectly for my first bite. How Kenny Vance flipped the world's largest pancake or how the gay baker punched holes in the doughnuts really didn't concern me.

Marge was the only real waitress at the café. She made small talk, took orders, delivered orders, and bussed tables at the same speed: full throttle. People always said, "Why does Marge stay at the café? She could make a hell of a lot more money someplace else," though they secretly prayed she would never leave.

Given the right opportunity, I would have asked the question everybody else was afraid to ask, but Marge moved too fast. She would fly by, slide a pancake and warm maple syrup on the table, top off a cup of coffee and be gone before you had a chance to speak. And once I laid eyes on my warm pancake, the reasons she had for working at the café no longer interested me. The grim reaper could have delivered the pancake for all I cared, as long as he moved as quickly as Marge and brought warm maple syrup.

My mom came in the door, holding my little brother, Matt. She weaved her way through the tables and sat down across from me. She had stopped next door at the bank—a Saturday morning ritual—and deposited Dad's paycheck, keeping a little spending money back for the week.

"Has Marge come by?" Mom asked as she slipped Matt's arm out of his jacket.

"Yeah," I said while looking at Kenny. He stood near the table of men, next to my dad, laughing over some gossip while wiping his hands on his apron. No ordinary apron, but one the size of a pup tent. And well stained from a morning of preparing breakfast and possibly years worth of preparing food. I wanted to yell at him to get back in the kitchen and flip my pancake. And if he wasn't cooking it, who was? I didn't want to think about that.

Kenny and his wife Phyllis filled my dad's requirement that a cook cannot be skinny. "What do skinny cooks know about cooking?" my dad had said a thousand times. And he was right. The food

Choking in Fear

at Vance's was awesome. And Kenny and Phyllis had not seen skinny since they were in utero.

I surveyed the cafe, trying to determine who was cooking my pancake. If it were anyone else but Phyllis, I would puke. It couldn't be Edna, I tried to convince myself. As far as I had ever noticed, she only bussed tables. But I had to admit I had never seen inside the kitchen.

Edna did a fine job of bussing tables. She did not speak in full sentences, but in short grunts that contorted her whole face like she was having an uncooperative bowel movement. Plus, Edna was the only woman I had ever met who had a Fu Manchu. I'm not talking about a few stray facial hairs. No, we are talking about a full blown Fu Manchu like elderly Asian men in Bruce Lee movies.

And Edna always determined when you were done eating. You could be driving a fork full of food toward your mouth but if she was ready to bus your table, she would grab the fork out of the air and throw it in her tub. Argue? Not unless you wanted to risk being bounced around the cafe like a basketball. This was her turf. She made the rules. So I learned to eat quickly.

My feelings for Edna were a bit conflicted. On one hand, I laughed at Edna because, well, she was funny. But on the other hand I felt sorry for her. Why? Because she was a single mom raising a boatload of kids in house that was more like a woodshed. I rode bikes and hung out with her youngest son Gary, who was my age. I remember the first time I walked in their house and noticed the dirt floors and old furniture. My parents had told me many times that they did not want me going in other people's houses, and I knew this meant Gary's, but I didn't know why. Were they scared that I would be bitten by the poor bug? I probably followed him home ten or eleven times and never found myself envious of his home. Deep down, I always felt a ping of guilt because I had a nice house, clean clothes, toys, and great parents who didn't have Fu Manchus (I'm not even sure if my dad could grow one).

"What did you order?" Mom asked. Matt was reaching for the salt shaker, sugar, and silverware—anything he could his little one-year-old hands on.

"Pancake and chocolate milk," I answered while watching Wally Poore make his way toward our table with his tub of dirty dishes. Wally looked like a Pez dispenser when he walked. With each step, his head moved forward, his neck would stretch to it full elasticity and snap back as his legs moved forward. Unfortunately, candy didn't pop out of his mouth.

"Hey, Tom," Wally said as Dad slid in the booth next to me.

"Wally Poore, howya doing?" Dad asked with a smile.

I looked at Wally and smiled because I couldn't tell if he was looking at me, my dad, or the table on either side of us. His eyes were crossed. The exact same thing that would happen to me if I didn't quit purposely crossing my eyes for a laugh, my mom said. But Grandpa Jim always chimed in and said that if they got stuck all you had to do was hit your head real hard and they would go back to normal. I could never figure out why Wally didn't try that.

Marge appeared at the table in a flash, slid my pancake in front of me, gave me a bottle of maple syrup, and filled two cups of coffee for my mom and dad before disappearing into the kitchen. Why was she always in a hurry when everybody else who worked for Kenny (including Kenny) was not? I heard many a farmer say you would have to light a fire under somebody's ass to get a cup of coffee refilled if Marge was not working.

"Hi, Sherri. Hi, Tom."

I recognized the voice and stopped, fork short of my mouth, frozen like an animal before being pounced on by a predator. Fight or flight? My brain was arguing with itself. It was a voice like none other, spoken through the nose more than the mouth. A little bit of a snort. It was "Wandering Wanda."

Well, that was her nickname because when she wasn't washing dishes at Vance's, she wandered the streets in town on foot, until recently when she purchased a powder-blue moped. I always found the moped an interesting invention since it had a motor and worked like a low-speed motorcycle, but was equipped with pedals to also work like a bicycle. Who in their right mind would pedal the thing around when they could fire up the motor and drive it? I guessed the pedals would come in handy if you ever ran out of gas.

"Hi Wanda," my parents said in unison, never making eye contact and quickly turning their attention back to the tasks in front of them, Mom feeding Matt, and Dad stirring his coffee. It was amazing how much concentration stirring coffee required.

I felt sorry for Wanda most of the time, because people made fun of her. Although my sympathy faded fast when she had me cornered in a booth at Vance's. I know, it doesn't make much sense to do something to hurt a person and then feel sorry for them, but I did it often. Cut me a little slack, I was nine.

Wanda certainly wasn't a cheerleader nor did she ever win any beauty contests. My dad said kids were ruthlessly mean to her in high school. But, it wasn't really Wanda's looks that drove people away; it was the fact that she would wear out her welcome. If you made eye contact or let her in your front door, she was prone to stay forever. It was the same rule we used with stray dogs and cats: don't feed them because they will never leave. With Wanda, never make eye contact or she will never leave.

I had also heard that you did not want to make Wanda mad. It happened once just outside the kitchen at Vance's and she flung a knife across the kitchen at the instigator.

"Wanda, they need some help in the kitchen," Wally said as he cleared the table next to ours.

I hate to even say this, but I was about to abandon my pancake after I did a quick glance at Wanda and noticed a booger dangling from her nose. Saved by Wally. I hustled to finish eating my pancake before she returned or Edna snatched my fork.

"I need to run to Crawfordsville and get some groceries," Mom said. She was wiping syrup and small chunks of pancake from Matt's face. He fought each wipe like she was using course sandpaper.

"Let's go after we finish breakfast," Dad replied. "I need to get back and put a uniform together before I go to work tonight."

Dad dropped Mom off at the Marsh Grocery Store and we drove

across the street to get some gas in his State Police car. Dad pulled up next to the pump at the Clark Station.

"I'll wash the windows," I said, while vaulting from the backseat of the car.

Dad walked around to the rear of the polished police car and removed the gas cap. I pulled the squeegee from the bucket of water and began cleaning the windows, as far as my nine-year-old arms could reach. The attendant made his way to the pump.

"Dan Stonebraker," Dad said with a smile.

"Hi, Tom," the attendant answered. His hair was long and parted on the side, and a bushy mustache swallowed his upper lip. He was much younger than my dad.

"Got anything other than gas for sale?" Dad asked sarcastically.

"Of course not," Dan replied as he watched the numbers rolling on the pump.

"Talk to Drollinger lately?"

"Yeah," Dan said.

"You better get your shit together," Dad said, but not in a harsh tone.

Dan did not reply. He watched the numbers rolling on the gas pump.

"Drollinger is going to take you down a road you don't want to go. Mark my word."

CHAPTER TWO

Promptly at 3:15 P.M., the doors of the school opened like a dam bursting, spewing children across the snow-covered yard. Children running, yelling, falling down on the ice-slicked sidewalk, book bags flying in the air. Hostages set free, pardoned for another day.

On most days, I would board bus number thirteen driven by Dean Norman. I always wondered why the bus was numbered thirteen since there were only three busses for the whole school. However, today, I had received word through the school secretary, Cora Robinson that my mother would be picking me up out front. I had no reason to doubt the message since Cora had been taking similar messages from the same office, same desk, and same phone since my father was in school.

The structure of the school had changed very little since my father graduated in 1962. The high school had been moved ten miles away to a neighboring town in 1972 when all of the small towns in the southern half of our county consolidated grades seven through twelve. It was the same red-brick building with creaky wooden floors and twelve-foot high ceilings. It was hot in the spring and fall, and cold in the winter. The gymnasium floor, where we now played tag and dodgeball, was the same floor my dad had averaged fifteen points a game during his high school basketball career. A large wooden marquee on the south wall of the gym proudly displayed the names of athletic record holders throughout the history of the school. My dad was listed twice, once for free-throw percentage in basketball and again for strikeouts in baseball. My Uncle Denny held the record for the fifty-yard dash. I can remember the first time I read the records, with Uncle Denny's name listed under track and field as the fastest man in the school's history at the fifty-yard dash. I was convinced it was an error or a joke. But Dad said it was indeed true. He used to be quite a runner. I figured fifteen years and a few too many brewskies had adjusted his adolescent physique.

After I navigated through the other kids sliding on the sidewalk, Mom leaned over and opened the passenger door of our brown Pontiac. My younger brother Matt sat beside her on the front seat, smiling from ear to ear as toddlers do.

"What's going on?" I asked. I was embarrassed that my mom was picking me up from school. I was too old for that. And right here in front of God and everybody. The least she could have done was parked down the street away from the buses and the bicycle rack.

"I thought we'd run to Crawfordsville and pick up a package at JC Penney's," Mom said as she looked over her shoulder and waited her turn to pull out into the traffic creeping out from the school. "But it's starting to snow. Better wait until tomorrow."

The last time Mom picked me up from school was last fall. It was still hot and humid and our car was dusty from traveling our gravel driveway. Mom had been standing outside the car, talking with Mrs. Link, my best friend Jerry's mom. My parents had been arguing the night before; Mom wanted to go to my grandparents' over the weekend. My dad said no because he had to work and didn't want to come home and jump right back in the car and drive sixty miles one way. The bickering went back and forth all evening.

As I stood outside the car on that humid fall afternoon, I listened to the song on the radio as Mom and Mrs. Link talked. Tammy Wynette was singing, "My D-I-V-O-R-C-E was final today." After the first verse, I wrote "My parents are getting a…" in the dust on the rear window and waited for the chorus again. As she belted out the spelling of divorce, I scribbled it on the back window. It seemed innocent enough until my mom found it two days later, while leaving Coleman's Grocery. It seems a small group of women were standing at the rear of our car snickering. My mom knew how fast stories moved through town and how each time the rumor passed from group to group, something new was added. By the time my innocent statement scribbled in the dust of our car ran full circle around town, the rumor would have my parents divorced, close to remarrying, with more children on the way. That's how things worked in Waveland. And for this reason, the red tab on my Levi's was warmed by Mom's hand.

"I need to stop at the library to drop off a book," I said while digging through my book bag, which was cluttered with spelling papers, pencils, Valentine's Day cards, and cookie crumbs from the afternoon party.

Mrs. Mitchell had marked off the last two hours of the day for a Valentine's Day party. Several kids' mom's brought red punch and cookies shaped like hearts, covered with red icing and Red Hots. We exchanged cards. I had spent the better part of the last evening sitting at the kitchen table, pencil in hand, personally endorsing cards for my thirty-two classmates and Mrs. Mitchell.

I liked Mrs. Mitchell even though she was not tolerant of goofing around. I had learned this the hard way one afternoon when I thought she was out of the classroom and I was laughing and telling a joke when I was supposed to be reading. She walked up behind me, never uttered a word, but wrapped her fingers around my collar bone. I slid out of my seat to the ground. She released me before snapping my collar bone like a chicken wish bone and I reclaimed my seat. I started reading and never looked up. She was "old school" and had been teaching since my dad was in school. I did not make eye contact. I knew this had been resolved. She would not be calling my parents. And I would not be telling them what happened.

Mom pulled up in front of the library. My door was already open, my foot skidding across the pavement before she came to a complete stop. I vaulted up the steps two at a time, through the first door, up another flight of stairs, and through the second door. The library always smelled the same, musty and old, just like my grandparent's house smelled. And it was dark. Funny that a place filled with books and designed to encourage reading would be so dark. The only time the lights were flicked on was during a dark, stormy day when there was little natural light.

I slid the book onto the left side of the librarian's desk, the area reserved for returns only. And heaven forbid the kid that laid a book on the other side of the desk. Librarians were scary people. They hated kids. That was a requirement.

The library was so quiet. The quiet always got me in trouble. Being at the library was a lot like being at church: no matter how hard you tried, you just couldn't be perfectly silent. It was too much to ask of anybody. It was just last summer, while at the library, that I decided to pass gas. Unfortunately, it wasn't a little swoosh of gas, but a long, piercing squeak like the shrill of a mouse caught in a mousetrap. My friend Jerry thought it was the funniest thing he had ever heard. Of course, what wasn't funny when you were expected to be quiet? He screamed, doubled over at the waist, tears falling from his eyes and saliva dripping from his mouth like a rabid dog. With one swoop of her hand, Mrs. Evans, the librarian, ordered us out the door without so much as a spoken word. We had committed the one unpardonable sin: noise. The laughter continued down the street, as we stopped every few feet to catch our breath, knowing full well that our parents would have already been notified of our deviant and unspeakable behavior.

The memory brought a slight smile to my face as I pivoted quickly on my right foot and started for the door. Mrs. Evans was nowhere to be found.

"Hi, young man," Mr. Simms said. He was sitting in the reading area, rocking back and forth in one of two wooden rocking chairs.

Mr. Simms had been coming to the library every day of his life to read the afternoon newspaper, except Sunday, when the library was closed. You could set your watch by him. Three o'clock every afternoon. He lived about two miles north of town and surely spent more than the cost of a newspaper in gas, or so my dad claimed, coming into town each afternoon to read the paper. I had never met Mrs. Simms, so he might have had an alternative motive. Or maybe he had a thing for Mrs. Evans. I've heard stories about librarians.

I descended the steps of the library two at a time and nearly broke my neck on the ice-covered steps. Clared Moore wasn't doing his job. As far as I could tell, it was Clared's responsibility to sweep the steps of the library in the fall, sprinkle salt on them in the winter, and mow the grass in the spring and summer. He had the same responsibility at the Methodist church where he was a member. When he wasn't tending to the library or Methodist church, he was at the Waveland Volunteer Fire Department behind Vance's Café. He was the assistant fire chief. I am not sure what his real job was. He rarely left town, except for Sundays, after church, when he would drive thirteen miles to the Holiday Inn in Crawfordsville for brunch. Sunday was the only day that Clared did not wear his trademark olive green work shirt and pants, but opted for a suit and tie. Every Sunday.

"What took so long?" Mom asked.

"Mr. Simms stopped me," I said while slamming the car door shut with both hands.

"Reading the newspaper?"

"Yep." I had never seen him reading anything else.

"Do you have any homework tonight?" Mom asked as she turned onto Main Street.

"Not really," I said while staring out the window at the line of dusty pickup trucks parked along the street. It was after 3:00PM and every farmer was drinking coffee at Vance's Café. Winter was their reprieve from the exhausting spring tilling and planting and the fall harvest. It was a time to make repairs, feed the livestock, rest, drink coffee at Vance's, and catch up on gossip.

"What's not really?"

"Well, I have a speech to write. I'm running for class president. We have to give a speech tomorrow." No big deal, I thought.

"And you waited until now to tell me?" she said with more than a hint of agitation. "How long have you known about the speech?"

I shrugged my shoulders. "Since last week sometime. I only officially declared my candidacy today, though." I laughed. She didn't.

We pulled into the driveway and parked next to Dad's state police car. Our home was a one-story farmhouse, gray with black shutters, shaded in the front by large maple trees and enveloped in the rear by rows of apple trees. The house had been abandoned for years until my dad, Grandpa McCarty, and Uncle Denny remodeled it two years ago.

I raced into the house, kicked my shoes off, slung my book bag on the bench on the back porch, and rushed into the kitchen. Dad was hanging up the phone, still dressed in his state police uniform.

"Did you learn anything today?" Dad asked.

"Not much," I said. "We had a party this afternoon."

"Mrs. Mitchell let you guys have a party?" he asked while stepping around the bar. "She must be getting soft. She wouldn't let us have parties when I was in school."

"There were only nine people in your class," I smirked. "That's not hardly enough to have a party." But it was the perfect number to allow my dad the distinction of telling everybody that he was in the top ten percent of his high school graduating class.

"Mrs. Mitchell was mean back then," he said. "Not nice like she is today."

I smiled. Yeah, I had heard this a million times. He had to walk to school uphill both ways; he mowed all day in the summer for a Coke and a candy bar; in his day teachers were mean and would hit the knuckles of your hands with a ruler as punishment; each year he only got one pair of jeans and three white T-shirts; he wore the same basketball shoes all four years in high school; he'd used the same baseball mitt since he was ten. I had the stories memorized, but was amazed at how they grew each time he told them.

"We aren't as mean as you guys were," I added.

I had heard all of the old stories from my dad's childhood. It seemed like my dad went to school with all of my friends' dads. And my friends' dads were always quick to tell a story on my dad, especially since he was now a police officer. There was the time they poured gas across the road and lit it as Charlie Stewart, the local sheriff, drove past. There was the story of my dad feeding a laxative to one of his cousins after convincing him it was a Hershey bar, and then watching as he nearly exploded in front of the potbelly stove. There were stories of my dad running from the local police in his 1964 Plymouth Fury (which he bought from a state trooper). And how he and his friends curled up a snake they found in the road and placed it on the floorboard of a friend's car only to later discover that the snake was not dead, but dazed. It had come to life while his mom was driving the car through town. And when Teddy Whitecotton climbed in the front seat of their music teacher's car, dropped his pants, squatted, and left a stinky surprise.

The stories had to be true because all of the old people in town always said, "I can't believe your dad is a state trooper." He never seriously harmed anybody. It was just part of growing up in a town where there were only two things to do: play sports or get in trouble. And my dad found the time to excel at both. Fortunately, sports kept him more occupied than the trouble did.

Dad took his gun belt off and placed it on top of the refrigerator. I knew he was probably not home for the evening; otherwise he would have taken the gun out of the holster, placed it high in his closet, and then changed out of his uniform.

"You want me to take the gun for you?" I asked with a straight face.

"Yeah, right," Dad said. His head shook as he laughed. "You'll be lucky to own a water pistol after last summer."

I laughed. It was easy to laugh now. Six months separated us from the incident. And yes, time was the best medicine for healing. However, there had been nothing to laugh about last summer. Mom and Dad had bought me a BB gun for my birthday and I took to cleansing the barn of barn swallows. As with all wars, there is friendly fire with innocent casualties and, in this particular war, it was every window in the barn. Ed Fowler, the old farmer who owned the property, had come to my dad one hot afternoon and asked him if he could investigate hundreds of small holes in the barn windows. It was Ed's nice way of alerting my dad to the damage. He didn't want to get anybody in trouble, but replacing windows each week was getting expensive and time consuming.

My dad remedied the problem (or so he thought) by bringing home some targets from the state police post. I put one on a tree near our swing, and proceeded to hone my skills. Unfortunately for my dad, I lacked skill. There was nothing to hone. The third shot missed the target, missed the huge trunk of the tree, and found its way to the soft spot just below my dad's left eye. I heard a big bellow, saw a puff of smoke come out of dad's ears, and watched as he dropped the bucket he was using to pick green beans and stormed toward me, gaining speed with each step. The old fight or flight theory isn't true. I had no intention of fighting, but I couldn't muster the strength in my legs for flight. In one movement, the BB gun was taken from my hand and wrapped around the tree, bent nearly in half. Thankfully, only the gun was punished.

The phone rang.

Dad stepped around the island bar and grabbed the receiver on the second ring. "McCarty's," he said. I could never figure out why my parents always answered the phone by saying our last name. I figured if somebody was calling our house, they already knew our last name.

My mom was now standing in the kitchen, cradling my half-asleep brother. She stood at the entrance of the living room, eyes focused intently on my dad.

"We don't know," Dad said as he leaned on the bar. "We're pretty sure the suspects live in the area. There's no way strangers could find that house."

There was silence as Dad listened to the person on the other end of the phone. I moved cautiously from the table to the rocking chair, which was closer to Dad. I was not sure what he was talking about, but if it had my mom's attention, I figured it should have my attention.

"Yeah," he continued. "The mother is Betty Spencer. You know, used to be Betty Miller. Herb's sister."

Silence.

"She survived," Dad said after a short pause. "Awfully damn lucky. Don't know how anybody could have survived that."

Silence.

"I'll let you know as we learn more," Dad said. "Take care."

CHAPTER THREE

"Mike, you need to get busy on your homework," Mom yelled through the door that connected the kitchen and the living room.

She was clearing dirty dishes from the kitchen table. Each time she turned from the table and trekked across the kitchen to the sink, my brother Matt, sitting in his high chair, would drop a Cheerio to the floor. He would lean over the side of the high chair like a scientist monitoring an exciting experiment, watching as each Cheerio fell and hit the floor. Then he looked at me, smiled proudly, and repeated his experiment.

"I will," I growled. We had every light in the house burning. Dad had already asked us sarcastically if we owned stock in the light company. Even though I didn't know what stocks were, I still responded, "Yes, I believe we do own stock in the light company."

"Now," Mom groaned. "We don't have all night." She turned from the sink and looked directly at me. I stood in the doorway, holding my ground (at least until I saw her move in my direction). Then she shook her head at the pile of Cheerios under Matt's chair and turned back to the pile of dirty dishes in the sink.

When she turned from me, I mocked a couple of smart remarks. I had learned over the years to only move my lips. Experience was a good teacher. Actually saying something out loud would get me smacked across the mouth or a night in my bedroom without TV.

"Tell Dad to get off the phone," I said as if it were his fault I had waited until the night before the election to prepare a speech. I stomped off into the living room and waited for her to yell again. I don't know why I didn't just do what I was supposed to do. For some reason I always felt the need to push my luck to the limit. Some called it headstrong. Others called it disrespectful. Looking back, I think it was both.

The telephone has been ringing nonstop since I had walked in the back door from school. It was the same conversation, with Dad saying, "We don't know" and "Must be locals." I had no idea what he was talking about, but people didn't call this often about stolen gas or a house that was robbed. Something big had happened. I knew that much.

Dad walked into the living room and plopped down in the green recliner. "So, you are running for class president, huh?"

"I guess," I answered without taking my eyes off of the television.

"Who's the frontrunner?" he asked.

I shrugged my shoulders. I didn't really care. "Probably Mike Mitchell or Shelly Brumbaugh." Women were on the move. Three of the four elected officials in the fifth grade were women. Heck, I was more than willing to concede victory to Shelly right now, the night before the election, if it saved me wasting the next two hours writing a speech.

"Well, there is nothing like waiting until the last minute," Dad sighed. The sigh was not one of disgust, but exhaustion. "Who's your running mate? We have to make sure the vice presidential candidate doesn't have anything in the closet that might come out. Is Jerry running with you?"

I laughed. "I hope Jerry doesn't come out of the closet. I think he likes girls."

"If little Jerry comes out of the closet you might as well kiss the election good bye," Dad laughed. "But seriously, do you have a partner?"

"No," I said. "We don't have running mates." I wished we did.

It was always easier to lose as a team than by yourself.

"Okay," Dad said, a more serious tone in his voice. "Do you know how long it is supposed to be? Or what you are supposed to talk about?"

I shrugged my shoulders again. I had no idea. It just seemed like a good idea when Mrs. Mitchell had asked us for volunteers. Actually, I had been daydreaming when she had asked for volunteers and Jerry had leaned over and said, "Raise your hand." I had, and here I was. Screwed.

"Well, let me call Mrs. Mitchell," Dad said as he stood and walked to the kitchen. I followed him.

Running for class president was uncharted territory. As far as I remembered there were no presidents, vice presidents, or cabinet members on either side of my family. A few policy violators but no policymakers.

"Hi Norma, this is Tom McCarty."

Norma? Who was he talking to? My Grandma McCarty was named Norma, but he wouldn't call his mom by her first name. "Who's he talking to?" I asked my mom.

"Mrs. Mitchell," she said.

"We're really not sure," he said. "Think it might be locals"

Silence.

Here we go again, I thought.

"I'll call you or Bernard as soon as we know more."

Silence.

"Yeah, I was helping Mike prepare his speech for tomorrow and we were needing a little direction." He looked at me. A look that said, "Pay a little more attention in class."

Dad listened as Mrs. Mitchell explained the project. I leaned on the wall, next to the living room door, upset with myself for having raised my hand and gotten myself into this mess. At a minimum the error would cost me a night in front of the television. More than likely, it would cost me an eternity of embarrassment after making a fool of myself in front of my classmates. I'd be shunned because I was goofy or because my pants were unzipped. I was tempted to tell my dad to relay to Mrs. Mitchell my withdrawal from the race. But I knew my parents would never let me simply withdraw. I had raised my hand and I would participate, like it or not.

Dad hung up the phone and turned to me. "The speech needs to be ten minutes long."

"Ten minutes!" I shrieked. The thought of standing in front of thirty-two classmates for ten minutes turned my legs to butter. I was terrified. Ten minutes was forever. I would get nervous walking in front of the class to sharpen a pencil, checking my zipper to make sure my barn door wasn't open (you don't want your horse to get out, Grandpa Jim would say). Now, I was going to have to stand there for ten minutes and talk with their eyes and undivided attention focused on me. I started to hate Jerry.

We spent the next forty-five minutes preparing a speech, my first public speaking engagement. I tried to identify the issues tearing at the hearts of my classmates, but drew a blank. Dad grabbed a pen and developed a list of issues he was certain would determine the outcome of the election: longer recesses, no homework, pizza for lunch every day, candy bars and Cokes instead of the traditional afternoon milk break. My dad, the trusted insider and advisor, asked me if I had done anything under the table in the last eight months, like stealing somebody else's girlfriend. If I had, he assured me, it would come back to haunt me. I told him my record was clean. Nothing in the closet to bite me in the butt.

"Now," Dad said, "You need to take this into your bedroom, close the door, and memorize it."

The phone was ringing again.

I scooped up the papers that were strewn about the footstool and headed through the house to the seclusion of my bedroom. I dropped the papers on my bed and walked over to my dresser and turned on the radio. I needed quiet, but not complete silence.

I sat down on my bed, on top of my comforter that was covered in American and National League Baseball logos, crossed my legs, and sorted through the papers. Under the pile of homework papers lay the afternoon newspaper, which I must have grabbed by accident.

My eyes were drawn to the front page. The picture on the front page showed two men removing a body bag from a mobile home while what appeared to be a detective stood at the entrance of the home, fedora on his head and a pen and paper in hand. He was looking beyond the front door, into the mobile home as the body bag on the stretcher passed by him. He didn't seem at all interested in the body passing by. His eyes were focused on the inside of the home.

My eyes moved from the picture to the headline, *Four Young Parke Men Executed*. Four men executed, I thought. Did they mean murdered? Executed is what they say on the news when a prisoner is "fried."

Directly below the photograph was another headline, much smaller: *Mother Injured, but Calls for Help.*[1] I read on.

> Four members of a rural Rockville family were forced to lie face down on the living-room floor of their mobile home and were shot to death by an unknown group of assailants...

Oh my God. My heart sputtered. Was this why our telephone had been ringing all afternoon and evening? Was this what my dad had been talking about?

I jumped from my bed and ran to the window and pulled the blinds. My heart was beating in my throat. I came back to the bed, but before sitting down, I opened the door leading back into the main part of the house, just in case I needed to run or scream for help.

I continued reading the article, though I knew I shouldn't because it would keep me from sleeping.

> The young men, ranging in age from 14 to 22 were all shot in the back of the head with a shotgun.

---

[1] Bill Runge, "Mother Injured, but Calls for Help," *Crawfordsville (Ind) Journal Review*, 14 February 1977.

Fourteen. He was only five years older than me.

> "Mrs. Spencer's life apparently was saved by a wig she was wearing," a trooper said. "Apparently when they fired, they weren't aiming directly at her head," Aldrich said. "The shot blew the wig off and they (the assailants) apparently thought they had blown her head off. She just laid there and pretended to be dead until they left."

I could feel my legs trembling as I continued reading the article, word by word, line by line, glancing back up at the photograph occasionally.

> "The telephone lines to the trailer had been cut and Mrs. Spencer ran about a quarter mile to the nearest telephone." Aldrich said.

This was exactly what my dad had been talking about on the telephone all evening. Mrs. Spencer. That was the name he had mentioned a hundred times on the phone already today. How did my dad know her?

I continued to grip the newspaper with trembling hands, certain that the evil that had killed the boys was lurking right outside my window.

> Police said they found the bodies lying in a pool of blood near a chair in the living room. Three of the bodies were next to one another and the other body was found about two feet away from the others. Police believed the space between the bodies was where Mrs. Spencer was lying. All four men were found face down and the sidewalls and ceiling of the room were splattered with blood.

A lightning bolt of fear shot through my body. I jumped from my bed and ran into the living room where my parents were talking. I climbed up on the sofa, newspaper on my lap.

"Who killed those boys in Rockville?" I asked.

My dad pressed his lips together. "I don't know," he said. "It actually wasn't in Rockville. It was near Hollandsburg. About four miles from here."

My mom shot him a look that said that was too much information. Don't scare him.

Too late. This was closer to our home than I first thought. Real close. "Why would they shoot the whole family?"

Dad shook his head slowly, back and forth. "I don't know. People do bad things from time to time. But it's nothing for you to worry about. It probably had something to do with a fight or drugs. Somebody trying to get even."

I hoped that was the case. I knew people did bad things from time to time. Heck, Jerry and I did bad things from time to time. We passed many a warm summer day down by the creek, smoking a cigar while thumbing through a dirty magazine, or a lazy August afternoon tossing rotten tomatoes at passing cars.

But this was a different kind of bad. It was unlike any other kind of bad I had heard about around the kitchen table as Dad and the other troopers and local police offers drank coffee and swapped war stories. Those stories generally centered on drug use, drunk drivers, traffic accidents, husbands who beat their wives, and fathers who beat their children. Murder only happened in Indianapolis, far from here.

I knew the troublemakers in town, who the oddballs were, who used drugs, who was crazy, and who was sleeping with whom (particularly if they were married). But I didn't know anybody who knew somebody who had been murdered.

"Are you ready for your speech?" Mom asked, changing the subject masterfully.

"Yeah," I said. "We can use our notes." The speech was the furthest thing from my mind.

"You need to be going to bed. It's past your bedtime," she said.

I stood up and walked toward my bedroom, but stopped short of leaving the living room and turned around. "Dad, those guys won't come here next will they?"

"No," he said. "They have no reason to come here. They're probably long gone by now."

I searched his face for reassurance, but could not read him, then wandered off to my bedroom. Scared to death. I turned the light on in my room and crawled under the covers completely, head and all. The fear was overwhelming. And the stranglehold would only strengthen as the details of the crime unfolded. Unfortunately, I would have to wait eighteen years for the real truth.

CHAPTER FOUR

I had timed my speech at ten minutes last night as I stood in my bedroom, facing a full-length mirror on the back of my door, and addressed my make-believe audience of classmates. But under the glare of my thirty-two classmates, the speech was delivered in less than five minutes and without the laughter my dad had predicted. It was the humor that I had counted on to get me through the speech and bring home the votes, even though I didn't care if I won or lost. All I really cared about was finishing the speech without peeing my pants or passing out. At one point, halfway through the speech, I glanced over at Jerry, who had a blank look on his face. The look drained the remaining drop of saliva from my mouth and left me speechless for a few seconds. Thank God for note cards. In the end, Mike Mitchell carried over half of the class, receiving seventeen of the thirty-two votes. He had concentrated on more class time devoted to homework. Realistic issues. My first taste of politics ended with a stinging defeat.

"Why'd you do that for?" Jerry asked as we jumped from the school bus.

"Cause you told me to," I snapped. "You idiot." I would have called him worse but we were in my mom's sonar range.

Jerry laughed as we walked up our gravel driveway. The kind of

Choking in Fear

laugh that said this was funny because it happened to you. "I didn't think you would be stupid enough to do it."

"Thanks." I kicked a rock and watched it bounce end over end down the long driveway. "Now I am the biggest idiot in the fourth grade."

"I don't know about the biggest," Jerry smirked.

We traveled the final fifty yards in silence. I grabbed the handle on the back door, pulled, and almost ripped my arm off. It was locked. That's strange, I thought. I smacked the glass twice with my fist and waited anxiously. We never locked our back door. What's going on?

"I'm sorry," Mom said as she unlocked the door, then hustled back toward the kitchen. My brother Matt was playing, carefree, on the kitchen floor, pushing a small plastic car in circles, no interest in anything going on around him. "I didn't see you guys coming. Well, are you the new president?"

"He got skunked," Jerry said as he grabbed a chocolate chip cookie off the counter.

"Skunked? What happened?" She asked in a concerned voice. "It didn't go so well?"

"No," I rested my elbows on the table. "Nobody laughed. Dad was wrong. I'm gonna kill him."

"Well, don't worry about it. I'm sure you did awfully well, considering you didn't write your speech until last night."

That made me feel a little bit better, but didn't eliminate the obvious: I would still have to face my classmates tomorrow and every day after that for the rest of my life. Losing the bid for the presidency didn't really bother me. Truthfully, I was kind of glad I didn't get it because from time to time the president and his cabinet would have to stay after school for meetings with teachers. And I had more important things to do…play ball, hang out at the creek, and ride my bike.

"Hey," Jerry said, cookie crumbs dropping from his mouth, "we going outside?"

"Yeah," I said, pushing my chair away from the table.

"Stay close to the house," Mom said. "Don't wander off too far."

"We won't," I said while running out the back door, forcing my fist and a chocolate chip cookie through the arm of my winter jacket.

We ran across the driveway, under the basketball goal, over the fence, across the field—careful to avoid the cow-made land mines that were everywhere—then down the hill through the thick woods. At the bottom of the hill, we followed the shale-covered creek back toward the main road.

Under the highway, the creek flowed effortlessly through a man-made culvert that was nearly eight feet tall. It was the perfect hideout. A place to sit and think, discuss girls and sports, plan our lives, thumb through the weather-soaked issues of *Playboy* we had lifted from our grandpas, and occasionally indulge ourselves in one of the finer things in life: a stale cigar. Because of the steep terrain, the hideout was safe from adults. We could puff on our stale cigar and enjoy our magazines on the bank of our lazy creek.

I sat down on a large rock near the edge of the creek. Jerry fumbled around in a crack in the wall—a secret hiding place for our stash of magazines and cigars.

"We still have one of your dad's cigars," Jerry said as he turned to face me, a half-smoked cigar dangling from his mouth.

"No way," I said. "My mom will smell it." My mom could smell cigar smoke on my breath or clothes a mile away. I only smoked when I knew my mom was not home and I could brush my teeth, rinse my mouth, take a bath, and hide my soiled clothes in the bottom of the hamper.

"You pussy," said Jerry as he rolled his eyes. "All we have to do is sneak in the house, rinse your mouth out in the bathroom, and we're fine."

"Do you remember last summer?" I replied. "Do you?" I knew he did. We were both grounded for over a month when Jerry's mom caught us smoking out back of their home. No bike riding, no swimming, no movies. Nothing for a month. That was one-third of summer vacation squandered on a Winston cigarette we stole from

Choking in Fear

his dad. It was a stiff penalty for a little puff.

Jerry shook his head while carefully placing the stale cigar back in the crack in the wall where it had been for the last two months. He walked over and sat down on the bank of the creek.

"Has your dad caught those killers yet?" he asked while staring at the ice-cold water flowing below him.

"I don't know," I replied. "I haven't talked to him today."

"My aunt went to school with the boys that were killed."

"I wonder why they killed them," I said. "Did your aunt know them?"

Jerry shrugged his shoulders. "Don't know."

"Are you scared?" I asked while skipping a flat rock across the surface of the creek.

Neither one of us spoke for several minutes. The hiss of the wind and splash of the creek were the only noises.

"A little bit," he replied. "My grandma and grandpa live right down the road from where it happened. One of my aunts told my mom there was nothing left of the bodies. They blew their heads off. That's what she heard at school."

"I keep thinkin' about it," I said. "If they like to kill kids, we might be next." I put my hands in my coat pocket and shrugged my shoulders so the collar on my jacket would protect my neck from the cold wind. A coal truck roared overhead, shaking the culvert.

"My aunt said she thinks it was somebody at school," Jerry said. "There was a big fight after the basketball game last week. Everybody thinks it had something to do with that."

I hoped that was true. Otherwise, there was no reasonable explanation for the horrible crime. And there had to be a reason. People didn't kill each other for no reason.

And the fear in the community was like nothing I had ever experienced before. I had been spooked in the dark. Or watched a horror movie and had a bad dream. But this was nothing like that. This was real. And nobody knew who the killers were. But we knew they were close and had struck once. The hiss of the wind, the sound of an approaching car, the look of a stranger all sent a ripple of fear throughout my body.

"Did your dad see the dead boys?" Jerry asked.

"I guess so. He hasn't said much about it, though. He did drive me and my grandpa by the house yesterday. It's spooky out there. Felt like the devil was watching us the whole time."

"You ready to go back to your house?" Jerry stood, brushing the dirt from his pants.

"Uh-huh," I said. I could tell Jerry was scared. And I knew I was scared. We were a long way from the house and easy prey if the killers were nearby. Dark clouds sailed overheard, mirroring the mood of the community.

We scaled the hill, looking around for any signs of the killers. There was nothing, so we walked through the thicket to the road.

"What are you boys doing down there?" a female voice screamed.

I snapped my head, looking for the voice. It was a deep, raspy, masculine female voice. One I didn't recognize. Then I saw her. She stood at the edge of her property, stretching at least ten feet in the air. It was Mrs. Trevillo, an old lady who hated kids. She fixed her beady eyes on me. I could feel the heat as her eyes burned holes through me. Dang, I thought, my Dad is right, Satan really is a woman.

As far as I knew, nobody had stepped a foot on her property. Or lived to tell about it. We had tried to muster the courage to run onto her property, knock on her door, and run. Just to spite her. But it wasn't worth the risk. Rumor had it she kidnapped kids and kept them in her basement. And I couldn't imagine myself living out the rest of my life in her basement. You just can't mess with pure evil.

"You boys get out of here," she said with a sweep of her hands, fingernails as long as her fingers. "You have no business down there."

We inched along the road, eyes on her, until suddenly, without provocation, and for no intelligent reason, Jerry screamed, "See ya, Mrs. Fat Ass."

My eyes almost fell out of my head. I looked at Jerry, who

smiled, then I looked at Mrs. Trevillo. Holy shit! She stood motionless for several seconds, digesting the insult hurled at her. Thoughts of whips and chains, of basements filled with bats and spiders, danced through my head. I could feel my heart beating in my throat.

She started toward us, slowly, like an animal preparing to pounce on its prey.

I took off. Smoke pouring from the soles of my shoes as I ran up the road as fast as my legs would take me. Jerry was close behind. At the top of the hill, we stopped briefly to catch our breath and laugh. But only for a split second until we noticed she was coming up the hill in her car. The smiles and laughter faded as we raced across my front yard. The back door was again locked. "Oh, crap," I said. Jerry was watching the road. I pounded on the door furiously. Mrs. Trevillo pulled in our driveway.

Bam! Bam! I continued to beat on the door. My mouth went dry. I had a lump in my throat that wouldn't go up or down. We're dead. We're dead. "Mom, Mom," I screamed.

Mrs. Trevillo was barreling down our driveway, her tires spitting rocks in all directions. Finally, just as Mrs. Trevillo leaped from her car, my mom opened the door. Thank God.

"What are you boys doing?" she asked, then noticed Mrs. Trevillo. "What did you boys do to Mrs. Trevillo?" Mom's eyes were focused on the giant of a woman who was shaking the ground with each step.

"Nothing," I lied as I ran past her.

"I called her Fatty Arbuckle," Jerry lied as we ran through the kitchen down the hall, and into my bedroom. We dove under my bed, scooting close to the wall, just in case she reached under the bed for us.

The fear of being killed by unknown killers disappeared as I pictured myself captive in Mrs. Trevillo's basement, chained to the wall, or maybe shackled to the bed. Homesick. Never to see my family again.

"Where's your walkie-talkie?" Jerry asked through gulps of air.

"On the dresser."

"Get it." We need to call your dad. Mrs. Trevillo is going to kill us."

"I'm not getting out from under this bed."

I heard my mom's voice.

"Those boys aren't bothering you," she said. "No, they did not. They wouldn't talk like that."

"Oh crap," Jerry said. "Get the walkie-talkie. We're dead. Hurry."

If my mom found out what Jerry called Mrs. Trevillo, I knew we were dead. There would be nothing left of us to chain up in Mrs. Trevillo's basement, nothing for the ghouls and gremlins to torture.

I poked my head out from under the bed and looked. Nothing. I jumped up, grabbed the walkie-talkie, and slid back under the bed as far as I could go.

"Can you talk to your dad on that?"

"I don't know," I said while turning it on. My hands were shaking so much I could barely keep my finger on the button long enough to depress it. I never tried."

"Try. Hurry." Jerry's voice cracked.

"Dad."

"Dad."

The radio was silent.

"Oh my God," Jerry said. "If your dad doesn't answer, we're done for."

I held the button down, ready to yell for my dad a third time, when I heard someone walk into the bedroom. "Mike? Jerry? Where are you hiding?" It was Mom, her voice stern.

I looked at Jerry, his eyes wide with horror. She knows Jerry called Mrs. Trevillo "Mrs. Fat Ass" and she is handing us over to her, I thought. How could she do this? Doesn't she know she'll never see us again? That we will be locked in her basement forever? We were only kidding. No harm intended. I'm sorry. Just give her Jerry. He said it.

"Come on out. She's gone."

I slid out from under the bed, walkie-talkie clutched in my shaking hands. Jerry followed, his eyes focused on the floor. We were both relieved.

"What did you say to Mrs. Trevillo?" her eyes were burning holes through me.

Jerry, still staring at the floor, shrugged his shoulders. "I just called her Fatty Arbuckle."

"Is that true, Mike?"

I nodded my head, unable to speak, convinced that she knew the truth and was setting me up. Everybody always said "honesty is the best policy," but I had never found that to be true. Whether I fibbed or told the truth, the punishment was always the same.

"Why? Why would you say something like that to her?" Mom pressed.

"She was just yelling at us for being down at the creek," I said. And I wasn't sure why Jerry had felt the urge to call her Mrs. Fat Ass. Well, maybe I understood the urge, but couldn't believe he had said it.

"You two need to stay away from her. She doesn't like kids."

Boy was that true, I thought. She kidnaps them. Probably eats them.

"Take your jackets off. Both of you. You're staying in the house."

Fine by me, I thought. I'd had enough excitement for one day in giving a disastrous speech and now nearly being killed by Mrs. Trevillo. But I noticed my mom seemed edgy. Preoccupied.

I walked in the living room, followed closely by Jerry, and sat down in front of the television. The newspaper was opened on the footstool. *"Boys' Murders May Not Be Solved Soon,"*[2] proclaimed the headline. I told myself not to read it. It would only heighten my fears. My nerves were already shot. But I couldn't resist. I had to know exactly what had happened to those boys.

I read the article, my mouth opened wide, chin touching my chest.

The sole survivor of the massacre, Betty Jane

> Spencer, 41, told police the men appeared to be in their early 20's. She said she didn't know the assailants. She told police late Monday that four men entered the trailer after her husband, Keith, had left for work at an Indianapolis television station. She told investigators two men entered the front door of the double-width mobile home and two others came in from the rear.

The words sent a chill down my spine, like a droplet of cold rain sliding down the back of my neck.

> The men ordered the five people to lie face down on their living room floor and then four of the five were executed. Police say they believe Mrs. Spencer was saved when a wig she was wearing was blown from her head and the assailants may have believed she was dead. She "played dead" until the assailants left and ran to a neighbor to call for help.[2]

The fear of being killed by Mrs. Trevillo faded. A worse fear replaced it. A fear of being killed by unknown assassins. As least with Mrs. Trevillo I could keep my eyes open for her, watch over my shoulder. I knew what she looked like, where she lived, what she drove. But protecting myself from unknown killers was impossible. They could be anybody.

---

[2] Bill Runge, "Boys' Murders May Not Be Solved Soon," Crawfordsville (Ind.) Journal Review, 15 February 1977.

CHAPTER FIVE

Grandpa Jim was sleeping in the green recliner when I saw him shift sideways, lifting one leg off the chair. It was a move I had seen him make a million times. Unfortunately, for me, I didn't have time to run or dive for cover. The gurgling sound started slowly, gaining momentum like a motorcycle accelerating, then peaked like a singer hitting her highest note. Jerry looked at me, his nose curled up and lips curled down in an expression of fright and disgust. This was a familiar sound from a familiar place. However, it wasn't the sound that concerned me. It was the impending smell that would get us. We were in that grace period. That time between sound and choking smell when you still had time to escape. Jerry knew it. I knew it. The sound was universal, the grace period universal, the smell personal and horrible.

I snickered, fighting off a screaming laughter that would wake Grandpa from his sleep.

"That didn't sound right," Jerry said.

"It sounded wet," I said while closing my mouth quickly to stifle the laughter. The laughter bounced off my pursed lips, then came out of my nose with a string of snot.

"Maybe you should get him some toilet paper," Jerry said.

"Why?" I asked. "You gonna wipe him? He's asleep."

We both burst out laughing.

Jerry was right, the noise did sound a little wet, like more than just air. But that was always the case with Grandpa. He had never been one to let a silent-but-deadly that strangled you without warning. His relief always came with a loud, slushy warning.

And I guess I shouldn't have worried so much about whether or not he had made an accidental deposit in his pants because Grandpa had told me that the anus was the smartest muscle in the body. It was the only muscle that could tell the difference between a gas, a liquid, and a solid, he had said. But I wondered if his anus had lied to him this time.

Grandpa rolled back over on his back, a slight grin on his face, then opened his eyes. "My belly growling again?" He rubbed his robust belly.

"I don't think it's your belly, Grandpa," I said. "I think you crapped your pants."

"Oh, no," he replied. "I wouldn't do anything like that. It's not nice to pass gas in front of company." He smiled, stood up, and then stretched.

Company, friends, strangers, the Pope, nobody had ever kept him from passing gas before.

"I think I will go out and get a little fresh air," Grandpa said.

Thanks a lot, I thought. You just made the living room smell like an outhouse in August and now you're leaving. "We're going with you." I took a deep breath and held it while running through the war zone.

My grandpa was very easy to approach and talk to. You could ask him anything. I mean anything. I remember one time when my cousin Kert asked him if he and grandma ever had sex. It was a reasonable question considering that they did not share a bedroom, bickered all the time, and never looked at each other with affection. But I couldn't believe Kert had actually asked him. I had held my breath awaiting his reply.

"Hell, no," Grandpa had replied. A look of disgust on his face.

Kert and I laughed uncontrollably. I think I laughed partly because it was funny, but mostly out of relief. I am not sure I could have handled the mental image of my grandparents sharing a bed.

My grandma was less tolerant of what she called "Grandpa's antics." She would scold him and tell him he was little more than an ornery child. And I knew it was the ornery child in him that I loved so much. He was liable to do or say anything. Many afternoons were spent on the banks of the Tippecanoe River, which ran behind their house, fishing and talking about baseball, girls, family, or anything that floated through our heads.

And there were countless stories passed down about Grandpa's behavior in his younger years. Many of the stories involved alcohol. Like one Christmas Eve when Grandma fumed because Grandpa was several hours late coming home. She had sent my Uncle Phil out to look for him and—lo and behold—he found him outside a bar, drunk as a skunk, with a parking meter zipped up inside his jacket to keep him from falling over.

Jerry and I caught up with Grandpa out by the barn, where he used the milk house to shield the cold wind. Grandpa pulled a pouch of Levi Garret chewing tobacco from his back pocket, dug three fingers into the foil package, worked the tobacco into a ball, and shoved it in his mouth. He used one finger to position the ball of tobacco in the perfect place in his mouth, chewing rapidly, and then spat a line of black juice across the gravel driveway.

"You boys want a little chewing tobacco?" Grandpa said while holding the pouch of Levi Garret open.

"No, thanks," I said. Last time I tried chewing tobacco, I swallowed a mouthful of the juice when my mom came out of the house unexpectedly. I could still remember the burning heat in my throat, the profuse sweating, and then the projectile vomiting. Grandpa always said chewing tobacco would put hair on your chest. I had come to the realization that hair on the chest was a little overrated.

"Sure," Jerry said. He was a sucker. He reached in the pouch, grabbed two leaves, wadded them up to the size of a marble, and stuck it in his mouth.

"Howya gonna' chew that?" Grandpa laughed. "That's not even a real chew."

Not to be outdone, he reached into the pouch, grabbed a larger wad, and shoved it into his mouth. He grimaced, then his mouth locked open. "This is burning my mouth." It sounded like he had a speech impediment. His tongue and lips didn't move.

Grandpa smiled. "Work it around a little bit and spit."

Jerry spit. Spit some more. I thought he was going to dehydrate if he kept spitting at this pace.

"Tastes better, dudn't it?" Grandpa said. He had only spit once since he'd first put the golf-ball sized roll of tobacco in his mouth. Experienced chewer, I thought.

Jerry nodded his head very slowly, but his face turned white. Barf time. He had that look on his face and in his eyes, that ashen look of those about to hurl or those that were already dead. His stomach muscles convulsed like the cowboys getting shot on television, twitching and twirling, before he bent his knees and blew the wad of tobacco across the ground. He heaved a couple more times, but nothing came out.

"I need a drink," Jerry said and back to the house we ran.

At 10:30 P.M., Mom ushered Jerry and me into the living room to settle down on the pallets she had made for us on the floor. Dad stepped from the bathroom dressed in his state police uniform.

"I need to get going," Dad said to my mom. "I'm not exactly sure where the house is at."

"Okay," Mom said, her voice weak and shaky. She looked away from Dad.

"There's nothing to worry about," Dad said. "Those guys are long gone by now. Anyway, your mom and dad are here."

Mom followed Dad to the back door and locked it, then went through the house double-checking the locks on all the windows and the front door. She made me nervous. I had never seen her like this before. She brushed past me, a look of concentration on her face, focused on fortifying the house. Did she know something I didn't?

Were they keeping something from me?

I walked back in the living room just as the evening news appeared on the television. The three composite pictures of the suspects were splashed on the screen. My heart sputtered as I looked at them, wondering who they were, where they were, if they were hiding out in the barn, waiting for my dad to leave so they could kill us.

The newscaster recapped the events of the week: four boys shotgunned to death; no apparent reason; no apparent motive; mother survives; mother able to describe three of the four killers well enough for detectives to develop composite pictures; eight hundred people attended the funeral for the four boys; state police calling in investigators from throughout the state to follow up on the hundreds of telephone calls from people who think they recognize one of the composites; and yes, they still believe the killers have local ties.

I grabbed the newspaper from the footstool. I cut out the front-page article, *"Officers Still Look for Clues,"* and put it in the manila folder with the other articles. It had been five days since the bodies were discovered and the detectives still didn't have any substantial leads. The murders were in my thoughts day and night. It didn't matter where we went—post office, grocery store, gas station, hardware store, school—everybody was talking about the murders. They were saying the same things: "must have been drug related"; "killers better not show up at my house, got the shot gun loaded and under the bed"; "had to install locks on my doors"; "got to be a reason this happened." I was scared to death and didn't know exactly who to be scared of.

CHAPTER SIX

The sun peeked over the ice-covered trees at almost the same moment I heard a loud knock at the back door. I sat bolt upright on the couch and looked at my mom. It had to be the killers, I thought. Mom ran to the kitchen window, eyes wide, and looked out. I was close behind. I wiped my eyes. The sun was reflecting off the iced cover trees and blinding me.

"It's your dad," she said, relief heavy in her voice. She went to the back door and unlocked it. We weren't accustomed to locking our doors and Mom had the only key on her key chain.

Dad rushed into the kitchen, making weird noises with his lips and rubbing his hands together. "I didn't think you guys were ever going to open the door. It's freezing out there."

"I didn't hear you pull in," Mom said apologetically.

This was hard to believe because last night she would fly off the couch, run to the window, and stare out into the darkness each time a car passed. Her jumpiness had only fueled my fears. I looked to her and Dad for comfort, to ease my mind. They were my protectors. But now, I could smell fear in both of them.

I was convinced there was more to the murders than my parents were telling me. Every time I walked into the room, the conversation would stop abruptly and they would glance at me. If there was nothing to worry about, like my dad said, then why had my grandparents driven down to stay the weekend with us while he guarded Mrs. Spencer?

"Where's Jerry?" Dad asked.

"His mom picked him up a little bit ago," I said. "They were going shopping."

"What are you going to do this morning, Tom?" Mom asked. "Are you going to sleep or stay up for a while?"

Dad smacked his lips together a couple of times while deciding. "Might go up to Vance's and get a bite to eat, them come back and lie down for a while."

"Okay," Mom replied. "Grandma and I are going to run into Crawfordsville and do some shopping. Why don't you take Mike and Daddy with you?"

Thank God, I thought. Shopping with Mom and Grandma was the last thing on the face of the earth I wanted to do. And I had been plotting all morning how to get out of going. Grocery shopping always took forever. Grandma would be armed with an envelope bulging with coupons and we would go from grocery store to grocery store, saving a nickel here and a dime there, but spending twenty-five cents in gas in the process. But it made Grandma feel better.

Vance's Café was packed. Marge rushed between tables, taking orders before dashing off to the kitchen. Kenny stood near the cash register talking about his collection of cookie jars on display throughout the café. Cookie jars shaped like houses, people, pigs—you name it, Kenny had it. Edna talked wildly to an empty table as Wally helped her clear the dirty dishes.

We sat down at the big round table in the center of the café. There were several men at the table, drinking coffee and talking about the scores from last night's high school basketball games.

"Michael," Slick said as I sat down beside him. It came out as "Myy-kel" with Slick's strong Southern accent. He was from Eastern Kentucky originally. Slick's real name was Darrell, but not too many people knew that. My dad and Slick had grown up together, got in trouble together, played baseball together, graduated high school together, and then started families about the same time. Slick was a carpenter, like his dad, and drove a school bus.

"The usual?" Marge asked as she poured Dad a cup of coffee.

"Yep," I said.

"Tommy, whadya know about those murders?" Slick asked while lighting a cigarette. The conversation at the table stopped and all eyes turned to Dad. "That's pretty damn close to home." Slick tilted his head toward the ceiling and blew a stream of white smoke from his lungs.

"Betty was released from the hospital yesterday," Dad said as he added cream and sugar to his coffee, more cream and sugar than coffee. "I've been guarding her for the last week, and will be until we figure out who did this. She's the only witness." Dad swirled the coffee with a spoon, then laid the spoon on a napkin. "Gotta make sure they don't come back and kill her."

"Wasn't her name Betty Miller? Isn't she Herb's sister?" Slick asked. "I thought she lived out in California or someplace out there."

"Yep," Dad said. "She moved back a year or so ago and married Keith Spencer." Dad sipped his coffee. He didn't add any more cream or sugar, so he must have found the right mix.

"Did she tell you what happened?" Slick asked.

"Yeah," Dad said. "I didn't ask too many questions because I didn't want to upset her. But she was up most of the night. Couldn't sleep. She has a pretty serious gunshot wound on her back and on the back of her head. Keith doesn't want to hear anything about how the boys died. And I think she just needs to talk about it. After Keith goes to bed, she comes out to the kitchen and we talk."

"She didn't know the killers?" asked Kenny Vance, who now stood next to the table.

"No. She said she was sitting in the kitchen. It was about midnight and Keith had just left for work. She heard the front door fly open and thought it was Keith coming back to get something he had forgotten. Then two guys came in the back door.

The one longhaired guy in the composite picture with the bushy hair and mustache, and the other one with long hair who looks like an Indian. The other guy in the composite picture, the clean-cut looking one, came in the front door. They were all carrying shotguns."

Dad sipped the hot coffee carefully.

"She said they ordered them into the living room, face down on the floor. Side by side. The two younger boys, Keith's kids, were in bed and they went back and got them and marched them out and ordered them onto the floor next to Betty and her son Greg."

"I thought there were four boys," Slick said.

The front page of the newspaper was lying on the table and the headline read: *"Police Believe Killers May Have Local Ties."*[3]

"One of the boys walked in from work while they were lining them up on the floor. He worked over at the Hollandsburg Restaurant. Cleaned up after they closed."

Poor timing, I thought. Too bad he didn't recognize what was happening before he walked in the house. Maybe he could have run for help.

I couldn't believe I was sitting here listening to the true story. If my mom were here, she would have scolded Dad for talking about this in front of me and escorted me outside. Wouldn't want my head contaminated with this stuff. That was the way it always worked. We went to the movies recently to see the latest Billy Jack release and every time a nude scene came on the screen, Mom would rush me out of the theater and into the women's restroom. Why watch it on the big screen when you can see it live?

"They just started shooting for no reason?" Kenny asked.

"Well, the fourth suspect came in the house and lined them all up execution style. That's why there are only three composite pictures. Betty didn't get a real good look at the fourth suspect because she was already on the floor, facedown. They ransacked the house and then the shooting started. They used shotguns. Betty said that her son Greg, who was lying beside her—" Dad took a pen from his pocket and drew a diagram of stick figures where the bodies were

---

[3] Bill Runge, "Police Believe Killers Have Local Ties," *Crawfordsville (Ind.) Journal Review* 17 February 1977.

lying and wrote their names above them: Ralph, Reeve, Raymond, Betty, and Greg.

"He was shot and raised up on his hands and knees screaming and yelling. He was saying. "I'm flying. I'm flying."

Marge slid my pancake in front of me, stopping momentarily to see why everybody was being so quiet and looking at my dad. I had lost my appetite.

"Holy shit," Slick said, talking more to himself than anybody else.

"She said," Dad continued, "that one of the killers came up and grabbed him by the back of his hair and shot him at point-blank range with a shotgun. I talked with a couple of troopers who were on the scene and they said they have never seen so much blood and guts. There was blood and brain matter on the floor, walls, furniture, and ceiling. The whole living room was covered in blood."

My hands were wringing wet with sweat. The images forming in my head were disturbing. I had seen lots of dead animals, but could not imagine what it must have looked like inside the home. Dead people. Boys about my age. I tried to imagine how bad it would hurt to get shot in the head with a shotgun. I had hurt myself before, falling while running down the gravel driveway, run my minibike into the barn, slipped off the seat of my bike. I couldn't relate to getting blasted in the head.

"How did the mother survive?" Kenny asked.

"She said that after the one guy shot her son Greg, he went down the row kicking them. She said she tried really hard to not be tense and play dead. But she heard him tell one of the other guys to shoot her again. The lights were out in the trailer. She said she braced herself and prayed that they wouldn't kill her because she didn't know if the younger boys were dead or only shot. She knew Greg and Raymond, on either side of her, were dead. Then she felt the pellets come up her back and blow her wig off. They must have thought it was her head because they left."

"Did they rob them?" Wally asked. He stood next to the table, white tub full of dishes in his hands. "Do you think that's what they were doing? Robbing them and then killed them?"

"Dunno," Dad said shaking his head slowly, looking up over his shoulder at Wally. "They didn't steal anything of real value. Other than a car. Buy they dumped it."

"People don't just kill for no reason," Grandpa said. He was a retired police officer himself. "Must have been about drugs. Especially since the boys were killed. And they say the killers are so young."

"Don't make a damn bit of sense," Dad said. "The kids all seemed to be good kids, made good grades, never in trouble. I just don't know."

The not knowing scared the Hades out of me.

CHAPTER SEVEN

"Where'n the hell is that apple pie?" Dade (pronounced day-dee) screamed as he sauntered in the back door, head cocked to one side, blue work pants caught up in his boots and his trademark John Deere green hat tilted off to the side of his head.

"Dade Wiser!" Mom snapped as she shut and locked the door behind him. "I told you to watch your mouth around these boys. These little ears pick up that language and you are in big trouble." She had one eye closed, her nose wrinkled, the meanest face she could muster.

I bit my lip to hold back a grin. I didn't want to let on like I knew what she was talking about, but I did. And I loved it when Dade was around because he was just like my grandpa. He would say whatever popped into his head. He and my grandpa were the only two men on the face of the earth who could get by with cussing in our house. And I don't mean the little cuss words. I'm talking about the big ones that send you straight to the devil.

"Oh, hell," Dade said as he lifted his hat with a shriveled hand and pushed his gray hair back with the other hand. "Matt ain't even talkin' yet and, holy crap, Mike already knows more than me. He was using bad words up at the restaurant the other day I'd never heard before." He flashed me a devilish smile. Agitating my mom, all moms, was his favorite pastime.

"You're rotten, Dade," Mom said. She slid a piece of apple pie in front of him. The only way to keep him in line was to feed him. "It's no wonder why you're always in trouble."

Dade was a retired farmer and reformed alcoholic who'd never married. He was childless, but he loved kids and kids loved him. Why wouldn't they? He always said bad words, let us sample his Copenhagen snuff (much better than Grandpa's Levi Garret), and had candy bars and bubble gum.

Whiskey, straight whiskey, had ruled much of his adult life. If he was this much fun sober, I could only imagine what he was like drunk. But one day, while tilling the spring soil, he pulled his bottle of whiskey out (because he carried the bottle everywhere) and instead of drinking it, he stared at the bottle. "This shit is killing me," he had said to himself, and tossed the bottle in the tall weeds. It was the last time his hands held a bottle of whiskey. No counselors, no Alcoholics Anonymous meetings, just sheer willpower. He said the choice was simple, keep drinking and die a young man or quit drinking and live. And that's when he really started living.

With an extra jingle in his pocket from giving up the whiskey, he started buying candy bars and bubble gum and handing them out to kids. Any kid. He had never met a stranger. He was a year-round Santa Claus. A Santa Claus that cussed.

We had met Dade two years ago while eating lunch at the Milligan Restaurant, a luncheonette catering to farming families, just down the road from where the boys were killed. The restaurant was owned by my friend Jerry's Grandma James, and offered a limited menu. Each day Mrs. James and Francis Thomas prepared a meat, two vegetables, and an assortment of pies. For one dollar and twenty-five cents, iced tea was included with the meal, but sodas and pie were extra.

I noticed Dade meandering between tables, passing out candy and advice. Before long he was at our table acting like he had known us forever. I hesitantly accepted two pieces of bubble gum and listened as he told Mom and Dad about his theories of the world. Within a week, our home was added to his weekly itinerary.

Mom went back to our bedroom to check on Matt, who was napping.

"Where's the ice cream for this pie?" Dade screamed. He smiled at me, a smile that said he had no interest in ice cream.

Mom did not answer until she had checked on Matt, and walked from the bedroom after carefully closing the door. "We don't have any ice cream. And if you wake Matt you won't be eating that pie."

Dade shook his head in disgust. "I've been drivin' around all god-d—"

"Dade!" Mom yelled before he could finish. "I hate that word. I don't say anything to you when you come in here cussing and acting foolish. But you can't take the Lord's name in vain. If you don't change your ways old man, you're going to Hell."

I put my hand to my mouth and coughed to mask laughter.

"God-darn, that's all I was going to say," Dade smiled. "But no, like all women, you had to jump my ass. Thinkin' I was going to say something else." He looked serious, but I knew he was smiling on the inside.

"That's not what you were going to say," Mom snapped.

"See what I mean, Mike," he said. He shook his head like it was no use arguing. "Anyway, me and the Man Upstairs have it all worked out."

"Yeah, a one-way ticket to Hell," said Mom as she poured a glass of iced tea for him. "Cause I'm telling you, that's where you're heading."

Dade winked at me as my mom's back was turned to us. "The Big Man Upstairs told me I was all right. Matter of fact, He said I had a better chance of getting into Heaven than you so-called Christians."

My jaw locked shut and I cringed, waiting for my mom's reply. Dade was treading on quicksand, something he had done before, talking about two topics he knew nothing about, women and religion. And he knew this. It wasn't the debate he enjoyed, it was seeing how worked up my mom got that satisfied him.

Dade took a bite of the apple pie and, after savoring it for a minute, continued, "I read my Bible every day, help little old ladies across the street, but I quit taking communion awhile back. Too much alcohol. You Christians like to drink too much. That's bad for your health."

"I know what your communion was," Mom said as she sat the glass of iced tea in front of Dade. "Jack Daniels. I've invited you to church a hundred times, but you always say no. The roof would probably cave in if you did show up."

"Aw, bullcrap," he said. "You could use a straight-shootin' man like me in the pulpit."

Dad walked from the bedroom where he had been sleeping all day after having worked all night. "What's all the racket out here?" His face contorted as he stopped near the bar to stretch.

"Hi, Tom," Dade said. "I was just trying to share a little bit about my religion with your wife. Tried to explain how a God-fearing man leads his life."

Dad laughed and sat down at the table. He had heard all of this before.

"Sherri giving you a hard time?"

"Damn right," Dade said. "She's mean, Tom. Don't know how you live with her."

"Dade, I am serious," Mom said. "You need to get your life together. You might pull out of our driveway today and get run over by a coal truck. You'd go straight to Hell. I'm going to quit baking you pies until you straighten up."

"I think I've seen the light," Dade screamed. "Now give me another piece of pie." My mom's serious talk always made him nervous.

Mom reached over and squeezed his stubbled face, then shook her head.

Dade turned back to Dad. "Tom, you guys got any idea who did them murders?"

"We've interviewed hundreds of possible suspects," Dad said. "But everybody checks out or has a valid alibi."

"Everybody down home is sayin' that it had somethin' to do with drugs," Dade said. "All these young kids is hooked on dope."

"Don't know," Dad said. "Nothing indicates that the victims had any drug problems. But who knows." The frustration and exhaustion were heavy in Dad's voice.

"I know one thing," Dade said while poking at another piece of pie with his fork. "Those young sons-a-bitches show up at my house and I'll blow their damn brains out."

CHAPTER EIGHT

Mom filled her cup, then set the coffee pot in the center of the kitchen table. Dad was sitting at the table with Dave Blue. It seemed that somebody was always sitting at our table drinking coffee: friends, neighbors, police officers. I would always gravitate toward the table when it was police officers. The stories they told were always captivating. Police officers were unlike any storytellers I had ever been around. They told stories of the darker side of life: car accidents, drug dealers, suicides, thieves, child molesters. There was hardly a topic that hadn't been discussed at our kitchen table over a cup of coffee. And I was often amazed with the humor officers found in the cases they worked, laughing about things that would cause most people to puke.

Today was no different. When Dave Blue came in the back door, I was sorting baseball cards in my bedroom. I was trying to put all of my cards in order, filing them by teams to make it easier to locate individual cards when I was trading with my friends. I left the cards on my bed and walked into the kitchen and sat down at the table. Of all the police officers that I knew, Dave was by far my favorite. He had been a police officer only a few years longer than my dad. He didn't ignore me because I was only a kid. As a matter of fact, he always included me in the conversation. He looked at me when he was telling a story. Some of the others would let their eyes pass right by me like I didn't exist while I sat at the table listening. And it wasn't beyond him to play a game of basketball, even in his uniform. As an added bonus, he was funny, and acted a lot like a kid. Maybe that's why I liked him so much. Dave was a lot like my dad, a police officer that cared about people and one that everyone liked.

Dad poured milk in his coffee and stirred it slowly, the black coffee fading from black to chocolate brown with each stir. "Nothing really new with the investigation. I did interview Stonebraker last night."

"Dan Stonebraker?" Dad asked, his eyebrows raised suspiciously.

"Yep," Dave said reaching for his cup of coffee. "Do you know Bill Stonebraker?"

"Yeah," Dad said. "He used to be the town marshal in Linden. Grew up just down the road in Marshall."

"That's him," Dave said. "He's now an officer on Lafayette Police Department. He and Dan are cousins. Anyway, Bill called me yesterday morning and said he was sure one of the composite pictures was Dan."

Dad frowned, then walked over to the rocking chair and picked up the newspaper. The composite pictures were plastered on the front page, the same place they had been for a week. He studied the three composites as he walked back to the kitchen table and sat back down. He pointed at one of the composites. "This one does look a little like Dan." But everybody in Indiana seemed to recognize one of the composites as somebody they knew. The state police were swamped with phone calls and finding it hard to follow up on every lead, most of which had produced nothing substantial.

"That's what Bill thought," Dave said. "I agree that it looks a little like Dan. Bill was convinced. Said he got a sick feeling in his stomach when he looked at it."

"I don't think Dan would do something like that, though," Dad said, still glaring at the composite picture.

"That's what I said," Dave replied. "But Bill said he was convinced. After seeing the composite, he called down to the Montgomery County Jail to see if Dan was still locked up on drug charges.

When they told him Dan had made bond a couple months ago, he was certain the composite was Dan."

"I guess Bill might know his own family better than we do," Dad said as he folded the newspaper in half and laid it on the table, composite pictures facing up. "But I still can't see Dan Stonebraker killing anybody. He's a cocky little punk. Involved in a lot of things he shouldn't be. But he's not a killer."

I was hanging on every word, consumed with each miniscule detail of the case. And I wasn't alone. Everybody in town was talking about the murders. It was the only news. And the fear was oozing from our community. You could feel it. Everyone was becoming irritable because we didn't know who the killers were and we didn't know why the boys were killed. Not knowing was eating us up inside.

And fear was going to get an innocent person killed, my dad had said. People were doing things they had no business doing: sleeping with their shotguns; answering the front door with a shotgun; distrusting everyone, friend and stranger alike.

Mom walked back into the kitchen and leaned against the bar, studying Dad and Dave, listening intently.

"I know," Dave said. "But Bill was convinced, so we came down to Crawfordsville and drove around looking for Dan. We couldn't find him, so we went over to his dad's bar. Stoney said he hadn't seen Dan. Bill told him some BS about it was important for Dan to come in and talk because if he got pulled over on a traffic stop and ran the police might shoot him because he looked like one of the composites. Scared the crap out of Stoney."

"Did you find him?" Dad asked.

"I dropped Bill off at the jail and was damn near home when the post called and said Dan was at the Crawfordsville PD and wanted to see me."

"Didn't take Stoney long to get the message to Dan," Dad said. He leaned back in the chair and crossed his arms.

"Stoney and his wife brought Dan down to the police department," Dave said. "We went back in the interview room and talked. I told Dan his cousin Bill thought the composite picture looked a lot like him. Then I asked him where he was Sunday night and Monday morning. He gave me the names and addresses of where he was. We ran by each address and confirmed everything." Dave shrugged his shoulders.

"I didn't think he would do something like that," Dad said. "He sure isn't an angel. But he isn't a killer. Big difference between selling drugs and killing."

"Just another dead-end lead," Dave said. "I bet I have interviewed a hundred people who look like one of the composites."

"Not to change the subject," Dad said while placing his spoon in the empty coffee mug. "But I saw where Drollinger was convicted of all the drug charges."

"Yep," Dave said. "Roger Drollinger is finally on his way to prison. Where he belongs. We won't be hearing his name for the next fifty years. I should be retired by then." Dave smiled.

CHAPTER NINE

Dad leaned against the bar, telephone up to his ear. It was the same position he had been in for the last three weeks. Our phone had been ringing nonstop since the day the boys were murdered. People in town assumed Dad knew more than the television or newspapers were telling.

I slung my book bag on an empty chair. Dad was half-dressed in his state police uniform. He no longer spent each night guarding Mrs. Spencer. The state police had her hidden to free up the three officers assigned to guard her around the clock. They were needed on the street, following up on the seemingly endless number of leads flowing into the temporary command center down the road, near Hollandsburg.

Mom was sitting in the rocking chair, rocking nervously back and forth, chewing on her fingernails. She forced a smile in my direction as I stopped beside her, then returned her attention to Dad. I could see her mind was racing.

"Hey, young man," Geno said as she walked from the bathroom back into the kitchen.

"Hi, Geno," I replied.

Geno was a surrogate grandmother to my brother Matt and me. She was widowed and childless. I think my brother Matt and I were the grandchildren she would never have. At sixty-seven years old, she was hardly the normal age of a typical babysitter, but she could do anything a teenage babysitter could do and more. She played basketball, baseball, tag, and hide-and-seek. And we didn't have to be careful with what we said. The words "hell" and "damn" flowed as easily from her mouth as from ours—or, at least, mine. Matt wasn't talking yet.

Geno, spry and ornery, had an unmatched mastery of the English language. She always corrected my lazy grammar. "Ain't is not a word," she would correct. "It's 'have to,' not 'got to.' She was a real stickler for proper grammar, but she made her corrections lovingly, and they were accepted without offense.

Geno was in great shape, which she attributed to the exercise she received from riding her bicycle. It was a green bicycle with a white front-end basket and horn, and it was her trademark in town. Most days, weather permitting, she would pedal her bicycle around town, first to Elston Bank, then to Coleman's Grocery, and last, to the post office (occasionally she went to the Narrow Door Liquor Store, but it was hard to fit a case of beer in the little basket). But when the weather was bad, she backed the Dodge Duster from the garage and scooted around town at about the same speed as her bicycle. Other than a small stint in Philadelphia, Pennsylvania, she had always lived alone in a one-story gray house on the east side of town. Her husband had passed away several years ago.

Geno sat down at the kitchen table and took a sip of beer. Actually, it was more like a gulp; sipping was not her style. The beer was part of the payment for babysitting. She charged one dollar a day and a can of beer. She always drank the beer from the can, wrapped in a napkin, to absorb the condensation, not to hide the contents. A nip of whiskey here and there was not out of the question either, but not while babysitting.

Dad hung up the phone.

"What's going on, Tom?" Mom asked. She had waited patiently to ask the question since getting home from the grocery store.

"They've made an arrest in the murders," Dad said. Now he had my attention.

"Thank God," Mom said. "Who did they arrest? Nobody around here."

A toothpick dangled from the corner of Dad's mouth. "Dan Stonebraker. Roger Drollinger. David Smith. And Mike Wright."

"The nightmare is finally over," Mom said. I shared the relief in her voice.

"Not yet," Dad said. "They can't find Drollinger, Smith, or Wright."

CHAPTER TEN

I glanced up from the living room floor, where I was doing my homework, as the evening news played out on the television. The newscaster declared there had been a major development in the Hollandsburg murders. Investigators had made an arrest last night and were now combing the Pine Hills Nature Preserve, an area about ten miles north of the murder site, for the weapons used in the killings. I looked up at the television just in time to see my dad bend over and point to a rusted shotgun lying next to a tree.

"Mom," I screamed. "Come here. Hurry."

"Shhh," she said while rounding the corner. "You'll wake up your brother. What's wrong?"

"Look. It's Dad. On television." I pointed to his rear-end.

Mom walked closer to the television, wiping her dishwasher-soaked hands on a towel. The four faces of the killers were splashed on the screen, replacing my dad's butt, as the newscaster read their names and mentioned that only one of the murderers, Daniel Stonebraker, was in police custody. The other three killers were on the run and feared to be out of state.

I heard a car racing down our driveway. I jumped to my feet in one motion, but still wasn't quick enough to beat my mom to the window. She was a step ahead and had the curtains parted with one hand. It was Dad. Another state police car followed close behind.

"Go unlock the back door for your dad," Mom said. "I need to check on Matt."

I rushed to the back door, unlocked it, and hung my head outside, staring at Dad and Dave Blue as they got out of their cars. "I just saw your butt on TV," I screamed, smiling from ear to ear.

"I'm famous," Dad said. He didn't know that his butt was literally the only part of him I'd seen on television.

I held the door while Dad and Dave came inside. "They had a good picture of your butt," I said. "You were bent over looking at the gun. I saw you, too, Dave."

"When you're good, you're good," Dad joked.

"I suppose you'll want an autograph," Dave said.

"I'll pass," I said.

Mom came out of the bedroom, taking great care to close the door without waking Matt.

"Hi Sherri," Dave said.

"Hi Dave," she said with a hushed voice, still only a few steps from the bedroom door. "I just made some coffee, you guys want some?"

"That'd be great," Dave said as he pulled a chair from the kitchen table and sat down.

"We just saw you guys on television," she said while grabbing two coffee mugs from the cabinet above the stove.

"That's what Mike said," Dave replied as he smiled at me. "He said they got Tom's best side on the camera."

Mom laughed.

Dad came out of the bedroom, grabbed the milk from the refrigerator and a spoon from the silverware drawer, and sat down at the kitchen table.

"I still can't believe Stonebraker was involved."

"I can't either," Dave said. "But I arrested him last night and listened to his confession."

Mom sat down at the table, clutching her cup of coffee, savoring the warmth of the cup.

"You just interviewed him a couple of weeks ago," Dad said. "Wonder why he didn't tell you then?"

"I don't know," Dave said with a shrug of the shoulders. "May have been partly the way I interviewed him. I didn't really think he was involved. I was just doing it out of respect for Bill Stonebraker. I guess Bill's gut instinct was right."

"I can believe Drollinger," Dad said as he added a dash of milk to his coffee and stirred it to a chocolate brown color. "Nothing he could do would surprise me. I told Stonebraker about a month ago that Drollinger was going to get him into some serious trouble."

Dave nodded his head then sipped his coffee carefully. "He did it this time. Four counts of first degree murder."

"How did Stonebraker's name surface as a suspect again?" Dad asked. "After you cleared him a couple of weeks ago."

"Scott Hamilton called me last night and told me he knew who had committed the murders. He was still hanging out with Stonebraker and was starting to think they had done the murders. Drollinger had told Hamilton that the cops couldn't put him at the scene."

"Him meaning Drollinger?" Dad asked.

"Yeah," Dave said. "Drollinger was careful enough to not be seen. A couple of nights ago, Hamilton asked Stonebraker if they did it and he all but said they had. I picked Stonebraker up last night and brought him to the jail to talk. Figured he would be the most likely to confess. Didn't know the other three had already fled the state."

"Stonebraker tell you everything?" Dad asked.

"Pretty much," Dave said. "I sat him down in the interview room. Stan Kenny, Loyd Heck, and Barney Thrasher were there. Do you know Heck or Thrasher?"

"Not that well," Dad said. "I know they're heading up the investigation."

"Anyway, they wanted me to start the interview since I knew Stonebraker. I just leaned over and asked him, 'Dan, do you believe in God?' Dan said he did. Then I asked him if he believed in confessions. He said he did. I said, 'That's good because God can forgive you for what you did, but the State of Indiana never will.'"

"I'll-be-damn," Dad said to himself as he sat back in the chair. I could tell he still found it hard to believe that Dan Stonebraker had participated in the murders.

"Dan asked me a couple of questions," Dave said. "He asked me if I thought he would do something like that. I told him I didn't think he would, but the evidence said differently. He then asked a couple of questions about what kind of a sentence a person convicted of this crime would get. Heck told him life in prison."

The telephone rang. I didn't move. I couldn't. I hung on every word coming out of Dave's mouth, half scared that my mom would send me to the other room because I shouldn't be hearing things like this. But I didn't budge. I had a right to know. A need to know.

Mom grabbed the phone, and said a quick hello, then apologized and said she would call back a little later, we had company. No time for small talk with details from the most horrific crime in the state's history unfolding at our kitchen table.

"Stan Kenny read Dan his rights while Heck went out and retrieved one of the shotguns that was used and came back in with it," Dave said.

"I thought you found the guns today," I said. I had just watched it on the news.

"We found the other two today," Dad said. "But one of the shotguns was found last night. Before the arrest."

"An employee of Shades State Park found one last night," Dave added.

I wondered how bad it must have hurt to get shot with a shotgun. I had been shot a few times with a BB gun while playing war out in the woods, or when I fired the gun too close to the barn and the BB bounced off the hard wood and pelted me. Each time the sting of the BB had brought tears to my eyes. But that was just a BB, fired from a gun not meant to maim or kill.

"Dan doubled over when he saw the shotgun," Dave said. "Apparently it was his shotgun. I think he was hyperventilating. Once he composed himself, we took a break and then he told us everything."

"Was it drug related?" Dad asked. "Or a robbery?"

"Nope," Dave said. He sipped his coffee. It seemed to take forever for him to raise the ceramic mug to his lips, sip the coffee, and put the mug back on the table. "It was purely a thrill killing."

Dad shook his head slowly and scratched his chin.

Thrill killing, I thought. What is that?

"He said they had been driving around, smoking a little pot and looking at houses. Dan thought they were going to do another home invasion robbery like they did a couple nights before the murders over near Kingman. Stonebraker said it was different when they drove past the Spencer home. Drollinger said that was the house, then pulled down a lane below the house and shut the lights off on the car. Drollinger started giving the orders. He kept telling them to 'seek and secure' and get everybody in a central location in the house."

Matt cried out from the bedroom. His nap was over. The timing of a toddler.

"Seek and secure, what's that crap?" Dad said as much to himself as to Dave.

"You know Drollinger," Dave said. "He's nuts. Anyway, while they were sitting in the car, Drollinger pointed a pistol at everyone and made them agree to shoot somebody or they would be shot. Then they went back to the house. Stonebraker and Smith ran in the back door, Wright went in the front door and got Betty Spencer and the boys on the floor in the living room, facedown with their hands behind their backs."

"Where was Drollinger?" Dad asked.

"Said he was going to cut the phone lines," Dave smirked. "But the lines were never cut. Just like Drollinger to stay back, let the other three go in and get everything under control. He could run at the first sign of trouble."

"Drollinger's always had a way of getting people to do things for him," Dad said. "The guy's just like Charles Manson. It's unbelievable the power he has over people."

"That's Drollinger," Dave said.

"Look at how many times we have arrested him," Dad said. "Statutory rape. Drug trafficking. Burglary. Throwing cement blocks from over-passes." Dad shook his head. The murders had been choking the life out of our community for nearly three weeks. And

Choking in Fear

now, even knowing who the killers were, there were still many unanswered questions.

"Once they had everybody lined up on the floor, Drollinger went through the house looking for valuables. Then he shut the lights off. He and Smith stood at the feet of the victims and Stonebraker and Wright stood to the left of the victims." Dave used his index finger to draw a diagram on the table. "Drollinger looked at Wright, nodded his head, and the shooting started. Wright shot several times, execution style. Stonebraker shot once and his gun jammed. Smith had a sawed-off shotgun and was shooting from the feet of the victims. Drollinger was orchestrating the massacre."

"Probably getting his rocks off," Dad said.

Mom shook her head as a tear slid down her cheek. "How could anybody do that to other human beings? They were just little boys. How could they kill little boys?"

Why did they do it? That was the question we all needed answered, me especially. Three of the killers were still on the loose.

"So Drollinger didn't shoot anybody?" Dad asked.

"He did" Dave said. "Drollinger shot the oldest boy, Greg Brooks, who was lying next to the couch and his mom. After Greg was shot the first time, he raised up on his hands and knees and Stonebraker said he screamed, 'Oh my God, I'm dying. Oh my God, I'm dying.' Drollinger took the sawed-off shotgun from Smith, walked up behind the Brooks boy, grabbed him by his ponytail, and stuck the shotgun right to the back of his head and fired. Stonebraker said he watched the boy's brain fly across the room and land on the coffee table."

Dad grimaced. I tried to visualize it, but it was beyond my comprehension. Mom fanned herself with the newspaper, then got up and took my brother into the living room. She had heard enough. My heart raced in my chest as I tried to imagine what it must have been like inside the Spencer home that night. It scared me. I loved my parents and my brother so much. And what could I do if somebody broke in and started shooting? Why did those guys think they had the right to kill people, to take those boys away from their mom and dad forever? And for no reason. It wasn't fair.

"Drollinger then went down the line," Dave said. "Kicking the bodies to make sure they were dead. He then went over to Stonebraker and told him to shoot the woman again. She must've flinched or something. Dan said his gun jammed. Drollinger cleared the jam and threw it back to him and told him to shoot her. Dan said he thought Drollinger felt like he hadn't shot anybody. Dan said he raised the gun and shot at the boy next to the couch, just beyond the mom because he knew that the boy was dead. Some of the trailing buckshot caught her wig and blew it off. They thought it was her head. They collected their spent shells and left."

"The motive was purely thrill killing," Dad said. "That means it could've been anybody around here."

"Drollinger wanted to kill somebody," Dave said. "He was just looking for the right house. This one was perfect. Out in the middle of nowhere, neighbors over a mile away. And they had several nice cars in the driveway. Stonebraker said that Drollinger figured they were having a party and they could go in, kill everybody, and then rob them. The only items stolen from the house were some T-shirts, a calculator—just small items. Murder was the motive. Robbery was only secondary."

"Betty Spencer told me that she thought for sure she was a goner when she heard them say shoot the woman again," Dad said. "She actually heard Drollinger order Stonebraker to shoot her again. She felt the buckshot climb up her back and head. She didn't know how badly she was injured. Once they left, she waited several minutes to make sure they were gone. She said it sounded like a train in the house. It was the blood draining from the boys. She ran out the back door, down through the woods to a neighbor's house, and called the police. Scared the hell out of poor Harold Escue."

"Good thing she was able to get to his house and call the police," Dave added. "Otherwise more people would have been killed."

"What good did that do?" Mom asked. She had made her way back to the kitchen. "They weren't caught until last night. Three of them are still free."

"Stonebraker said Drollinger's plan was to kill two families," Dave said. "Just like Manson and the Tate-LaBianca murders. The only reason they didn't kill anybody else was because they had a portable scanner and heard the police being dispatched to the Spencer home."

We sat silently for several seconds, shocked. I felt like pinching myself to see if in fact this was true and not a dream. But I knew this was not a dream. It was a true-to-life nightmare that we had lived for almost a month.

"What do you know about Smith or Wright?" Dad asked. "I don't think I ever arrested either one of them."

Dave poured himself another cup of coffee. "Smith is only seventeen years old. He's Drollinger's right-hand man. I don't know Wright that well. He's only been back in the area a short while after getting out of the Navy. Kind of a hothead, I hear."

"I'll be doggone," Dad said.

I didn't think anybody had a clue the murders would turn out like this. We sure didn't think the killers would be members of our community. At some level I think we all wished there were a plausible explanation for the murders. Like drugs, or a fight—something that said it couldn't happen to us. But this was like a plot out of a good novel, not a true story playing out in our community.

"You want to know what's disturbing?" Dave asked. "Drollinger was on trial for his drug charges when he committed the murders."

"That's right," Dad said, shaking his head. "How did he get out of jail to begin with? Wasn't his bond fifty thousand on the drug charges?"

"Yeah," Dave said. "His dad posted the bond. Put up some property."

"He was in jail six or seven months before he bonded out," Dad said. "I didn't even know he was out until his drug trial started."

"He made bond exactly one month before the murders," Dave said. "The judge lowered his bond."

"Lowered his bond?" Dad asked mockingly. "The guy had been arrested for everything but murder. What more does it take to keep somebody locked up? Don't the courts have an obligation to protect society? I bet the judge is feeling pretty crappy about that move. I hope he is."

Dave nodded his head. "What is unbelievable," Dave said, "is that Drollinger was actually on trial when the murders happened. He took the stand on the Friday before the murders in his own defense. Court was recessed for the weekend. The murders happened early Monday morning on the fourteenth and he was back on the stand less than eight hours after killing four people. An officer in court that day said Drollinger was alert, calm, probably more articulate than he had been the Friday before."

"A true sociopath," Dad said. "No remorse. No fear. That's Drollinger. I'm not at all surprised he would do something like this."

"Stonebraker said that a couple of days after the murders, they all met at the Captain's Table for lunch: Drollinger, Stonebraker, Wright and Smith. Drollinger grabbled a French fry and told them that after the murders, when he got home, he was undressing and a piece of brain fell off his collar. He swiped the French fry through the ketchup, said he had fed the brain to his cat, and then he ate the French fry, smiling from ear to ear."

Dave finished his coffee and placed the cup in the sink before leaving. I walked into the living room, dazed by all the information and the images flooding my head. I grabbed the newspaper. The headline read, *"Four Montgomery County Men Face Charges in Parke Massacre"*[4] I studied the pictures of the four killers. They were the first killers I had ever seen. And they didn't look much different from most people I knew. They didn't look the way I pictured the boogeyman looked. I studied the pictures hard because I wanted to make sure I had plenty of time to run if I saw them.

I cut the article out of the paper and was taking it to my bedroom where I kept the other articles in a manila folder when I saw Mom sitting on the edge of their bed while Dad changed out of his uniform. Thank God he was home with us tonight.

---

[4] Dick Robinson, "Four Montgomery County Men Face Charges in Parke Massacre," *Crawfordsville (Ind.) Journal Review*, 19 March 1977.

I walked into their bedroom. Dad pulled his pistol from his holster, but instead of putting it high in the closet as usual, he laid it on the nightstand on his side of the bed and finished changing his clothes.

CHAPTER ELEVEN

The Coca-Cola deliveryman pushed the door open with his back and stood against the door long enough for us to enter, balancing a red hand truck stacked full with cases of Coke. We sidestepped to the left to clear a path for people leaving while Mom unbundled Matt. I unzipped my coat, took off my stocking cap and gloves, and shoved them in my pockets. Mid-March in Indiana meant the cold days were offset by a warm day now and then. Some of the worst snows in the state's history had happened in March when we were all worn out with winter and longed for the warmth of spring and summer.

As I waited impatiently for mom to peel the layers of clothing from Matt, a flood of memories from Coleman's Grocery Store raced through my head. Not all of them necessarily good. It was the fall of 1971 and I was much younger. Traffic in and out of Coleman's was much heavier than usual. Mom and I walked inside, stopped to figure out where to go, then went down the middle aisle. The shelves were filled with every canned good imaginable. We worked our way to the end of the aisle and found the end of the line which snaked through part of aisle three and wrapped around to the back of aisle two. It looked like everybody in town was here.

"Let's go," I said. "We don't have to waste our time."

"No." Mom said, licking her fingers and running them through my hair. "We're here. And we're getting your pictures taken."

"Ugh," I moaned through gritted teeth.

"It won't take that long," she said.

I raised my eyes just high enough to see if I recognized any of my friends in front of us. Nope. Thank God. Then I put my head back down, like an ostrich burying its head in the sand. I couldn't afford for one of my friends to walk through the door to buy a candy bar and see me standing in line to get my picture taken. My life would be over.

I stared at a loaf of Wonder Bread, praying silently that the camera would break, while Mom checked the prices on several items on the other side of the aisle. Mom had me dressed like a goofball in a brown and yellow striped sweater, brown pants, and brown dress shoes. I didn't dress this well for church. What's so special about this guy up there with the camera? He looked like a pervert. Telling stupid jokes and flashing a fake smile.

Finally, after what seemed like a year, our turn arrived. Mom signed some papers and up on the carpeted platform I went, in front of God and country. As the Olan Mills photographer situated me on the platform, he tried his hand at humor, hoping I would smile so he could snap a couple quick photos and move on to the next kid. I didn't smile. I wasn't happy. And he sure wasn't a comedian, either. I also realized I would be sitting on this platform all day if I didn't smile. Mr. Photographer might give up, but Mom wouldn't. So I flashed a couple of cheesy smiles. He took the pictures. Mom was happy. The photographer was happy. And I was more than happy to exit center stage. Mom grabbed a gallon of milk, and my first photo shoot was over. However, by next summer's end, the pain of the photo shoot would be replaced by something far worse.

I had the window rolled all the way down and my head sticking out of the car like a dog lapping at the summer air as Mom pulled into the gravel parking lot at Coleman's Grocery. My cutoff shorts were still wet from playing in the hose. As Mom slowed the car, I vaulted out the door before she could slide the transmission into park.

The gravel was hot against my bare feet. My only hope for survival was to run, lifting my feet high with each step. I figured it to be ten steps or less to the row of railroad ties that served as parking barriers. I could hop the railroad ties and walk them to the shade in front of the store. Coleman's was a customer centric store, no goofy rules about having to wear a shirt and shoes to shop.

I glanced down at the gravel as my left foot started back down. No! I saw the broken pop bottle, directly below where my foot would plant, but I couldn't stop my momentum. The last minute lunge pushed my foot forward, but not enough to miss the broken bottle. The soft flesh of my heel sliced like a ripe tomato from the knob on the inside of my ankle to the knob on the outside of the ankle as my foot smashed against the jagged piece of glass. I jerked my foot high in the air and stared in horror as the back of my heel flipped back and forth. Then the blood began pouring from the massive cut.

Serious pain is a weird thing. It tricks you for a few seconds before attacking you. That false moment of hope between accident and pain. Just when you think you have ole Mother Nature fooled. Then, *boom!* The pain swallowed you. It was like sliding off the seat of my bicycle and landing on the bar (a bar found only on boys' bikes...I never could figure that one out), smashing my jewels (or so Grandpa Jim called them). It never failed, I always had time to stop, get off the bike, and lie down on the ground before the gut-wrenching pain burned in my abdomen.

Mom walked around the front of the car at that exact moment the false hope fled and the pain arrived. I screamed—a stinging, visceral scream like Ned Beatty's in the movie *Deliverance*. My mom was horrified. She swept me up with one quick movement, put me in the front seat, and wrapped my foot with a beach towel. I held the towel tight against my foot, writhing in pain, as Mom drove the thirteen miles to Dr. Millis' office. Dr. Millis, who had delivered me as an infant and who had stitched the back of my throat after I ran into our neighbor's door with a peace pipe in my mouth, stitched my foot and covered it with a gauze bandage. Saved again by Dr. Millis, my own personal seamstress.

A few months later, I would jump the fence and test my luck as a hardened criminal at Coleman's Grocery.

"No, you can't have the bubble gum," Mom said. "Put it back."

I turned to stomp off to the front of the store and put the gum back on the rack. What the heck was a little bubble gum going to hurt? It only cost twenty-five cents. But no, "It'll rot your teeth out" was all I ever heard. Who really cares about teeth? I thought. You can get fake ones. Grandma Mett and Grandpa Jim had. Grandpa carried his around in his front pants pocket.

Betty Coleman was standing at the cash register talking with Mrs. Johnson. I started to put the gum back on the shelf, but something came over me. I really wanted the gum. I could taste the sugar and sweetness of the gum exploding in my mouth. I could feel the sensation of chewing on the gum, blowing bubbles. I deserved the gum. Yes, I did.

I shot a quick glance over my shoulder. Mrs. Coleman was not looking, so I stuck the gum in my pants pocket.

Mom turned the corner with her groceries and started placing them on the counter to pay for them. She made some small talk. The bubble gum was burning a hole in my pocket. I could already taste the explosion of sugar in my mouth. Mom paid and we left.

I climbed in the car and sat down before turning sideways in the seat and fishing the gum from my pocket. I unwrapped the gum and threw a piece in my mouth. I was chewing on the gum like a cow chews its cud. Stupid.

Mom put the groceries in the trunk and slammed the trunk shut. As she backed from the parking lot, one hand on the back of my seat, she slammed the car to a stop. I felt the heat of her eyes, but I didn't look at her. I did stop chewing.

"What's in your mouth?" she asked sternly.

"Nothing," I said through pursed lips.

"Don't lie to me," she said. "You know where you go for lying."

I knew exactly where she was talking about. It scared the bejesus out of me. Just any day now the ground was going to part and I was going to be swallowed into Hell, punished with eternal damnation for all the things I had done that I wasn't supposed to. I didn't say a word.

"Open your mouth."

I opened my mouth about the width of a piece of paper.

"All the way, Mike."

The thought of swallowing the gum came and left. Too much gum to swallow. It would probably get lodged in my throat, and then I'd choke to death and be sent off to Hell. I reckoned owning up to what I had done would be better than meeting Satan today. I opened wide, gum resting on my tongue.

"Where'd you get that?" Mom's eyes glared at me.

I shrugged my shoulders like I couldn't remember. Alzheimer's. Didn't work.

"Inside," she gritted. "You stole that?" Her voice raising with each word. "You stole that gum from Coleman's!"

I didn't answer. The word *stole* stung. Did I steal gum? It felt more like borrowing.

She was out of the car, eyes glaring through the front windshield as she circled the car to my door and jerked me out by my arm. I had a fleeting thought of resisting, maybe letting my legs go limp, but a little voice—a wise voice—in the depths of my brain said, "Go. Don't be stupid."

To make matters worse, as we stormed back into the store, Mrs. Coleman was helping a customer, bagging the remaining groceries. So now I had to stand at the end of the counter, Mom with a death grip on my arm like she had caught me robbing an old lady in the parking lot, and Mrs. Coleman looking at us for some indication of why we were back so quickly, and why Mom was holding me like an escaped felon.

As soon as the customer gathered her bags and left, Mom looked at me and said, "Don't you have something to say to Mrs. Coleman?"

I felt like I had the whole pack of gum lodged in my throat. What could I say? I'm a thief? Sorry?

"Mike," Mom said sternly. "Go ahead."

Mrs. Coleman had a perplexed look on her face.

"I'm sorry," I whispered, my eyes burning holes in my tennis shoes.

"Sorry for what?" Mom asked. "Look up."

I laid the sweaty pack of bubble gum, which I had been clutching in my shaking hand for the past five minutes, on the counter. "I took this. And forgot to pay."

"You took it," Mom said. "After I told you that you couldn't have it. You didn't forget to pay."

Mrs. Coleman stood silently.

"I'm sorry."

Mom fished a quarter from her purse, laid it on the counter, told Mrs. Coleman she was sorry, and we walked outside. Before we turned the corner of the store to the parking lot, she tossed the four remaining pieces of gum in the trash. Pocketing anything that wasn't mine never crossed my mind again. Lesson learned.

Mom stopped at the meat counter in the back of the store. Matt was sitting up in the cart, his hair still standing straight up from the static electricity generated when Mom had removed his stocking cap. Mr. Coleman, known as Forest to the townspeople, was slicing a pound of ham for a lady I didn't recognize. Ethel Calvert stood a few steps behind Forest, carving on a chunk of meat.

"Hi, Sherri," Ethel said, wiping her bloodied hands on her apron and walking towards us. Ethel's voice was as kind as her spirit. As far as I could remember, nobody ever said a bad thing about Ethel or the meat she cut.

"Hi, Ethel," Mom said. "What's good today?"

"Have some nice steaks."

"That sounds good. And I'll take half of a pound of bologna."

Forest wrapped the ham methodically in white paper, weighed it, and sat it on the counter before writing the price on the wrapper in black marker. He asked the lady if there was anything else he could get for her. She said no and left.

"Hi, Sherri," Forest said. He wiped his hands on his apron.

"What's Tom know about those boys wanted for the murders?" Ethel asked as she pulled the roll of bologna from the meat counter.

"He knows a couple of them real well," Mom said. She rested

one hand on top of the meat counter. Mr. Coleman listened intently. His wife had slipped away from behind the cash register in the front of the store and now stood beside Mom, listening intently, occasionally glancing over her shoulder for people wanting to check out.

"Sure never thought boys from around here could do something like that," Ethel said. "Wish they'd find those other three." Ethel wrapped the bologna and wrote the price on it before sliding it across the counter. She turned to get the steaks.

"Me, too," Mom said. "This has been going on forever. I can't remember ever being this scared before. I haven't slept solid for the past month."

"At least they know who they are," Ethel said while sliding the packaged steaks across the counter.

"Yeah," Mom said. "I still don't think I'll sleep any better until they find the other three."

CHAPTER TWELVE

For six weeks a dark gray snow sky hung low as the heavens mourned the loss of four innocent boys. My community was weary from fighting the cold and fear. We needed some good news and some sunshine.

Thankfully, today, the sun was burning through the clouds. The light and warmth would help. The birth of spring brought with it a renewal of hope that all would be normal again. We would be allowed out of our parent's reach—able to ride bikes, play baseball, swim in one of the local lakes or streams, and camp in the woods out back of our house.

I also knew that for summer to be normal, the final three killers must be captured. Otherwise, I would be stuck at my parent's side all summer. There would be no carefree days of playing outside. No running through the woods or riding my bike in town. And there was no way I would sleep out back of the house in a tent with killers still running free. The killers had something against kids and I was going to do everything within my power to make sure I wasn't another notch on their belt.

And sadly, it did not look like they would be caught any time soon. I might as well forget about summer. I couldn't stomach the thought, after all the fun of last summer.

I watched as the marshmallow on the end of the stick I had whittled caught fire and turned from pristine white to charcoal black in seconds. I jerked the stick toward my mouth, blew out the flames, then blew on the scorched marshmallow a few more seconds before pulling it off the stick and popping it in my mouth. After three roasted hot dogs, Jerry, Robby Bazzani, and I were sharing a bag of marshmallows.

"I wish we had some cigars," Jerry said with marshmallows stuck to the corners of his mouth. "One of those Swisher Sweets."

"Dad didn't have any," I said. My dad smoked cigars off and on, not as a habit, so it was unpredictable when a box of cigars would be lying around the house. And this would be a good time for a cigar; with all the campfire smoke, we wouldn't have to worry about my mom smelling smoke on our clothes or breath. But not tonight.

"Didya check his old truck?" Jerry asked.

"Yeah, dipshit," I said.

Robby walked to the edge of the woods and watered the grass under his feet.

"You guys want to throw some apples at coal trucks?" I asked while standing from the log I was using as a chair.

"Hell, yeah." Jerry answered.

"Wait for me," Robby yelled while trying to run and zip his pants at the same time.

I stopped under a row of apple trees, pulled my shirttail out, and held it with one hand while filling the makeshift basket with apples from the ground, softened by a couple of days of rotting. I had already learned how loud a freshly picked apple sounded when it hit a coal truck. Down the edge of the woods we went, weighted by the apples. There was a large maple tree close to the road, perfect cover. We dumped the apples on the ground and waited for a coal truck.

"Don't hit the cab of the truck," I instructed. "It'll make too much noise. Only hit the trailer."

"I'm aiming for the driver," Robby laughed.

"I'm serious," I said. "The trucker might stop if we hit the cab. He'll never hear the apple hit the trailer."

"I know," Robby said. "I was only kidding."

Then I heard the familiar hum of an approaching coal truck,

backing his way through the gears, the hiss of the air brakes as he slowed for the S curve and the acceleration as he negotiated the final curve. We crept up toward the ditch like marines preparing to overtake an enemy camp.

The excitement was unbearable. I couldn't stand still waiting for the truck. A surge of adrenaline shot through my body, making me feel as if I could throw the apple through the steel trailer. Chill out, I told myself. Don't get too excited and bounce one off the windshield. Just last year I got so excited I pelted the driver's door of a car and, before I could turn and run, the car was peeling down our driveway, throwing gravel in all directions. That one apple and split second of pleasure cost me my freedom for over two months, grounded at home, with no friends, no swimming, and no camping. I wasn't even allowed to eat apples.

As the cab of the coal truck passed, we jumped to our feet and pelted the trailer with apples. After smacking the trailers of three coal trucks, we were bored. The rush of excitement in throwing apples was the possibility that the driver might stop. Either the truckers didn't hear the apples or they didn't want to waste the time and energy required to stop. That's when I came up with a brilliant idea. "Let's throw one apple at a car," I said. "Then we'll go back to the campsite."

"Okay," Jerry said.

"All of us throw an apple at a car," Robby said.

"No way," I said. "We'll get in trouble. I'll throw one apple. I've done it before." Clearly, I was the most experienced apple thrower.

I heard a car accelerate out of the S curve, so I began my low crawl toward the road and hid behind a small tree. I cocked my arm like a shotgun and fired the apple. In slow motion my life passed in front of my eyes as I watched the apple float through the air and impact with the front hubcap.

BAM!

The sound was deafening.

The driver locked the brakes on the car, the tires screeched against the dry pavement, and a billow of smoke drifted skyward.

"Way to go numb-nut," Jerry screamed as he turned to run into the thicket of the woods.

"Kiss my butt," I mumbled as I bolted through the woods, thorn bushes and briars scarring my skin. Why did I throw that apple? Stupid. Stupid. The warning from my parents had been specific and with grave consequences (I stress the word grave).

Robby, Jerry, and I were sitting around the campfire, talking nonchalantly, though I was visibly shaken, as I watched the approaching shadow of my dad. If we acted stupid, maybe he wouldn't think we did it. The problem was I was sweating like I had just finished the Boston Marathon and blood oozed from numerous fresh scratches on my arm. And the front of my shirt was stained from the rotten apples.

"Mike," Dad said, his voice stern. I could tell he was holding back a loud tongue-lashing for the benefit of Robby and Jerry and the lady standing in our front yard whose car I pelted. "Get up to the house. Now!" he talked through gritted teeth.

I'm dead. I walked to the house in silence.

Jerry and Robby, loyal friends and brave souls, stayed behind until Dad turned around. "Jerry. Robby. Come on."

I apologized to the lady. And thankfully, the apple hadn't done any damage. It didn't even dent the hubcap. She left. Dad extinguished the campfire, drove Jerry and Robby home, then came home and warmed my hind end a little bit with his hand. I finally realized there wasn't a real market in this world for experienced apple throwers.

I followed Dad inside the hardware store and was temporarily blinded as my eyes adjusted to the darkness. The store was as quiet as the library. Always quiet. The only sound was the creak of the wooden floors as we walked to the rear of the store where all business was conducted. On most days, a small group of local contractors, jacks-of-all-trades, would be huddled around the cash register talking about their most recent projects, or who was building an addition onto their

Choking in Fear

house and didn't have the money to do it. But that wasn't a real problem because Larry Servies did most local business on a tab that could be paid off with no interest.

Slick was sitting in a wooden chair between the counter and the desk that served as Larry's office. Larry was sitting behind the desk, straight-faced as always.

"Tom." Larry said evenly. He never showed the slightest hint of excitement or disdain. And he never said hi. Just your first name and a slight nod of his head.

"Hello Mikey," Slick said.

"Whatta you need, Tom?" Larry asked as he stood up. He appeared to be all business to the foreign eye.

"Need some more paint," Dad said as he handed Larry the paint chip.

Larry stuck the paint chip in his breast pocket—probably remembered the paint exactly as he had mixed it last week. "I told you that wouldn't be enough." A smirk appeared on his face, then disappeared.

Larry marched off to the paint section at the front of the store. I turned from Dad and Slick and fell in behind him so I could watch him mix the paint. A splash of this color, a dash of that color—colors you could never imagine being combined to make a gallon of tan paint. He put the lid back on the can, smacked it with a rubber hammer, then secured it in the shaker and turned it on.

Larry was middle-aged and single. He'd always been single, at least as long as I had known him, a whopping nine years. He lived alone in a white two-story home on the west end of town. Each summer his yard was freshly cut and a sprawling garden grew out behind his house. He was a good man, humorous in a dry way, like the time he walked into Vance's Café, pulled his tape measure from his belt, and started measuring Grandpa Jim. He never said a word. Just recorded the measurements on a piece of paper. But Grandpa Jim, like everybody else in town, knew Larry also owned the local funeral home. Larry joked that he would eventually get the business of everybody in town. Grandpa didn't appreciate the mortuary school of humor. And it wasn't just the hardware store and the funeral home Larry owned. He owned pretty much everything including Machledt and Servies Lumber Yard and Machledt and Servies Furniture Store.

I had never met this Machledt character whose name was on all of Larry's businesses. It didn't make much sense to me because everybody knew that Carl Morgan was Larry's business partner. But when I had asked Dad who this Machledt guy was, he had said that he was dead. Why was a dead man's name still on the businesses? I had asked. Dad said it was a bunch of legal stuff; Larry and Machledt had started the businesses together. And I figured if it was a bunch of legal stuff then I didn't really care anyway.

Besides owning everything in town, Larry was also the Chief of the Waveland Volunteer Fire Department. It was hard to believe that one man had time to do all these things and run all the businesses. But with no wife or kids, I guess it was possible. One minute he was pulling you from a burning house, saving your life, then the next, he was embalming you for burial. A true jack-of-all-trades.

When he wasn't driving a fire truck or his gold hearse, he was tooling around town in his silver pickup. Only on rare occasions, usually on a date, would you see Larry back his polished gold Cadillac from his garage. You could tell a lot about the goings-on around town by what Larry was driving. If it was the fire truck, we knew there was a fire. If it was the pickup truck, we knew it was business as usual. If it was the Cadillac, we knew he was socializing. And if it was the hearse, we knew somebody had died.

I made my way toward the rear of the store, where Dad and Slick were talking.

"Heard y'all arrested another one of those killers," Slick said. He reached in the breast pocket of his flannel shirt and retrieved a cigarette, then turned sideways in the wooden chair and fished the lighter from his pants pocket.

"Uh-huh," Dad said. "The FBI picked up Mike Wright in California."

Slick held the pack of cigarettes out to me. I smiled. "No thanks."

Choking in Fear

Slick turned back toward my dad and lit his cigarette. He blew a line of smoke toward the ceiling. "Wonder how they found him in California. Somebody rat him out?"

"He'd been calling Stonebraker to see what was happening back here," Dad said. "That's how he found out Stonebraker was arrested. One of our troopers—Dave Blue—got a phone bill from somewhere...Wright or Stonebraker's family. It had the number Wright had been calling from. He'd been calling collect. From San Jose, California."

"Why'd the FBI get involved?" Slick asked. "State police won't send you to California to pick him up?" He grinned.

"Heck, it's all they can do to send me a paycheck twice a month," Dad said. "Since three of them—Drollinger, Smith, and Wright—had fled the state, we needed some help finding them. Fleeing across state lines makes it a federal crime. Two of our detectives—Heck and Thrasher—flew out and interviewed Wright and brought him back to Indiana."

"What about those other two?" Slick asked. "Drollinger and Smith. Have any ideas where they're at?"

"Headed south," Dad said. "Probably Florida. Stonebraker last saw Smith and Drollinger with a woman from Crawfordsville who was on her way to Florida."

"Have you talked to either one of the killers that were arrested?" Slick asked.

Larry walked around the cash register and set the can of paint on the counter. He stood there like the marine guarding the tomb of the Unknown Soldier.

"I haven't talked to them since they were arrested," Dad said. "But I have known Stonebraker since I became a trooper."

"They must've drove right through town," Slick said, cigarette dangling from his lip, eyes squinted to avoid the smoke.

"Right through town," Dad said. "Drove right down 59, past our house, and just found the Spencer house by mistake. Heck, you can't find the Spencer home if you know where you were going."

Dad turned and pulled his billfold from his rear pocket and paid

Larry for the paint. Slick stood up and walked behind the counter, toward a door in the rear of the store.

"Well, I better get some work done," Slick said. "Just put the materials on my bill, Larry." He slipped out the side door where his truck was parked in the alley.

We walked out the front door of the hardware store. Pickup trucks lined the street. It was four in the afternoon and everybody who was somebody was drinking coffee at Vance's Café. With the gallon of paint in Dad's hand, I figured we would be skipping social hour. Then again, I guessed we'd just had it.

CHAPTER THIRTEEN

Mom stood in the doorway of my bedroom, hands resting on her hips as the light from the rest of the house flooded past her. I could barely make out her silhouette through my sleep-filled eyes. It was the third time she had opened my door and asked me to get out of bed. I always played possum. Don't move. Act like I am dead or at least can't hear her and maybe she would forget about me and let me sleep. I hated getting up early.

"Mike, get up," she said. "We are going to be late for church."

Who cares, I thought, but was smart enough not to say. Plus, I knew being late would not keep us from going. We were always late. Every Sunday we walked in late and had to parade in front of the packed church looking for empty seats.

I swung my legs from the warmth of the covers, let them dangle over the side of the bed, then sat there for a few minutes clearing the sleep from my eyes and trying to remember how to walk. I wasn't old enough for coffee and the bowl of Fruit Loops and glass of orange juice each morning weren't enough to get my engine going.

It was 6:30 A.M. Easter Sunday. And as ritual would have it, we were on our way to the sunrise service, which started at 7:00 A.M. The high point to the early morning service was always the sunrise breakfast that followed the sermon. Then it was back home for a late morning Easter egg hunt, weather permitting. The Easter Bunny, who looked a lot like my dad and seemed to have a love interest for my mom, would hide the colored eggs around our yard. After all the eggs were collected in my plastic grass-lined basket, Mom and

Grandma Mett would prepare an Easter feast of turkey, noodles, mashed potatoes, corn, sweet potatoes, and an assortment of desserts.

I brushed my teeth and then dressed in the clothes my mom had arranged for me on my bed: white oxford shirt, yellow tie, blue dress pants, and black shoes. You can't wear brown shoes with blue pants, my mom had told my dad many times. Mom and Dad were walking toward the back door when I came out of my bedroom.

"Mike, put your lightweight coat on," Mom said as she walked from the kitchen toward the back door. "And pull the back door closed. I have already locked it."

The street in front of our church, the Waveland Christian Church, was lined with cars on both sides of the street. Dad pulled into an empty space in front of the Cunningham's house. I followed Mom and Dad across the street, peeling off my jacket. As we entered the vestibule, Mom and Dad stopped momentarily to speak with Rich and Jeannie Dickerson before taking Matt to the nursery. I slipped around them into the sanctuary, and followed the wall around to the southwest corner of the church. The two back rows of pews were reserved for older kids. You had to be at least nine. No adults. Once you graduated from high school you had to move up a few rows. Usually it was hard to find a seat because there were more kids than seats. And the most humiliating childhood experience was having to sit with your parents during church. So most Sundays, we sat squished together like sardines. Better to be utterly uncomfortable than to sit with your parents. Today, though, there were plenty of seats. Many of the kids (or their parents) had elected to sleep and come to the normal 10:30 A.M. service.

Norman Walker played a soft hymn on the organ, one I did not recognize—or spend much time trying to recognize. At exactly 7:00 A.M., Reverend Winger spoke of the crucifixion and resurrection of Jesus Christ. I nodded in and out, having heard this sermon a hundred times. A chilly spring breeze squeezed under the cracked window to my left and provided just enough bite to keep me from a deep slumber. Normally, we would play tic-tac-toe, dots, or hangman, but it was too darned early today. We couldn't concentrate long enough to draw the grid for tic-tac-toe or the noose for hangman. Staying awake demanded all of our energy.

I opened my eyes and noticed my mom glancing my way, making sure I was not sleeping or goofing around. Fearful she had been watching me sleep, I closed and opened my eyes several times like I had dirt in them. Then I smiled. She smiled back. Thank God, she hadn't seen me slumped over the arm of the pew, spit dripping from the corner of my mouth.

As the early morning service drew to a close, my dad, along with several other men of the church, walked forward and received the offering and communion trays from the two elders, Roger Johnson and Russell Fisher. Jeannie Dickerson played softly on the piano as the offering was collected. Thankfully, Mr. Walker was sitting at the organ today. It took him forever each Sunday to put his twenty-dollar bill in the offering plate and fish out his change. Then the communion was passed pew-by-pew, person-by-person. First it was the bread, representing the body of Jesus Christ, then the grape juice that represented the blood of Jesus Christ. It was a time of quiet reflection on the sacrifice Jesus Christ had made for us. I didn't really need quiet reflection. My mom reminded me almost daily what a sacrifice Jesus had made as she scolded me for being bad. Reminding me I was going to Hell if I didn't straighten up (maybe that's why I have good posture).

After the closing prayer, I sprang from my seat like a launched rocket and wove my way through the slow-moving traffic toward the front door. It would be at least a half-hour before breakfast was ready. A feast of eggs (fried or scrambled), pancakes, bacon, ham, sausage, sweet rolls, muffins, and toast. All you could eat.

I slipped out the front door. The sun was warm. Buds were slowly opening on the trees, the grass was turning green from the dormancy of winter, yellow crocuses were in full bloom around several houses in the neighborhood, and the birds were chirping a song of spring. The temperature would become consistently warm in a few weeks. And what a welcome relief from the blustery, cold and snowy winter we had just survived. A week of seventy-degree weather would erase from our memories the frigid temperatures and blizzard-like conditions of the past winter. But the warm weather could never erase the memory of what happened to our community.

I moved around to the west side of the church and sat down on the steps. The town was quiet; no horns blowing, no lawnmowers mowing, no kids playing, only the sweet music of birds chirping. The townsfolk were either in church or still in bed. The saved or the sinful, as my mom would divide them.

All the men of the church gathered at the foot of the steps, some sneaking a quick puff off a cigarette away from the watchful eyes of their wives. There were few things I would rather do than sit and listen to the older men talk.

Rich Dickerson's stomach growled as loudly as a bear defending her cubs. He patted his stomach with one hand and said, "Hang on. I'll feed you in a minute." The men laughed, which wasn't anything new. We were always laughing at Rich. The more we laughed the more exaggerated and ornery his stories became. It wasn't uncommon for grown men to be doubled over at the waist, tears pouring from their eyes as Rich finished a story, straight-faced as a preacher in the pulpit. His wife, Jeannie, tired of his orneriness, would shake her head and leave, long since giving up the hope of changing him. Rich was a big man, but he was all boy.

Rich told stories about growing up in the small town of Lebanon, Indiana and his favorite hangout, the funeral home. I'd heard Dad and his friends talk about their hangouts, like the soda shop, or a lake, but never (until I met Rich) had I heard anybody talk about hanging out at a funeral home. I had asked him what he did when there was a dead body. He said without hesitating, "We dealt him a hand and put a cold beer in the coffin. We ain't too good for nobody."

"Did Margaret cook anything?" Dad asked Russell Fisher.

"No," Russell said while cupping a cigarette in his hand. "I'd warn you if she did."

Everybody laughed.

Russell was a dedicated family man and an obedient man of God. But his dedication to his wife, Margaret, ended when it came to her cooking. It wasn't that she was a bad cook; that would be too nice. She was the worst cook ever. Couldn't ask for a nicer person, but she couldn't spread peanut butter on a slice of bread without making it taste like tar paper. About one Sunday a month in the summer, the members of our church would gather for a potluck dinner, rotating the host each time. The first thing anybody did at the dinners was search out Russell to find out what Margaret had brought. The hushed whispers spread throughout the crowd, "Don't eat the chicken salad. It's Margaret's." Identifying Margaret's contribution was as much a survival instinct as breathing. Thanks to Russell's kindness and understanding (Lord knows he understood, he ate her food every night), many a sour stomach was averted and many a dog made happy.

"You guys ever going to catch Drollinger?" Roger Johnson asked.

I was sitting at the top of a series of steps that led into a never-used side door of the church.

"He's up to somethin'," Dad said, his foot resting on the bottom step, hands buried in his pants pockets. "You know they found Smith last week in Lexington, Kentucky?"

"Yeah," Roger said. "I read that in the paper."

"They were hopping trains," Dad said. "Heading back this way."

My body shuddered, like from a cold chill. Drollinger heading back this way?

"Coming back to Indiana?" Rich asked, his stomach growling louder than ever.

"I don't know what the hell they were doing," Dad said. "I think they were heading back this way."

I cringed, waiting for a bolt of lightning to part the sunny sky and zap my dad dead. Slipping and using cuss words was a forgivable sin (thank God), but I didn't want to test my luck on the steps of the church. Sacred ground. The house of God. That's not to say from time to time that sinful thoughts didn't run through my head while sitting in church. They did. But I fought them off, knowing good and well that if I continued to undress women in my mind, the floor of the sanctuary would open and swallow me into Hell.

"Where had they been hiding?" Russell asked.

"Florida," Dad said. "Right before Stonebraker was arrested, Drollinger and Smith caught a ride to Florida with a lady Drollinger was messin' around with."

I scooted away from Dad. Love ya, dude, but if lightning strikes, you're going on to the next life by yourself. I had too much unfinished business in this life.

"They stayed in the Daytona Beach area with her until the FBI found out where they were staying. I think it was one of her relatives. Smith and Drollinger had already fled. The lady had called home to check on her older daughter and Smith's stepbrother said Drollinger and Smith were wanted for murder. The local police actually had Drollinger and Smith surrounded in a swamp, but they got away somehow. Then they started heading north for some reason."

"How did they end up catching Smith?" Russell asked.

"I guess they got separated," Dad said. "They found Smith walking along the railroad tracks in Lexington, Kentucky. He's pretty young-looking. Couple railroad workers thought he was a runaway."

"Sure was," Rich said. "Running away from murder."

"Do you think Drollinger is back around here?" Russell asked, his voice an even mixture of concern and curiosity.

"Wouldn't put anything past Drollinger," Dad said. "Never know what's going through that boy's head. It would be hard for him to hide around here. His picture had been plastered on the television and newspapers for the last two months."

Jeannie Dickerson raised a window on the church and hung her head out, "Breakfast is ready, you guys. Let's eat."

I stood and descended the steps while brushing the dirt off my pants. Russell flipped his cigarette butt across the street. I watched it bounce, end over end, sparks flying each time it touched the asphalt pavement.

"I've been living around here all my life," Russell said. "And I still can't believe something like that could happen here."

CHAPTER FOURTEEN

Dad was sitting in the green recliner in the living room, newspaper spread across his legs like an apron, a cup of coffee in hand. I walked into the living room and plopped down on the couch, still clad in my Dallas Cowboy pajamas. The Phil Donahue Show was on the television, holding Dad's attention as Donahue sprinted up and down the aisle, throwing his microphone to people in the audience for their comments.

"Hey, sleepyhead," Dad said when he finally saw me. "Think you can sleep all day because it's spring break?"

"It's only nine o'clock," I said, wondering why I had gotten up so early. "Where's Mom?"

"She went shopping," Dad said as he folded the newspaper in half and laid it on the table. "What do you want for breakfast?"

"Cereal," I said.

"Cereal?" Dad asked. "That's all? Don't you want some eggs or pancakes?"

"Only if we're going to Vance's," I said. "Not if you're cooking."

"Oh, you're nuts," he said. "I'm a good cook."

"I don't think so." I sat up. "Last time you cooked eggs, I had to eat them out of the pan." I remembered it like it was yesterday. Mom had gone to Florida with some of her friends and I nearly starved to death over the next few days. If it hadn't been for Kenny Vance, I wouldn't have made it.

"Okay," Dad said and threw his arms up in the air in defeat. "If that's the way you are going to treat me, then get dressed and we'll go up to Vance's for a pancake."

I dressed quickly and met Dad outside. He stood next to his police car, watching the cows file into the barn to eat. The sun was shining but there was a chill in the air. The chill of an early spring morning. I figured by lunch it would be warm enough to play outside in a sweatshirt. Baseball season was around the corner and I needed to start loosening my arm for the grueling Little League season.

Vance's Café was as quiet as the funeral home, except for the occasional clank of a pot or pan being washed in the kitchen. The dirty dishes were the only evidence of a morning rush hour. I ordered a pancake and a glass of chocolate milk. Dad drank coffee and made small talk with Wally Poore and Kenny Vance. I devoured the pancake like I hadn't seen a meal in weeks, chugged the chocolate milk, burped quietly to myself, and then waited at the front door for Dad to pay. Then it was down the hill to Wart Weaver's Filling Station for a splash of gas.

Dad parked his car at the pumps and we walked inside the station which was more like a condemned building. Wart was sitting behind the counter, red faced as usual. He didn't jump to his feet like a man grateful for a little business. As a matter of fact, he never made a movement other than to nod his head as we walked inside.

I walked over to a chair near the door and plopped down. Dust exploded from the pillow. That pillow had probably been sitting in the same chair since Dad was a kid. A trip to Wart's always involved more than a tank of gas and a clean windshield. It was a place to test out new gossip from Vance's. It was the perfect place to pass along the rumors as townsfolk gassed up for a trip to Crawfordsville or on their way home.

Out of boredom, I glanced at the newspaper lying on the makeshift end table. Just as I was starting to look away to find something else to idle my time, my eyes locked on the photograph on the front page. I picked up the paper slowly, eyes focused squarely on the photograph; all else around me faded away. There he was, the man (beast) that had masterminded the slaughter of four boys less than four miles from my house. His hair was long and greasy, and parted perfectly down the center. A bushy beard hid most of his face. But his eyes—piercing evil eyes—glared from behind his prescription glasses. No way of hiding those eyes. Even a black and white photograph captured the evilness inside this man.

"Hey," I yelled, interrupting Wart and Dad's conversation. "Drollinger was arrested."

"I know," Dad said. "I forgot to tell you. That's what Wart and I were just talking about."

The headline read, *"Drollinger Arrested by State Police after Hearing in U.S. Court."*[5]

> Roger C Drollinger was arrested by the Indiana State Police last night after a hearing in Federal Court in which the suspect in the Feb. 14 multiple slayings in Parke County pleaded unsuccessfully to be kept in Federal custody.
>
> Drollinger had surrendered to Federal authorities about six hours earlier, emphatically maintaining his innocence.
>
> Chief Federal Judge William E. Steckler released Drollinger on his own recognizance on a charge of unlawful flight to avoid prosecution, clearing the way for his arrest by state authorities in connection with the shotgun slayings of four members of a Hollandsburg family.
>
> The ruling came despite claims by Drollinger that the state police "would shoot me on sight" if he entered their custody.
>
> The twenty-four year old Waynetown man's attorney, Nile Stanton, expressed the same fear and claimed that the F.B.I. had assured him before Drollinger's surrender that he would be kept in Federal custody.

---

[5] "Drollinger Arrested by State Police after Hearing in U.S. Court," Indianapolis Star, 12 April 1977.

Choking in Fear

I felt a rush of cool air and heard the birds chirping as Dad and Wart walked out the front door of the station. I leaned up and looked out the window to make sure they weren't leaving me here by myself. Wart removed the gas cap on Dad's car, turned the pump on, and began filling the car with gas. God only knows what they were talking about now, I thought. I doubted it was Wart's son Gordon, better known as Gordy, who was notorious around town for window peeping with a mask and cape. A perverted version of Zorro. I turned back to the article.

> Another request from the defendant was, however, when Stanton, in a telephone call from Steckler's chambers, obtained an order from the Parke County Circuit Court stipulating that Drollinger be kept in the Marion County Jail pending trial in the slayings.
> Drollinger and Stanton had told Steckler the defendant would not be safe in jail in Parke County, where the murders took place.
> Drollinger, the last of four suspects in the slayings to be captured, surrendered at Stanton's office at 115 North Pennsylvania Street shortly before 1 p.m. yesterday. He said he was innocent of the crime and was returning to face the charges because he wished to be with his wife and young daughter and feared for their safety.
> At a brief press conference in the attorney's office prior to telephoning the F.B.I., Drollinger said his family had received many threats since a warrant was issued naming him as one of the suspects in the slayings of teen-agers Ralph, Reeve and Raymond Spencer and their stepbrother, Gregory Brooks, 22.
> Drollinger said he and David Smith, 17, Wingate, who was arrested March 31 at Lexington, KY, in connection with the slayings, were together on the

night of the crime and were not "close to that" (the murder scene).

Dad followed Wart through the front door and leaned against the counter as Wart ran the state-issued credit card through the imprint machine. Dad signed the receipt and grabbed his copy.

"What are you reading?" Dad asked as he sat down on a stool, forearms resting on his thighs.

I turned the paper and pointed to the picture of Drollinger. "Do you have a quarter?" I asked. "For the paper."

"Why?" Dad asked. "If I sit here long enough you can read the story for free." He flashed a smile in Wart's direction.

"Might as well," Wart said. "Everybody else reads it for free."

"I want to cut the article out," I said. "Put it with the other ones."

"Why are you saving all those articles?" Dad asked.

I shrugged my shoulders. I wasn't really sure myself. It just seemed like the right thing to do. I had been doing it since the first article was printed in the local newspaper. I could not explain why I was keeping the articles or why I watched the evening news on television each night. I had never read the paper (except the comic page) or watched the news before the murders. I'd rather have had Dr. Perry drill and fill a tooth with no painkiller than watch the news or read the paper three months ago.

But there was something different about this crime. It was more brutal than anything I'd ever heard of before, and close to home. I was almost the same age as the victims. There was something in the back of my head telling me to save all the articles, tuck them away, that one day I might better understand what had happened.

"I've got that paper at home," Dad said. "It's lying on the footstool in the living room."

"Okay," I replied. "Give me a minute." I scanned the article, searching for a the spot where Dad had interrupted me.

"There is no way I murdered anybody," said

Choking in Fear

Drollinger, his voice nearly breaking and barely audible much of the time.

He said he fled the state solely because he was not given the opportunity to have counsel present during a parole revocation hearing on March 2.

Drollinger was on parole on charges of assault and battery and intent to gratify sexual desires in connection with the statutory rape of his second and present wife, Kathy, 16.

The revocation was initiated because of later drug charges on which Drollinger is awaiting trial.

Drollinger said he fled to avoid revocation because "I felt I was being trapped. I wanted to get away and have an opportunity to think. I felt my family was in jeopardy."

Drollinger refused to disclose where he had been since fleeing the state except to say he had spent three days prior to his surrender in Stouffer's Inn on the near-Northside, where he stayed in his attorney's room.

Drollinger also described as "crazy" the first two suspects to be captured in the Hollandsburg case—Daniel Stonebraker, 20, Darlington, and Michael Wright, 21, Crawfordsville.

"They scare me," he said.

Asked if Stonebraker, an acquaintance who was linked to Drollinger by authorities in a Montgomery County theft ring, may have implicated him in the murders, Drollinger replied, "He's done it before in Montgomery County."

"You ready now?" Dad asked as he opened the door of the gas station.

"I reckon," I said. "You sure you have this paper at home?"

"Yep," Dad said out of the corner of his mouth, credit card clinched between his front teeth.

I jumped in the passenger side of the car, my mind spinning in multiple directions. Dad slid behind the wheel, pulled a magnet clip from the side of his police radio, and clipped the gas receipt to several others.

"Drollinger said he didn't do it," I said. "He said Stonebraker and Wright are lying."

Dad rolled his eyes and exhaled while he waited for a car to pass, then pulled out onto the highway. I stared at the hill above Wart's Station, where my great grandparents had lived, wondering about what kind of people they had been. Dad talked so fondly of his grandpa, a man I never met. Their house was long since gone, but I could picture my dad running around the hill, next to the pond as a kid.

"That's Drollinger," Dad said. "He's a liar. Lies about everything. Thinks the whole world is out to get him." Dad waved at Ed Cunningham as we passed the grain elevator. "He did it. I guarantee it."

I turned my eyes from Dad and stared out the passenger side window of the car, looking at the passing houses, the steep hill behind Cora Robinson's where we went sledding in the winter, thinking about the murders. Drollinger's arrest was indeed a relief, a weight lifted from my spirit. He was the leader, the mastermind, the one we feared the most.

My head hurt. Not like a headache or a migraine, but more like an overexerted muscle. My brain was tired, having focused so heavily on the murders for the past three months. The stranglehold had been released, but it would take days—maybe weeks—of breathing to recover. Yet in the depth of my mind, I knew we would never fully recover. Return to some sense of normalcy and function? Yes. Forget? Never. It happened here once and that meant it could happen here again.

CHAPTER FIFTEEN

Christmas Eve arrived quickly in 1977 according to my parents, although Christmas could never arrive fast enough for me. I loved Christmas. There were parties night after night for the week leading up to Christmas, mostly just get-togethers except for the annual school program, which consisted of well-rehearsed Christmas carols. And it was two weeks of no school. Two weeks of sledding out behind the house or behind Cora Robinson's house, drinking hot chocolate with marshmallow cream at the kitchen table while Mom baked, listening to Christmas music. And snooping for presents.

Mom and Dad scurried around the kitchen preparing for the Christmas Eve party we hosted each year after our church's candlelight service. Mom basted a ham that would be sliced for sandwiches while Dad mixed Seven Up, ginger ale, and sherbet in the punch bowl. By nine tonight, our two-bedroom house would be bulging with as many as forty friends and family members. Mardi Gras had nothing on a McCarty Christmas. I slipped stealthily from the watchful eyes of my parents into their bedroom for some last-minute snooping, just looking for confirmation that they had followed the Christmas list I had spent weeks preparing for them.

I looked under the bed. No, that was too obvious. Nothing. Then their closet. Wow, there it all was. Boxes stacked to the ceiling, all neatly wrapped. Then I remembered their hiding place last year and tiptoed across the bedroom to peek behind their cherry dresser and mirror. Last year, I found an orange boat-sled propped up behind the dresser. It was so well hidden that Santa Claus forgot to put it out Christmas morning and I had to remind my parents after all the gifts had been unwrapped. Nothing today. I had waited too long.

"What are you doing?" Mom asked. I jumped, startled. She was standing next to her bed, arms crossed, a stern look on her face.

Quick, come up with something, I thought. I shook my head like I was trying to orient myself. Yeah, I was dazed, delirious, lost.

"It's a little late for snooping," she said. "Everything is wrapped." I didn't fool her.

"I wasn't snooping," I lied and looked away. Why the heck did I say that, I thought. Why else would I be in their bedroom? Oh, maybe I should have told her I was checking Dad's dresser drawers for the latest issue of *Playboy*.

"You're busted." She grinned. "The presents are all wrapped. Now go get ready for church. Grandma and Grandpa will be here any time. Jeff just got here. He's out in the kitchen."

I walked out of their bedroom and into the kitchen. Dad and my cousin Jeff were sitting at the kitchen table talking.

"Nice haircut," I said sarcastically.

"How you doing, Bubba?" Jeff asked as he stood up and wrapped his arms around me. "You like that haircut? We can give you one for Christmas."

Jeff had joined the Marines last spring after graduating from high school in Rawlins, Wyoming. He was nine years older, but we had practically gown up together until Uncle Phil got a wild hair up his butt and moved Jeff and his brother Kert to Wyoming. We only saw each other once a year now, usually at Christmas. And it looked like this would be the last Christmas he could make for a while because he was shipping out to Okinawa after the holidays.

Jeff, Kert, and I had spent countless hours at our grandparent's home on the Tippecanoe River, some sixty miles north of here. It was a paradise on earth. Our grandparents lived on Tecumseh Bend, a winding drive that followed the course of the river. Small cottage-like houses lined the riverbanks. There was a nice balance of full-time residents and weekend retreaters. On weekdays, we owned the river: fishing, swimming, inner tubing, diving for shells. Weekends had a party atmosphere, as weekend retreaters arrived ready to unwind from a hectic week at work.

The riverbank sat not more than thirty paces out my grandparent's back door. It was a perfect location. A small tributary, never more than knee deep, separated the riverbank and a large tree-covered island. Just beyond the island was the heart of the river. After a week at Grandma Mett's and Grandpa Jim's, my skin would be leathery and bronzed from the sun and water. Every waking moment was spent in or near the water. The peacefulness and tranquility of the river permeated my body. The subtle comfort of being alone, floating on the water, with birds dancing overhead and singing happily and fish jumping from the water. It was a place to dream, to be anything in the world I wanted to be. And except for an occasional fishing boat, nothing to disrupt my dreams.

"Mike, you and Jeff need to get ready or we'll be late," Mom said as she hurried across the hallway from their bedroom to the bathroom.

Jeff handed me a duffel bag and asked me to take it into my bedroom. He went back out to his car to get the rest of his luggage. I slipped out of my sweatpants and sweatshirt and left them in a pile at the end of the bed. I dressed in blue dress socks, khaki pants, white oxford, and a red sweater before Jeff returned.

Jeff piled his belongings in one corner of the bedroom and then carefully unzipped his hang-up bag and retrieved his Marine uniform with the care of a surgeon's hands. He dressed slowly, meticulously, checking to make sure his button-up shirt lined perfectly with his zipper (he called it the gig line). How impressive. The toes of his shoes were polished to a mirror finish. All the gold and silver on the uniform sparkling in the light.

Grandpa Jim and Grandma Mett were sitting at the kitchen table when I came out of my bedroom, two steps ahead of Jeff. Grandma stood up and started breathing deeply as she looked at Jeff. I thought she was going to pass out. Wouldn't that make for a memorable Christmas, I laughed to myself. Grandma had a knack for the exaggerated.

"Why don't you wear something respectable?" Grandpa Jim asked.

Jeff smiled. "It's all I got."

Grandma hugged him. I stood still for several seconds. I wasn't quite sure what I was supposed to do. Crack a joke, hug Grandma, salute Jeff, or commit hara-kiri.

Grandpa broke the silence, a knack he was known for. Usually the silence breaker came from below his belt. Thankfully, tonight, he used his mouth. "Uncle Sam treatin' you okay?"

"He is now that boot camp is over," Jeff said. "No more drill sergeants up my rear end."

"Oh, just give them the old one finger salute," Grandpa said as he raised his middle finger to demonstrate.

Mom walked out of the bathroom just as the finger was fully erect.

"Daddy! What are you doing? It's Christmas Eve."

"I wasn't doing anything," he lied like a child caught with his hand in the cookie jar. "Mike and Jeff wanted to see my finger that doesn't have a fingernail."

Quick thinking, I thought. Good answer. He had a flair for saying just the right thing or saying it at the right time to get himself out of a pickle. Quick wit must be like fine wine, its gets better with age. Grandpa was Dom Perignon and I was still Boone's Farm.

Then again, it didn't hurt to have a middle finger missing a fingernail. I'm not saying it didn't hurt when a sewing machine ripped it off when he was a kid, but even Grandpa admitted those few days of pain were well worth the usefulness it had provided over the years. He had hundreds of photographs buried in shoeboxes with him flying the one finger salute just as the camera flashed. "Nope, I wasn't being a dirty old man," he said. "Just showing my disability."

As a matter of fact, just last week, Grandpa had been taunted into flying the one finger salute. We were parked outside Service Merchandise in Lafayette while Mom, Dad, and Grandma did a little last minute Christmas shopping. Grandpa and I stayed in the police car, tired of shopping. A carload of teenagers kept circling us, working up the courage to make a smart aleck remark, as usual. Then on the third pass, a pimple-faced kid hung out the passenger side window and screamed, "Pigs!" How creative, I thought. I was only ten, but I knew people didn't use the word *pig* anymore. Anyway, before the kid could finish, Grandpa leaned across the seat and flipped them off. The look on the pimple-faced teenager was one of stunned disbelief. I'm not sure if he was stunned by being flipped off by an old man in a state police car or if he was stunned by the stumpy middle finger with no fingernail staring at him.

That wasn't the first time Grandpa and I had had a little fun in the police car at Dad's expense. Last summer, we were packed in the car like sardines. Mom, Matt, and Grandma were in the back seat. Dad, Grandpa, and I were in front. The good ole days before the safety and security of seatbelts. Grandpa leaned over and dared me to hit the siren. It seemed like a heck of an idea and, since it was grandpa's idea, I leaned down and twisted the knob to "Yelp." Well, I should have given it a little more thought. Not so much because of how Dad would react—I knew that he'd be ticked off. It was one of those things you weigh quickly in your head: does the fun outweigh the consequences? Yes, in this case it did. However, I should have at least looked to see who was driving the car in front of us. The poor old lady was nearing ninety (Grandpa said she was darn near pushing up daisies after that). The minute I twisted the knob to "Yelp" and the siren screamed, the old lady almost dove through a chain-link fence at Alcoa. Steam rose from Dad's head like a teakettle about to sing. That's the moment I knew my butt was about to become his bass drum. I hoped he'd use his hand and not his foot to play it. Dad stormed up to the car, apologized for the mistake while flashing his angered eyes in my direction, waited for her pulse to drop below a thousand beats per minute, and then stomped back to the car. Grandpa stared out the passenger window, whistling nonchalantly like he had nothing to do with the present predicament. The scolding lasted all the way home—forty miles. Then Dad fired up my bass drum.

"Is everybody ready for Church?" Mom asked.

"Your dad says he doesn't feel good," Grandma said sarcastically. "He's going to say here and rest."

Here we go, I thought. Grandpa always got sick during the holidays, before church, before a family reunion or party. And he always recovered from the self-diagnosed cases of food poisoning, E coli, salmonella, and even cancer, faster than anybody in the world.

"Oh, get your butt up," Mom said. "It's Christmas Eve. You're not going to die."

"No," Grandpa said. "I better not take any chances."

Dad smiled at me.

"All right then," Mom said. "We'll be home in an hour or so."

"I don't feel good, either," I said. It was worth a try.

"You're going, young man," Mom snapped.

Grandpa walked into the living room, holding his belly with one hand. The piece of acting deserved an Oscar. I followed him into the living room just to let him know I knew he was full of crap, envious that he didn't have to go. "You don't look sick."

"It's a stomach thing," Grandpa said while contorting his face. "I nearly crapped my pants on the drive down here."

"You could put on one of Matt's diapers," I said. Then I remembered how much noise he made when he was in the bathroom. Not the kind of interruption we needed at the candlelight service.

"I'll stay here and guard the house," he said. "May have a beer to settle my stomach." He grinned. I figured he'd be two sheets to the wind before we got back home.

"Come on, Mike," Mom yelled. "We're going."

The candlelight service was moving, as always. The church glowed from the white candles standing on each of the windowsills, the piano, the organ, and the elder's table. The candles added to the warmth of the season. I sat with my parents. This was the only service each year when we kids relinquished our rights to the back two rows. The service was not prepackaged, but informal. The men of the church stood and told of how God had blessed them and their families in the past year. Communion was passed and we concluded the service with several Christmas carols, ending with "Silent Night, Holy Night," which we sang while holding burning white candles. Scalding hot wax dripped slowly onto my hand, making it hard to concentrate on the lyrics or Baby Jesus.

Fifteen minutes after leaving church, our house bulged with friends and family. My first order of business, against my mom's direct order, was to peel my dress clothes off and put my sweats back on. She'd be too busy to notice anyway. A ham sandwich, handful of potato chips, couple of gulps of punch, and then it was time to party. The adults congregated in the kitchen, dining room, and living room, talking, laughing, and telling stories. The alcohol wouldn't surface until later in the evening, when most of our friends had retreated home to wait for Santa Claus. The rear of the house, the two bedrooms, was the designated kid hangout. We ran, whistled, played games, listened to records, and talked about what we hoped to get the next morning for Christmas.

At 11:30 P.M., the party took its final breath. I was lying on the couch in the living room, hung over from playing hard and eating too many sweets, exhausted, but excited about Christmas morning. I watched the taillights disappear on the last car as the Kings pulled out of our driveway. Mom and Dad were cleaning up the remaining mess of paper plates, plastic cups, and napkins. I had already cleaned the bedroom area.

Dad walked into the living room with a half-filled garbage bag in one hand. He fished several old newspapers out of the wooden magazine rack next to the recliner and looked through each of them before throwing them in the trash bag. As he started out of the room, he dropped a paper on my chest and said, "you may want to cut that article out." He pointed to an article.

I glanced at the headline of the article, *"Stonebraker Gets Life Terms."*[6] It was yesterday's paper. I walked in the kitchen, grabbed the scissors from the utility drawer, and cut out the article. I wadded up the rest of the paper in a ball, screamed to get Dad's attention,

---

[6] Dick Robinson, "Stonebraker Gets Life Terms," *Crawfordsville (Ind.) Journal Review*, 23 December 1977.

and then shot the make-believe ball across the kitchen, off of Dad's chest, and into the garbage bag he was holding.

"You need to get to bed," he said while tying the top of the bag. "Santa won't stop if you're still awake."

"I'm going," I said, playing along even though I knew the real Santa Claus was holding the garbage bag in our kitchen. I staggered off to my bedroom. I retrieved the manila folder of articles and laid it on my bed before plopping down on the bed to read the new article. The murders were still headline news, but not daily front-page news since the arrest of all four suspects. It seemed each month there would be several days of coverage during a trial. The trials had been scattered all around the state because of some crazy legal claim that the killers couldn't get a fair trial around here. I'd heard many a man in town say he could institute a little justice. I reckon they'd received better treatment than they'd given Greg, Raymond, Reeve, Ralph, and Betty Jane nearly ten months ago. The joy of the evening evaporated as my heart ached for Mr. and Mrs. Spencer. Their first Christmas since the murders.

I turned the reading light on next to my bed and adjusted the pillows under my back before reading the article.

> Almost 11 months after the bloody massacre of four Hollandsburg brothers, Clelland Hanner, Parke County prosecutor and John Dowd, his deputy, closed the case Thursday in Decatur County when Daniel Stonebraker of Darlington was sentenced to life in prison.
>
> Stonebraker was the last of the four defendants in the case to be sentenced for the Feb. 14 shotgun slayings of Raymond, Ralph, and Reeve Spencer, and their stepbrother Greg Brooks.

"Are you still awake?" Mom asked as she peeked into my room.

"Yes," I said. "I'll go to sleep after I read this."

"What are you reading?" she asked.

"This article on Stonebraker," I said pointing at the black and white print. "He was sentenced to prison last week."

"I don't think there is anybody on the face of this earth that knows more about those murders than you," she said. "Hurry up and read that and get to sleep. It's after midnight."

"I'm almost finished," I said. "Good night. Love you."

"Love you, too," she said and then left. I turned my attention back to the article.

> Stonebraker's plea agreement. He was sentenced to two life sentences and two fifteen to twenty-five year sentences for his participation in the murders. Then the judge granted the request of Stonebraker's attorney that his client be confined in a different institution than Roger Drollinger, since Stonebraker had testified against Drollinger. The judge agreed.

"Lights out," Dad said as he passed by my door on the way to bed.

"Okay," I said, meaning "Don't rush me." "Okay."

I read quickly, before Mom and Dad came in and shut off the lights.

> In an interview on the jailhouse steps, Stonebraker admitted he was fearful for his life and didn't want to be in the same prison as Drollinger. Gibson (Stonebraker's attorney), in his comments to Judge Westhaver, said Stonebraker was the only member of the gang who tried to talk Drollinger and the others out of "killing somebody" and only agreed to go along with the others after they made a pact to "kill or be killed." Stonebraker said he knew Drollinger was not kidding when he pointed a gun at him and ordered him to shoot.
>
> "I don't know what it was like," Stonebraker

said commenting on the murders of the four Parke County brothers.

"It was weird and kinda strange. I just can't say what happened. Sometimes I think it didn't happen."

"If I had it to do all over again, I would not have gone into that house," said Stonebraker.

I put all the articles back in the envelope and laid my head on the pillow and stared at the ceiling. The envelope was bloated from the articles. There were articles collected from the day of the murders, the manhunt, and the arrest through both of Drollinger and Smith's two-week trials, and now to Stonebraker's plea agreement. I still didn't understand how people could kill just for the heck of it. What leads people to kill? I had learned a lot about the murders over the past ten months, but I still had a ton of unanswered questions that I needed answered for my own peace of mind. And I finally realized that the only people who could answer those questions were the four guys convicted of the murders. I couldn't quite picture myself talking to any of the killers.

I decided to sleep in my sweatpants. It was easier and it would make opening presents in the morning much quicker because I wouldn't have to waste five minutes getting dressed. Plus, if I had to get up in the middle of the night and flee, I was ready.

I reached up and shut the light off. The house was quiet; there was not a sound. I started my nightly prayers: "Now I lay me down to sleep, I pray the Lord my soul shall keep, if I should die before I wake—"

I stopped as my mind drifted back to the murders. The prayer was more than words. Dying was actually a possibility. It did happen to kids my age. Quit thinking about it, I thought. The killers are all locked away securely in prison. But a part of me knew that this story would never really be over until the haunting questions in my mind were answered.

"I pray the Lord my soul shall take." And I wasn't convinced the Lord would want me.

PART TWO

RESCUED ADOLESCENCE

CHAPTER SIXTEEN

I was sitting on our front porch, my back against a brick pillar, when I heard the familiar engine race. Grandpa Jim sat back in the porch swing, arms stretched across the back of the swing, chomping on a wad of chewing tobacco. He and Grandma had moved to Waveland last year after he retired and bought a small house at the bottom of the town hill, next to Cunningham's elevator. Since that time, Grandpa had been coming to our house every afternoon to sit on the front porch, drink iced tea, gossip, and watch the even flow of traffic on Main Street. Grandma always stayed at home to watch her "stories" on television in peace and quiet.

The silver Buick threw gravel from the neighboring driveway as Carl negotiated the change from horseshoe-shaped gravel driveway to asphalt pavement at full throttle, never slowing to check for an oncoming car or a mother pushing a baby stroller on the sidewalk. The engine roared like an airplane taxiing down the runway preparing for takeoff. Townspeople stopped dead in their tracks when they heard the roar of Carl's engine, a sound as unique as Elvis's voice. Being a neighbor and knowing Carl better than most, I was even more cautious. I always stopped at Carl's trailer, like at a street corner, looked down the driveway for any sign of Carl. Then walked past. Chuck Yeager had nothing on Carl Hannah. I did worry about the poor visitors wandering through town, though. They were vulnerable to becoming Carl's hood ornament.

As Carl drove past, he smiled and waved before blasting the horn. Not an ordinary horn, but a horn that played the Dixie fight song like on the television show *Dukes of Hazard*. He was pushed all the way against the back of the seat, standing straight up in the car, accelerator smashed between his foot and the floorboard. He had two speeds: stopped or breaking the sound barrier.

"I'll be damned," Grandpa said. "Whatya think his hurry is?"

"Probably going to the grocery store," I said while I watched him disappear up the street.

"Carl's gonna kill somebody one of these days," Grandpa said. He leaned forward and spit a line of black tobacco juice off the porch into the shrubbery. "Boy's nuttier than hell behind the wheel."

"Or kill himself," I replied.

We had adopted Carl as our neighbor almost four years ago, shortly after my eleventh birthday. My parents, tired of living in a rented house in the country, had purchased a two-story brown house on Main Street. It was the first house that was really ours. It was great. The house came with my own bedroom on the second floor, complete with a walk-in closet and an exterior door with an attached staircase. My bedroom used to be the kitchen for an upstairs apartment. I thought the attached staircase would be my pathway to freedom, but my parent's first home project put an end to those dreams. They tore it down and put a window where the door used to be. Escape route sealed. My social life destroyed.

Carl, in his mid-thirties, lived next door in a yellow mobile home with his parents, Raymond and Mildred. Raymond was a soft-spoken man who moved gingerly around their property in his trademark faded blue overalls and white T-shirt. I'd never seen him dressed any other way. Mildred passed the days keeping an eye on the neighborhood while running her full-time garage sale called Millie's Place and smoking Winston cigarettes. Carl relied heavily on his parents for food, shelter, and clothing. Raymond and Mildred relied on Carl for transportation. And boy, did they get their money's worth.

Carl could drive, though that was open for debate, but he didn't have the capacity to live on his own. He depended heavily on medication to keep his thoughts balanced. And invariably, once a year, Carl would become belligerent and refuse to take his medication. This would lead to a frantic knock at our front door. On one occasion, it found Carl standing at the foot of my parent's bed in the middle of the night, crying uncontrollably before running out of the house. Dad had given chase, but Carl had gotten a sizeable head start since Dad had to get dressed first.

It seemed Dad was the only person Carl trusted at these times. Often, Carl would run off into the woods behind their mobile home. I would scurry throughout the neighborhood rounding up my friends for a game of hide-and-go-seek Carl. We never actually found Carl on these missions and were not sure what we would have done if we had. However, the incidents always ended the same way, peacefully, with Carl loaded onto a stretcher and into the back of an ambulance, carted off to the Veteran's Hospital to get his medication regulated.

Some rumors in town had it that Carl was drafted in the Army to go to Vietnam and was so overcome with homesickness when he was shipped off to boot camp that it screwed up his mind. Others said that idea was crazy, that Carl had always been that way. It was just something he was born with, no fault of his own or the government. Either way, Carl was Carl and it didn't really matter to us why he did the things he did. We liked him no matter what.

Almost as soon as Carl's car had disappeared, it reappeared. He was smiling from ear to ear as he flew past the house. At the last possible moment, he locked the brakes. It was like watching an airplane land, when the tires make their first contact with the pavement. There was a screech and a cloud of smoke, then the Buick disappeared on the other side of the mobile home.

"He's hard on brakes," Grandpa said, still staring off into the distance where Carl had just landed only seconds before.

"You ever ridden with him?" I asked.

"Hell, no," Grandpa said, like I was nuts. "Nobody in their right mind would get in a car with Carl."

"I went fishing with him once," I said. "Down at Tannenbobs."

"Your mom and dad let you get in a car with him?" Grandpa asked.

"Yeah, they didn't care," I said. Maybe they really didn't like me. "We were going so fast on the gravel road that the trees were a blur. I just closed my eyes and started praying."

"Tannenbobs?" Grandpa asked. "Where's that at?"

Grandpa and I had done a lot of fishing since they'd moved to Waveland, mostly out at Lake Waveland. I'd never taken him to Tannenbobs.

"It's out in the middle of nowhere. Not far from the Spencer house. Where the boys were killed a few years ago."

Grandpa raised his eyebrows and puckered his lips together like a fish. He knew exactly where I was talking about.

"Did you catch any fish?" Grandpa asked.

"Heck, no," I said. "Didn't have time to catch a cold. I barely got my line baited when he got bored and was ready to leave. My heart was still beatin' hard from the ride over there. Back we went, pedal to the medal. Praying all the way."

Carl walked around the side of the mobile home. He had an unusual gait. With each step he would rock from his heel to the tip of his toes. He was still smiling from ear to ear. If a stranger had just witnessed Carl's driving escapade, they would be convinced he was showing off. But we all knew he drove like that all the time. Rain or shine. Ice or snow. School zone or interstate.

"Hello, Carl," Grandpa said as Carl walked onto the porch and sat down in a folding chair.

"Hi, Jim," Carl replied. "Hi, Mike." His voice was childlike.

"Where'd you just go?" I asked.

"Grocery store," he said. "I was out of Cokes."

Carl placed hundreds of people at risk every day when he slid behind the wheel and made one of his many trips through town to the post office, the grocery store, gas station, or for a fifteen minute visit at a friend's or family member's house. The visits never exceeded fifteen minutes. Carl would be up, out the door, and squealing his tires. But that was Carl. And we all knew that if we had anything important to tell him, we had better do it quickly.

"How'd you like my horn?" Carl asked. "It's like the *Dukes of Hazzard*."

"It's pretty cool," I said. It wasn't me and I didn't see myself asking for a horn like that next fall when I got my driver's license. But I had to admit it was unique; nobody else in town had one.

"It plays seven different tunes," he said.

"Cool," I said again for lack of anything better to say, certain that before the day was over, I would hear the other six tunes.

"Did you ever think about becomin' an ambulance driver?" Grandpa asked.

Carl laughed, sort of a "tee-hee" kind of laugh. Then he jumped up. "Here, Mike, I got something for you."

I waited for him to fish the surprise from his pocket. Carl always had gifts to give away, especially at the first of each month when his disability check arrived. He would spend most of the money on cheap jewelry. By the end of the month he would try to pawn the stuff, but always ended up giving it away because nobody wanted it. Like the time he tried to sell Grandpa McCarty a watch for twenty dollars. Grandpa said no, he didn't need a new watch, his was fine. Then Carl came back twenty minutes later and lowered the price to ten dollars. Grandpa again said no. Then Carl came back an hour later and tried to give it to Grandpa.

"Here," Carl said. "It's an Indian necklace."

"Thanks," I said and looked at the turquoise rock shaped like an arrowhead hanging on a long chain. I could picture the rock splitting my head wide open as I forgot I was wearing it and took off running.

"Hi," Grandpa said and I turned my head to see who he was talking to. It was Stan Ivy.

Stan was walking down the sidewalk, delicately, like he was walking on thawing ice. Too much pressure and he would fall through. His lips were pursed and arms swinging back and forth, wrists cocked upward. The perfect stereotype.

When Stan was out of listening range, Grandpa said, "He's a little light in his loafers, ain't he?"

"Grandpa," I said. "Don't make fun of him. That's Carl's boyfriend."

Carl laughed, tee-hee. "He ain't my boyfriend." He squirmed in his seat nervously.

"That's not what I heard," I said. "I heard he likes your butt."

Carl was moving nervously, though he never was one to sit still very long. To the best of my knowledge, Carl had never been with a girl and I sure couldn't picture him with a man. Anyway, we all knew that Stan had a boyfriend. They would walk past on the weekends. His boyfriend didn't live around here.

"Is that right?" Grandpa chimed in.

"I better go," Carl said as he fled the porch like it was on fire. "See ya later."

"Stay out of trouble," I said.

"Carl's all right," Grandpa said. "When he's not driving. He means well."

We sat in silence for a few minutes, listening to the sounds of summer. Lawn mowers humming in the distance. Children playing. Birds chirping. This hiss of lawn sprinklers.

Dad interrupted the silence when he walked out of the house and sat down in the chair Carl had just vacated. He was still dressed in his state police uniform and clutching his handheld radio. "What's going on out here?"

"Hello, Thomas," Grandpa said with a salute. "Take anybody to jail today."

"Almost," Dad said. Then he burst out laughing.

"What's so funny?" I asked.

"I almost locked your buddy Roland up," Dad said. "Shoulda put his little butt in jail."

"What for?" I asked.

"Smoking pot," Dad said while shaking his head. "He was up at the grocery store, talking on the pay phone and smoking pot. Broad daylight. I know he can't see, but everybody else in town can see."

What was so funny about that? I thought. We all knew that Roland smoked a little pot. "Did he try to run away?"

"Roland?" Dad asked rhetorically as if I had lost my mind. "Where would he run to? He didn't even see me pull up next to him. I could have run him over and he would have never known what hit him." Dad laughed again, one of those guess-you-had-to-be-there laughs.

Roland and I had attended school together since the first grade. He was a good-natured young man considering the disadvantages life had thrown his way. We were still in grade school when his father passed away on the couch in their living room. Roland had tried to wake him for dinner. This loss put a real financial burden on the family.

But Roland's real problem was his eyesight. He was legally blind. Could barely see five feet in front of himself. I had seen him ride a bike into trees and telephone poles because he didn't see them in time to swerve. So it was not surprising that he hadn't seen Dad pull up to the pay phone.

"Did you take him to jail?" I asked.

"No," Dad said. "I just scared him a little bit. Took him for a long drive around town. He thought he was going to jail. I tried to get him to tell me who was selling him the pot."

"Are blind pot smokers the only kind of druggies you can catch?" I asked.

Dad grinned. "You remember when you guys played Little League together?" Dad asked. "The game down at Marshall?"

"Yeah," I said. How could I forget? The first three innings of the game were fairly uneventful. They had one of the fastest pitchers any of us misfits had ever seen. My buddies and I were more concerned with getting hit by the ball than hitting the ball. Then, for no apparent reason, the opposing coach took the pitcher out in the third inning. My dad saw this as a great opportunity to get Roland some playing time. He had to be careful because of Roland's poor eyesight. But every kid deserved to play. Roland was the first batter to face the new pitcher. Our mouths were hanging wide open when the pitcher threw the first pitch. He threw faster than the pitcher he replaced. The first pitch landed upside Roland's head. Sounded like somebody thumped a watermelon. Roland went down, spread-eagled. I was convinced he was dead. By the time we reached him, Dad had asked him if he had even seen the ball. Roland said, "No, but I sure felt the wind." Then he jumped up and ran to first base like nothing had happened. He shook it off; we shook it off, returned to the dugout, then started laughing. There was one thing for sure, Roland would not get the signal to steal second base. Then again, it wouldn't matter if he did; he couldn't see my dad giving the signal from the third base coach's box.

During the same game, Richard Brown was playing left field. Or, I should say, he was standing in left field talking to his dad who was standing along the left field line. The batter hit a line drive that was headed straight at Richard's head, which was turned, facing his dad. We all screamed. Richard turned and in self-defense caught the ball with is bare hand. An amazing catch. I guess he had forgotten he had a baseball glove on his other hand.

But Richard had always defied the odds. About this same time, rumor had it that Mikey from the Life Cereal commercial had died after eating Pop Rocks candy and drinking a Coke. Richard ate two packages of Pop Rocks, drank a coke and did flips around his front yard. Several of us had gathered on his porch, anticipating an explosion.

My thoughts were suddenly interrupted by the sound of a Buick taxiing around the gravel driveway. Carl was off and running again. This time his horn sounded like a cow in heat. I made a mental note to tell Carl not to play that when he was driving through the country. He might cause a stampede. And I wasn't sure what the mix between a silver Buick and cow would look like.

CHAPTER SEVENTEEN

The heat on the pavement was hot enough to fry an egg. Welcome to July in Indiana, with temperatures averaging near ninety with smothering humidity. Occasionally, Mother Nature would tease us by exhaling slightly, stirring the humid air, and ruffling a few leaves in the trees. Just enough to break the stillness and raise our hopes.

I walked out our back door, basketball shoes in one hand and a bottle of water in the other. I sat down on the top step and laced my shoes, looking around the neighborhood for any sign of life. Nothing was moving. Smart people were inside enjoying the air conditioning or out at Lake Waveland swimming. Didn't matter a lick to me; since we didn't have air conditioning, it was as hot inside as outside. My small window fan, as noisy as Carl Hannah's car, circulated the hot air in my room all night while I tossed and turned on top of the sheets.

I was sixteen and facing my final two years of high school. Working on my basketball skills this summer was going to pay off, my coach Ron Henricks claimed. It would make the difference between me attending college on a basketball scholarship or on a parental scholarship. My parents favored the basketball scholarship. We all knew academic scholarships were out of the question. There were just too many things to do other than spend every night studying.

I sat the bottle of water on the picnic table, in the shade, and jumped up and down on the basketball court to stretch my legs. Dad and I'd had a lot of fun pouring the court by hand last July. How could I forget the fun?

"Mike get up," Dad said, standing in my bedroom doorway dressed in

Choking in Fear

blue jeans and a white T-shirt.

I looked across the room at my alarm clock with one eye.

"It's only seven," I said. "You trying to kill me?" I closed my eyes.

"Get up," he said. "Grab some breakfast. I'll be outside. We gotta beat the heat."

I stumbled out of bed like a drunkard and wobbled to the bathroom. I had slept in a pair of shorts, so I grabbed a T-shirt and my tennis shoes and headed downstairs, one step at a time like a baby learning to walk. Mom had left a blueberry muffin on the stove. I ate it, gulped down a glass of orange juice, then headed outside to meet Dad.

Dad was removing the framing around the cement we had poured yesterday. "You ready to go?"

"Not really," I said.

"Well, let's go get a load of sand before it gets too hot," he said.

I walked across the driveway to his green truck. And what a Cadillac of a truck it was! It had a top speed of thirty-five miles per hour because it hadn't seen a front-end alignment in years. Any speeds above thirty-five would cause the truck to shake violently. The brakes barely worked, and with a ton of sand in the back, they didn't work at all. For Dad, this wasn't a problem, but a challenge. All you had to do was throw the truck in neutral a half mile before stopping if somebody pulled out in front of you. But that was part of the excitement, Dad claimed.

"I'll be glad when we're done," I said, leaning against the passenger door, wind blowing through my hair. I had already offered to quit basketball if we just didn't have to pour the basketball court. Dad said that was my choice (before he knew I could get a scholarship) but that we would still pour it for Matt.

Dad tuned the AM radio to a country station - Conway Twitty, Merle Haggard, Tammy Wynette and the likes - and off to Herman Teague's we went like we had done every day for the past week. A twenty-minute drive, Dad endured it because Herman only charged a dollar a ton for sand if you scooped it yourself. The key was getting to the sand early in the morning before the sun had scorched it. By mid-afternoon, a single bead of sand could burn your flesh like a hot coal.

We loaded the truck and drove home. Dad worked the mixer, adding equal parts of sand and concrete mix with water. Then we poured it into the frames. It was hard work.

"That's it," I said as I watched Dad work the trowel over the final section of the basketball court. "We're done."

"Could you get me the broom?" Dad asked. "It's over by the truck."

I grabbed the broom and gently pushed it across the freshly poured cement for texture." How long before we can play on it?"

Dad wiped the sweat from his forehead with the back of his hand. "Probably need to cure for a week or so." He said it matter-of-factly, like he'd poured cement all his life.

I faked right, spun left, and drove to the basket. Then I retrieved the ball, made the same spinning move, but pulled up for a fifteen-foot jump shot. The sun was so hot I could feel it burning through the layers of my tanned skin. That was really all the discomfort I needed to call it day. I loved to play basketball, but hated to practice, especially in the summer when the sport of the season was swimming and chasing girls in two-piece bathing suits at the beach at Lake Waveland. Come on now, we all know there's more to life than bouncing a rubber ball and shooting it through a ten-foot basket (but you better be careful saying that in Indiana or, for that matter, around my dad).

As the ball swished through the net and bounced across the pavement, I saw Grandpa Jim putt-putting down the back street in his blue station wagon. The only time the car shifted out of first gear was when Uncle Phil was in town. He prided himself on blowing the cobwebs out of Grandpa's cars. Unfortunately, he'd wrecked a couple of them in the process. Grandpa Jim parked behind Dad's police car, got out, and walked on bowed legs over to my other grandparents' home behind ours.

Grandpa McCarty was sitting on the front porch, where he spent

Choking in Fear

most days, in the shade of a huge elm tree, sipping on a plastic cup of Pabst Blue Ribbon Beer and listening to the Chicago Cubs on his portable radio. It didn't even matter if the game was on television; he preferred to listen to the game on the radio like he had since he was a kid. When fall rolled around, he would move inside his car to listen to the games, his plastic cup of beer resting on the dashboard and bottle of whiskey under the front seat for those particularly cold days during the play-offs. He used the whiskey to warm up his beer.

Beads of sweat trickled down my face and fell from my chin. I figured that was enough training for one day. I rolled the ball toward the back door and wiped the sweat from my face. I walked across the back street, which dead-ended in front of my grandparents' home, and sat on the wooden fence surrounding their front porch.

"I bet you don't even make the team this year," Grandpa McCarty said without so much as raising an eye. He was hunched over the radio and looked like an old man that didn't have the strength in his neck to raise his head. A piece of rusted wire served as the radio's antenna.

"Bull crap," I said. I had to sneak visits with Grandma and Grandpa McCarty since Dad and Grandpa had a falling out a year ago and weren't speaking. Not any easy thing to do when we almost shared a driveway. I knew the issues ran much deeper than the minor spat that precipitated the silence. When Dad was at work, I'd slip over and talk with Grandma or shoot the bull with Grandpa. And I knew Grandpa listened to my ball games on the radio, my Aunt Tracy told me that much. I watched the strained looks on Dad and Grandpa's faces as they tried to ignore each other while practically living together. Whatever their problems were, they weren't mine.

Grandpa McCarty raised one eye and smiled. "You'd never have made the team back in my day. Ain't that right, Jim?"

"Hell, no," Grandpa Jim said. "You had to be a man to play ball back in our time. Probably wouldn't even let you carry our jock strap."

I rolled my eyes and told myself I would never tell my kids or grandkids that things were tougher when I was a kid. But I knew I probably would. That's how things worked. Teasing was the way we men expressed our fondness and love for each other.

"Who's winnin'?" Grandpa Jim asked, taking a seat in a fold-out lawn chair.

"Cubs," Grandpa McCarty said. "At least right now. It's only the sixth."

"I'm going to get something to drink," I said. That excruciating twenty-minute workout had drained my body of vital fluids. A cold glass of water and a few minutes in front of the fan and I should be fine.

"Here," Grandpa McCarty said as he raised his cup of beer. "This is what you need."

I nodded my head in a manner that said, "Yeah, right." "You'll be coming up to Servies's to view my body if Mom and Dad smell beer on my breath."

"You don't know what you're missing," he said while shaking his head.

"That stuff you drink isn't beer," I said. "That's deer piss."

"Oh, that's good beer," Grandpa Jim said.

I smiled and shook my head. It was hard to take the word of a man who drank Red White & Blue beer, a brand the groceries practically gave away on sale. I said good-bye and was on my way back across the basketball court when Matt came roaring across the back yard on his minibike. He was trailing Mikey Reynolds.

"Did Grandpa tell you what happened?" Matt asked through bursts of laughter.

Before I could say no, Mikey shouted, "We ran into your grandpa's car!"

"Which one?" I asked.

"McCarty," Matt laughed. Spit was flying from his mouth every time he tried to talk.

"Did you hurt the car?" I asked, then thought about what I had asked. Grandpa McCarty prided himself on never spending more than five hundred dollars on a car. A bulldozer couldn't hurt Grandpa's car.

Choking in Fear

"No, but it scared the shit out of your grandpa," Mikey said, smiling from ear to ear. Streaks of dirt painted his face.

Surprisingly, hearing Mikey cuss like a sailor didn't shock me, even though he was only four years old. He was a little turd. I think the "f-word" was the first thing Mikey said as a toddler. Then he graduated out of diapers and into smoking his dad's cigarettes out behind the church. Mikey had no fear of church or God. Just last year, he was straddling the armrest on a pew near the front of the church, facing backwards, riding it like a motorcycle while Glen McFarland, our preacher, gave the sermon. Then we made eye contact and he gave me the one finger salute. Every woman in the church turned to the back row to see who was corrupting this poor innocent child. There was also the time he was standing in the vestibule of the church while his mom talked with Glen McFarland. Mikey tugged on her coat, tired of waiting, then said, "Hurry up, Mom. I'm freezin' my ass off." I nearly bit a hole in my lip.

"Was he sitting on the porch when you hit the car?" I asked.

"No," Matt said. He was laughing so hard that spit was bouncing off my chest as he talked. "He was driving down the street."

"How the heck did you hit him?" I asked.

"We were coming out of the alley by the church," Matt looked over his shoulder and pointed in the direction of the church, "I looked back and didn't see him coming. I smacked right into his driver's door. I was going like a hundred."

"You're probably lucky he's had a couple beers," I said. "Otherwise he'd have had a heart attack."

Matt laughed, kick-started the minibike, and threw dirt as he went up the hill in our backyard, across the basketball court and down the back street.

I walked in the back door, through the laundry room, and into the kitchen. I was standing at the refrigerator, door open, searching for something to drink, but nothing really appealed to me. Dad walked into the kitchen.

"That's not an air-conditioner," Dad said as he sat down at the kitchen table and started shining his black uniform shoes. He had to go to work in an hour.

"Who's out front?" I asked, grabbing a bottle of orange juice and tilting it to my lips.

"Don't drink out of that," Dad said. "Get a glass. We don't want your germs."

I gulped several more times, then placed the orange juice back in the refrigerator. "Who's outside?" I asked again. He hated it when I ignored him. And he especially hated it when Matt or I would drink out of the milk and juice containers. Mr. Particular.

"Betty Spencer," Dad said. He was shining the toe of a shoe. "She's talking to your mom."

"From the Hollandsburg murders?" I asked.

"Uh-huh," Dad said.

It had been six years since the boys were murdered. And though time had passed, the memories of the crime were still fresh in my mind. There were constant reminders. Like Geno's neighbor, Harold Escue. Every time I mowed Geno's yard, I would watch Harold as he piddled around in his yard or helped his wife Para run her store, Para Lee's, in their garage. I always wanted to ask Harold about the night of the murders. What it was like to have Betty Spencer at your front door in the middle of the night, towel wrapped around her head to stop the bleeding, shotgun wound to her back and screaming that her four boys had been killed. I wanted to know how scared he was that night and every night after that, because he moved to town shortly after the murders. No doubt because of the murders. But I never trekked across the street to ask Harold the questions. I knew they were personal. And I didn't know exactly how to ask such personal questions of someone I don't know that well. A lot of people had tried to forget about the murders, or acted like they'd forgotten about the murders. Harold was one of them. I knew he and all the others might have stopped talking about the murders, but they could never erase it from their memories.

"What's Mrs. Spencer doing here?" I asked. I would have been less surprised if he had told me that President Reagan was on the front porch.

"Talking with your mom," Dad said as he dipped the tip of an old T-shirt into a glass of water and worked the black polish into the toe of his shoe until he could see his reflection. "She's trying to get your mom to come down to Rockville and work with her."

"Work with her doing what?" I asked.

"She has started a group to work with victims," Dad said. "I'm not exactly sure what else."

Grandpa Jim walked in, said hi to Dad, poured himself a cold glass of tea, and started for the front porch. His afternoon hideaway.

"She still lives around here?"

"Yep," Dad said. "Still lives in the same house where her boys were killed."

How creepy, I thought. I walked through the dining room, the living room, and out the front door. Grandpa was rocking slowly in the porch swing, not interested in what Mom and Betty Spencer were talking about. I took a seat on the cement edge of the porch, across from Mom and Betty.

Mom and Betty looked up when I sat down.

"This is our oldest son," Mom said, "Mike."

"Hi, Mike," Betty said. "Nice to meet you."

"It's nice to meet you," I said. I felt myself staring. I studied her face, comparing it to the pictures I had cut out of the newspapers six years ago. She looked about the same. Memories of the murders flooded my mind as I looked at her. This was actually the mother of the murdered boys, I told myself. Sitting on our front porch.

What must it have been like? I thought. I was not listening to Mom and Betty talk. Betty had testified that she felt Greg, her biological son, die next to her, defenseless to do anything about it. My heart was thumping like it had six years ago when every sound in the night would fill me with terror.

My thoughts were interrupted when Carl pulled from his driveway, motor racing, and blared his horn. Grandpa saluted him. Mom didn't even look up.

Betty told Mom about what she had been doing since the murders. She had created a nonprofit program called Protect the Innocent that provided assistance to victims of violent crime by lobbying for changes in laws. She was starting a new program, Protect the Innocent Victim Advocate Foundation, which would provide direct services to victims of crime in an eight-county area. She wanted my mom to come work with her.

Mom administered the Victims' Assistance Program in our county prosecutor's office. She worked with victims of crime, mostly domestic violence victims, preparing them for court and directing them to social service agencies. She also served as an adjunct probation officer for some of the first-time offenders (theft, bad checks) who were placed on pretrial diversion.

Grandpa stood up. I held my breath for a second, waiting for him to hike his leg and make the sound he called "tree frogs chirping." Thankfully, he didn't step on a tree frog, but walked to the edge of the porch and spit a line of tobacco juice. "Do you want some?" he whispered in my ear, and laughed.

I shook my head. Heck, no. From time to time, when Dade stopped by, I would take a pinch of Copenhagen snuff. But not chewing tobacco. I had learned my lesson years ago, and Grandpa knew it.

Betty stood up and asked Mom to consider coming to work with her. She said she and Keith were planning a move to Hawaii so she would need somebody to run the programs. I wanted so badly to open the floodgate of questions in my head, to ask her everything about the murders. To find the answers to the questions that had been tugging at me for six years. But, just like with Harold Escue, I didn't know how to ask such personal questions of Betty.

Betty turned to walk away, then stopped and stared at me for several seconds. I didn't know exactly what to say. I felt awkward. Her eyes were distant; she had the look of a person daydreaming. She didn't say anything. Then she snapped out of it, smiled, turned, and walked to her car. She had noticed something in me. Maybe I reminded her of somebody. Then it hit me. I was about the same age as her youngest stepson Ralph. She probably wondered what he would be doing today.

CHAPTER EIGHTEEN

The light from the street lamps strained its way through the low-hanging branches. There was just enough light to see, but not too much light to expose us. The shrubbery jutted out from the house, forming an L-shape, providing more concealment. Perfect. Let the games begin.

Jerry crouched on the far side of the street, near my front porch. Calvin Hubble and I were in the shrubbery across the street, next to Hunt's house. The black string in my hand was attached to my mom's purse, which lay in the road with play money hanging out.

Noel Porter was our first victim and I wish he had been our only victim. I had known Noel all my life. We went to the same church, the same church functions, but I really didn't know him at all. Actually nobody knew Noel. In my sixteen years, I had never heard him speak a word. I wasn't sure if he could not speak or merely chose not to speak. An "odd bird" was how I'd heard him described around town.

Noel drove past. His brake lights blazed as he slowed to turn around. I was so excited I almost jerked the purse from the street. I could hear my heart thumping in my chest. He came back, stopped in the middle of the road, and rolled down his window, inspecting the purse with the same intensity a bomb expert studies a bomb, searching for clues or booby traps.

My heart raced, waiting for Noel's next move. Then he pulled his car to the side of the road and stepped from behind the wheel. He paused, looked in every direction, then walked over to the purse, no expression on his face (there never was). My sweaty hands had a death grip on the string and I could feel my heart beating in my clenched fingertips. Noel glanced around again, then bent over to grab the purse. I pulled on the string gently. The purse scooted slowly across the pavement. Only a few inches. Not enough to frighten him. We didn't want him to run. Not yet. Noel bent over, stepping closer to the purse, surely thinking he had just miscalculated how close he was to the purse. It was dark.

When he bent over the second time, intending to pick up the purse with both hands, I jerked the string like a fisherman hooking a fish. The purse jumped through the air and landed in the shrubbery. Jerry howled like a hyena. Noel, startled, sprinted to his car, made a U-turn and threw gravel as he sped away. Calvin and I rolled over on our backs, screaming in laughter.

We threw the purse back in the street and waited for the next victim. Several cars passed without even tapping their brakes to inspect it. A large truck ran over the purse and I wondered how I was going to explain the scuff marks to my mom. That's when we moved to plan number two. We cut the string in half and tied each string around the neck of a Coke bottle. Jerry was responsible for the traffic heading west. Calvin and I handled the eastbound lane.

I heard the hum of an approaching car, but didn't have time to look up at the vehicle. I was concentrating on the tires and timing the jerk of the string to coincide with the arrival of the tires. Perfect timing.

BOOOM! It sounded like a shotgun exploding.

"Oh, crap," Jerry yelled from across the street.

I leaped to my feet, scared that we had punctured the tire on the car.

"Son-of-a-" Calvin said. "That was Rosco."

"We need to get the hell out of here," Jerry said.

"No," I said. "Wait." I watched the car disappear down the street.

"He's not coming back. He probably thinks he just ran over a bottle." Which he had. But we needed some reassurance he had not seen us or the string on the bottle before we hunkered back down in the shrubbery and waited for the next victim.

Jerry shrugged his shoulders and placed his bottle back in the road.

We waited and waited, but no cars. My legs started to cramp from crouching so long. But before I could stand, a monstrous shadow leaped through the shrubbery. I froze in my tracks for a split second before the shadow reached out and grabbed Calvin and me by our shirt collars and banged our heads together.

"Quit, you asshole," Calvin hollered. The monster banged our heads together again. All I could make out between head knocks was a badge and a gun belt. The gun belt was brown, so I knew it wasn't Dad. Plus, Dad wouldn't bang our heads together. It wasn't his style. Then the gorilla-like person stood us up, still holding our shirts tightly, and led us from the darkness, across the street toward my house.

It was Paul King, better known as Rosco, after the bumbling deputy sheriff from the *Dukes of Hazzard* television show. Paul was the town marshal of Waveland, which meant he had police powers only within the town limits and at Lake Waveland. It was a part-time position, mostly nights and weekends. Waveland didn't have enough crime to justify a full-time position. Town marshal pay was very low, but that didn't keep Rosco from taking his job seriously.

"Rosco, let go of me," Calvin said as we were being marched across the street. "I'll kick your ass." Paul and Calvin knew each other well enough for Calvin to talk like that. Paul cracked our heads together again.

It had only been last summer that Calvin's oldest brother, Junior, nearly killed Paul. I was outside that night when people came running up the street, screaming for Dad, freaked out because Junior had Paul in a headlock, screaming he was going to kill him. Off I went, running down the street as fast as my legs would carry me. It had been a long time since anybody around here had been killed. Seven years to be exact, since the murders down the road in Hollandsburg. But this night, there was nothing strange about the crime. Paul King and the Hubble's were like family. This was a domestic dispute.

Halfway down the street, I could see the throng of people standing at the mouth of the Hubble's driveway. Sure enough, there were Junior and Paul locked in a position you were accustomed to seeing in a bedroom, not a driveway. Yet there was no mistaking that this wasn't a love grip. There was an electricity in the crowd, a mixture of fear and humor. Some laughed or smiled. Others yelled at Junior to let go of Paul. But I don't think anybody really thought Junior would kill Paul. Maybe whip his butt. Then again, if Junior was tripping on something heavy, you never knew what could happen. And Paul had a gun in his holster.

Dad negotiated with Junior, in his aw-shucks Andy Griffith voice and one hand in his front pocket. Junior finally let Paul go and was carted off to jail. Paul had barely caught his breath when the gathering of townsfolk started taking shots at him: "Watch out, Rosco or I'll sic Junior on you." Paul would never live this down. Small towns have long memories. Anyway, it had been the most excitement in town since the last time Carl had run off into the woods.

But this time, Paul had won. As we stepped onto our porch, Dad was standing there with Jerry.

"I've never seen Jerry's fat butt move that fast," Dad laughed. "He actually vaulted the fence in the backyard."

"Why are you staring at my butt?" Jerry asked.

Dad laughed. "Couldn't miss something that big."

"You boys need to get home," Paul said with the same authority as the President of the United States declaring war. "I oughta take you to jail."

What for? I thought but was smart enough not to say. I didn't want Paul to bang my head with Calvin's again.

"Okay, Rosco," Calvin said, using the voice of Rosco P. Coltrane from the *Dukes of Hazard*. He walked off the porch, toward home. Jerry was off the porch and heading the opposite way toward home.

Paul put one leg on the porch and began scratching his butt. No, not scratching. You scratched a mosquito bite. Paul was digging, really digging. Nothing casual about it either, like when your underwear rides high and you make one quick, unassuming motion to release the death grip your buns have on your underwear. No, Paul was onstage, digging so hard at his butt that I was afraid he would loosen his gun belt and drop his pants so he could use both hands. I waited for him to stop so I could inspect his fingernails. From a safe distance.

"Got an appointment over at Mooresville," Paul said. "These freakin' hemorrhoids are killing me."

Dad laughed. What else could you do? Definitely avoid shaking his hands for one thing. Ooh. Then I thought about how Paul's hands had been all over my head, face and neck as he dragged us from the shrubs across the street. And he had been driving around town all night with his hands up in his small intestines.

"You oughta see this thing I got in my car," Paul said. "I use it to scratch my ass."

I wrinkled my nose. Why the heck would anybody want to see the tool he used to scratch his butt? I could only imagine what it smelled like after weeks of soothing his aching hemorrhoids. It reminded me of a kid I had played basketball against last season. He was wearing a white uniform but had a large brown skid-mark up the back of his shorts. I assumed he had been doing some digging in the locker room and forgot he was wearing a jock strap, not underwear.

Mom walked out onto the porch.

"Hi, Sherri," Paul said, still clutching his butt with one hand.

"Hi, Paul," Mom said. "Mike, phone's for you. It's Darin Gregg."

I walked in the house, picked up the phone, and then asked permission from Mom to stay over at Darin's. She said yes. I gathered an overnight bag of clothes and left out the back door. Darin was standing up town, on the corner where Vance's Cafe' used to be. Kenny and Phyllis had closed the restaurant and started a catering business. Two more restaurants had opened, the Money Tree, better known as Wild Bill's, and the Waveland Cafe', though neither would ever compare to Vance's. The food was okay, but you could never duplicate the atmosphere at Vance's. It was hard, I had to admit, to beat the portions of food at Wild Bill's. I'd never seen that much food on a plate before. And Bill had as much grease in his hair and under his fingernails as he had in the food. I always kind of had this mental picture of him out back, changing the oil in his baby-poop green van, when his wife hollered out a food order. He'd wipe his hands clean of engine grease on his soiled apron, step back in the kitchen, and prepare the food to order. And boy did he hate the idea of competition. To heck with capitalism and a free market. He was a darned Nazi, eager to kill off the competition and anybody else that got in his way. I found out the hard way one day when he saw me coming out of the other restaurant (I only ate there because Wild Bill's was closed). He refused to serve me after that. That ticked me off. Wild Bill had never heard the phrase "the customer is always right." They'd never mentioned that at the mental hospital before his escape. Eventually, he went so far as to issue membership cards to his loyal customers. Waveland's first version of a country club.

"What's up?" Darin asked.

"Not much," I smiled. "My head's killing me. Rosco just bashed my head in."

Darin laughed and asked what had happened.

I told him what we had done. He laughed harder, said he wished he had been there. Then he told me how he and Sean Moser had almost gotten caught spying on Julie Johnson earlier in the evening. Darin and Sean had been outside talking to Julie. When she went inside to bathe, Darin climbed the television antennae to look in her bedroom window. Unfortunately, Julie's sister Janie saw Sean, yelled, and then gave chase. Poor luck for Sean since Janie ran cross-country. Darin kept quiet, waited for the smoke to clear, and walked back home across the street.

I smiled, glad they hadn't seen anything since I wasn't there.

We were in no hurry to get to Darin's, so we walked down Main Street to the northwest corner, across from the Narrow Door Liquor Store. Ruby Dale was standing behind the counter, staring out the window. I waved; she smiled and waved back.

We sat down on the edge of the building that protruded out. No way of telling how many hours I had spent sitting on this corner, watching traffic pass through town, talking with my friends, pondering the future, what we were going to do after high school. I figured I'd go to college, then come back to Waveland and raise a family.

This was the greatest place on earth and I couldn't picture myself anywhere else.

Darin and I sat side-by-side, tossing rocks into the road. Traffic was sparse, an occasional eighteen-wheeler grinding through the gears climbing the town hill. The street was empty, except for Elmer Huxhold's orange Chevy Vega. Elmer and the orange Vega were as much a nightly fixture on Main Street as the street lights themselves. I don't think he ever went home, except maybe when his wife wasn't around, to shower and change clothes. He did have a home, a wife, and two sons. But he always chose to sleep in his car along Main Street. It didn't matter if it was one hundred degrees or sixty below zero. He just enjoyed the freedom of the street, I reckon.

Darin's older brother Mark came roaring down the street in his car and locked his brakes when he saw us on the corner. I stared at him as he rolled the window down. "Darin, Mom said you guys need to get home." He squealed his tires and disappeared over the town hill. No wonder he'd wrecked so many cars, I thought.

The clock above Elston Bank read nine-thirty. Too early to go home. Then we saw Paul King's small squad car turn onto Main Street. We weren't doing anything wrong-it wasn't past curfew-but after my earlier head knocking party I didn't want to test my luck. My head ached. We jumped up and hid behind two large trash cans, moving slowly around the cans as Paul drove past. As his taillights disappeared over the hill, we shot across the street and down the alley next to the town hall. Party's over, I thought as I ran down the dark alley. Boy was I wrong.

We were standing in the street in front of Darin's house under the streetlight when Mark opened the door and yelled, "Mom said to get your asses in the house."

"Shut up, Mark," Darin yelled.

I knew Judy, their mom, had not said asses. She didn't cuss (or if she did, I'd never heard her). She probably hadn't even told Mark to yell at us to come in. But Mark had been drinking a little bit. He disappeared into the dark house. A split second later he was back, standing in their front door, dressed only in white briefs, a shotgun in hand. A real Kodak moment. I ran across the street, behind a large tree in Johnson's front yard. Darin was on my heels.

"Get your asses in here," Mark screamed. His voice carried through the still night. I figured lights would be coming on in neighboring houses.

I peeked around the corner of the tree just as Mark leveled the shotgun at us. I drew my head back and held my breath as the still of the night was shattered by the explosion of the shotgun. Branches in the tree, only inches above our heads, were falling, landing on our heads.

"Mark's lost his mind," I said, my heart beating so hard in my chest that it hurt. "Run before he loads the shotgun again." I ran down the street, not a straight line, but in a zigzag pattern so it would be hard to shoot me.

We stopped and caught our breath about two blocks away, behind Russell and Margaret Fisher's house. Then we heard the roar of a car. It was Mark.

"We need to get to my house," I said.

"He's drunk," Darin said. "Mom's gonna kill him."

"The hell with your mom," I said, my tongue so dry it stuck to the roof of my mouth. "He's gonna kill us."

We sprinted through backyards, hands in front of us to ward off low-hanging clotheslines. When we made it uptown, we had no choice but to run out in the open, well-lit-street. I listened for the sound of his car, but didn't hear anything. That didn't mean he wasn't close, though. He could be sitting around the corner, ignition off. Plus it was hard to hear over the beating of my heart and our panting breaths.

"Let's run toward the store," I said while pointing. "It's dark on the other side."

Darin nodded his head. I surveyed the calm night, looking and listening for a sign of Mark. No sign of him.

"Let's go," I said.

We ran across the street and were walking close to the front of Hunt's Electric toward the grocery when I heard the squeal of Mark's tires as he pulled onto Main Street. I dove behind a trash can, next to a Coke machine, and hit my already aching head on the metal can. Darin squeezed in tight behind me.

The engine screamed as Mark flew down the street, then slammed on his brakes. The squeal of tires was deafening. I could see smoke rising from the street in front of us. I didn't move. I couldn't; my legs were shaking and weak. If I heard his car door open, we were out of here.

Where was Rosco when you needed him? Probably parked in a dark alley soothing his hemorrhoids.

After a few seconds, which seemed like hours, he drove off. Darin and I ran around the corner of the store and sprinted the three blocks to my house.

Dad was sitting in the kitchen, television on, finishing some paperwork and listening to his police radio. "What are you guys doing out this late?"

"Nothing," I said, still panting.

"Mark tried to kill us," Darin said. "He shot at us with a shotgun."

I was amazed that nobody in town had called the police. It wasn't every day that somebody fired a shotgun in town at midnight. Not since Drollinger, Smith, Wright, and Stonebraker busted into the Spencer home just past midnight, lined them up on the floor, and executed the four boys and left their mother for dead. Since that early morning, when a shotgun was fired out of context, like late at night, people heard it and took notice. That's why I couldn't believe our phone wasn't ringing off the hook. Better safe than sorry. But nobody called. Maybe they had pushed the murders out of their memory. Yet, I couldn't imagine that ever happening.

Dad shook his head, thinking we were exaggerating.

"Call your mom," I said to Darin. "Tell her you're staying here."

I slumped down in the rocking chair near the television. Legs shaking. Exhausted. But glad to be safely at home. Glad to have survived.

CHAPTER NINETEEN

Snow floated from the dark, gray, wintery sky like leaves from trees in the fall. I stood on our basketball court, mouth opened wide, catching as many of the snowflakes as possible. Though it didn't quench my thirst after a two-hour basketball practice, the cool wetness on my face was refreshing. The peacefulness and tranquility of the nighttime snow shower was revitalizing. The stillness and solitude of winter. It was so quiet it seemed I could hear the snowflakes landing on the ground. The snow also carried with it the hope that school would be cancelled in the morning. That hope always put a bounce in my step.

I walked in the back door, slung my mesh bag of sweaty practice clothes on the bench, and went into the kitchen. Dinner sat on top of the microwave, the plate wrapped in plastic wrap. I removed the plastic wrap, slid the plate in the microwave, and went to the refrigerator for a glass of iced tea.

"Are the roads slick?" Mom asked as she walked in the kitchen.

"Nah," I said. "It's not that bad." I had finally gotten my driver's license three months ago. What a relief. I was one of the youngest people in my class and, while everybody else had been driving to school and going on dates, I was still being chauffeured by my parents. I warmed the plate of fried chicken, mashed potatoes with white gravy, corn, and a roll in the microwave and ate it like it had been months since my last meal. Then it was off to the living room for a little television. I had purposely scheduled a study hall first period so that I wouldn't be burdened with a lot of homework. I hated carrying all those books home. And I would much rather lounge on the couch

Choking in Fear

or in my room with a true crime book or a Joseph Wambaugh novel.

I was sitting on the bench of the bay window in our living room, waiting for the evening news to end, when I saw something move out of the corner of my eye. It was Carl Hannah. He walked back across the street, toward his parent's mobile home. He had just left the Payton brothers' house.

Carl was the only person I knew who had been inside the Payton house. At least, he was the only one who had lived to talk about it. The Payton house was an Alfred Hitchcock kind of place that townspeople avoided at all costs. Not once since we had moved to town, five years ago, had I seen a Girl Scout approach the house to make a cookie sale. I had watched people cross the street to avoid walking directly in front of the house. But Carl Hannah was a different story, a trusted insider. I reckoned the Payton brothers might have been the only two people in town who really understood Carl. And Carl was definitely the only person in town who understood the Payton brothers.

Bill and Bob Payton were interesting characters. They lived catty-cornered to us in a dilapidated house. At a glance, it looked to be abandoned. The house was always dark; there was never a glow from a reading light or even a candle. The front porch leaned to the east. The moldy, gray look of the rotting wood added to the aura of the house. The raw wood had not seen an ounce of paint in decades. I could only imagine what the inside looked like. Unkempt, bushy shrubs grew around the porch, adding to the intrigue. You never quite knew what was on the other side of the bushes.

However, it wasn't the spookiness of the house that scared most people. It was the Payton brothers themselves. They lived in near total seclusion. The first day of each month was the exception, when they would pull from behind their house in their beat-up yellow car and make the rounds. They'd pick up their disability checks from the military and social security at the post office, go to the bank to cash them, to the liquor store for a month's supply, and then back home. Most of their food was grown out back of their house. They didn't smile or wave as they drove past, but looked straight ahead. On a mission. Uncomfortable with being out in the light.

Like bats, the Payton brothers conducted most of their business after dark, fearful of the light. Many a hot summer night I had lain awake in bed listening to them mow their yard at midnight, hitting sticks, rocks, and anything in their way (thank God they didn't own a weed eater). Drunker than Cootey Brown. And it was so dang normal, nobody complained. Some nights they got so drunk they needed some fresh air, like the night they took their car for a spin in the pasture out behind their house with no headlights, and hit a tree stump at thirty miles an hour. We didn't hear much out of them for a few weeks.

Then there were the nights they would scream out - deep, stinging, visceral screams. Subhuman noises. On one such occasion, I sneaked across the street and tried to peek in a window. My heart was beating as loud as a drum, fearful they would throw open a window and shoot me with their shotgun. I knew they owned a shotgun because they had used it to kill a rabbit recently (unfortunately, the rabbit had been tucked against Hunt's house when they splattered it). That night I had fought off my fears and stayed at the window, dying to know what in the heck went on inside the house. It was so dark inside and out that I couldn't see anything. After a few minutes of futile staring, I ran back across the street to the safety of our front porch where Matt and our cousin Mark were waiting, wide-eyed, certain I wouldn't survive the mission.

"What'd you see?" Mark asked.

"They're corn-holing," I lied. Matt and Mark's eyes bulged as they looked at each other, mouths hanging open, then back at me. "Never seen anything like it."

"I thought they were killing each other," Matt said.

"Nope," I said. "Must be out of Vaseline."

Matt and Mark stared at the dark house, unable to speak, no doubt picturing the Payton brothers wrestling naked. Truthfully, nobody in town knew why the Payton brothers screamed out in the middle of the night. I tended to think it had to do with their homemade brew. But the unknown left a lot to our imaginations. And at

Choking in Fear

sixteen, I had quite an imagination.

"Mike," Mom said, interrupting my daydream." I need you to carry in a box out of the car."

"All right," I said and stood up.

I walked out the back door, across the snow-covered basketball court, to the trunk of mom's car. I lifted the trunk lid and stood still for a moment, head tilted toward the sky, mouth open. The snowflakes landed cold against my face and melted quickly. The sky was dark. There was nothing more peaceful than a snowy, winter night.

Headlights interrupted my thoughts.

Dad pulled into the driveway and shut off his state police car.

"What are you doing?" Dad asked while stepping around the back of his state police car.

"Grabbing a box for mom," I answered.

He was adjusting the volume on his portable police radio.

"How are the roads?" I asked.

"Pretty slick," he said.

Not the response I was hoping for. Horrible. Drifting shut. Impassable was what I wanted to hear. "Good," I said. Slick could always turn into impassable. "I could use a day off from school."

"It's hard to say," Dad said. "They are calling for high winds later on tonight, though. If that's the case, the roads will drift shut."

"That's what I wanted to hear," I said.

"You can ride with me in the morning," Dad said. "I go on duty at eight in the morning."

"No, thanks," I said. "I still have nightmares about Exit 25."

"Oh, you big wuss," he said. "That was nothing. We made it didn't we?"

"Barely," I said. "After the state highway snowplow pulled us out of the snow bank."

Dad shook his head, smiled and headed toward the back door and the warmth of our house. "Let me know if you change your mind," he said over his shoulder.

There would be no reconsidering.

The Exit 25 fiasco happened in late January 1978 during the famous blizzard of 78'. School was closed for almost two weeks starting on January 23 when five inches of snow fell on central Indiana. The initial burst of snow was followed up with another fifteen inches of snow over the next two days, wind gusts up to sixty miles per hour, and wind chill temperatures as low as fifty below zero. We had a snow drift in front of our house that reached over ten feet high. Nothing moved for many days. The only way to rescue the sick, injured or elderly was by snowmobile.

After several days trapped in the house, the state highway plow made its way to our driveway and dug us out so my dad could get the state police car back in service. Dad invited me to go to work with him even though it violated the Indiana State Police policy about riders (let alone the fact that I was only ten years old).

We cruised the main roads since none of the secondary roads were open. Then we got onto I-74 heading westbound. That's when it all happened.

"Do you think we can make it?" asked Dad. He pointed to where an exit ramp was supposed to be.

He's kidding, I thought. I could barely see the exit sign peeking out of the snow. It looked like a buoy floating on the water.

"I think we can make it," he said.

I felt the car accelerate and veer toward the exit.

"No way," I screamed. The snow looked to be five feet deep.

"We can do it," Dad said.

I had a fleeting thought that he was kidding. Of course a professional law enforcement officer would not endanger his son and himself. He had to be teasing.

Then the car veered right quickly and the nose burrowed into the snow.

Total white-out. The police car stopped. Complete silence.

When my heart rate dropped below seven-hundred beats per minute, I asked, "What are you going to do now?"

Dad grinned. He thought we should have made it. He grabbed his police radio and requested a snow-plow to Exit 25.

I smiled to myself and shook the snow from my hair and

reached back into mom's trunk for the box she had asked me to bring inside. I clutched the box in one hand, slammed the trunk lid shut with the other and jogged through the snow to the house.

"Here's the box," I said after slipping my snow-covered shoes off on the back porch and setting the box on the kitchen table.

"Thank you," Mom said. She reached into the box and pulled out a stack of old, yellowed newspapers. "Here, these are for you. Geno wanted you to have them. She found them in her basement."

"Okay," I said. "Thanks." I wondered what newspapers Geno thought I would want. Maybe the sports page if my picture had been in it while playing basketball.

I retreated to my room with the newspapers tucked under my arm, turned on my stereo and plopped down on my bed to study the old newspapers. I thumbed through each paper, reading the banners on the front page. The newspapers were over seven years old and chronicled the Hollandsburg murders. I had saved many of the articles as a young child, but there were several here in the stack that I had missed. I adjusted the pillow behind my head, leaned back, and began a journey back to a time we would all liked to have forgotten, but couldn't.

CHAPTER TWENTY

I walked through our back door and dropped a bundle of dirty clothes on the laundry room floor. The house was still, no music blaring, no voices from the television. That's strange, I thought. It was Friday afternoon. Mom worked Monday through Wednesday at the prosecutor's office. Dad was supposed to have a rare weekend off. Maybe they ran into Crawfordsville for some groceries. Nobody shopped in Waveland any longer since the Coleman's sold their grocery.

I poked my head into each of the downstairs rooms - living room, dining room, front room - checking for any sign of life. Nothing. Mom's car was parked in the driveway, you couldn't miss it. The mocha brown Buick Electra was the size of a Sherman tank. I remembered the day they brought the car home. I was standing on the basketball court when Mom pulled in the driveway, her head barely visible over the dashboard. I doubled over at the waist, laughing uncontrollably.

I was one of the few kids in high school who never asked to borrow their parents' car. Driving it wasn't so bad, but parking the beast was another thing all together. Parallel parking a semi would have been easier. Actually, it was a dating machine for a teenager. There was enough room in the backseat to do wind sprints from door to door. As a matter of fact, the owner's manual even boasted that the car would sleep six, four comfortably. And that's the reason Dad had bought the car in the first place.

He didn't need anything fancy (though Grandpa Jim likened the

Choking in Fear

car to a Cadillac). It was economical. And with the state-issued police car, my parents only needed a second car for Mom to drive and for vacations. Plus, this car doubled as a recreational vehicle.

I vaulted up the steps two at a time, around the corner and into my bedroom. Nobody was upstairs. My bedroom was starting to look more like Matt's room since I had moved back to my college dorm room. He was moving in slowly, a piece of furniture here and there, staking his claim on the bigger room.

Two bags were lying at the foot of my bed. They weren't mine, and I didn't recognize them. Maybe Matt had a friend over for the night, I thought. No. He wasn't even out of school for the day. Plus, it looked like girls' clothing. Girls' clothing? In my room?

I walked back downstairs, turned the television in the den on, and plopped down in the gold love seat. I figured my parents would explain the bags in my room when they got home.

It wasn't long before I heard the crunch of gravel under the weight of Dad's patrol car as he pulled in the driveway. I walked out the back door and met them halfway across the basketball court.

"Whose stuff is in my room?"

Mom grimaced. "I forgot to call you." She glanced at Dad.

Dad flipped the trunk button and walked around to the rear of the car.

He didn't intend to tell me anything. I couldn't tell by the look on his face whether this was something serious or simple. Either way, he always passed the baton to Mom when it came to explaining certain things. I moved around to the side of the car, trying to get a better look at Dad's eyes. If it was serious, he'd avoid eye contact, like the time he came out of the bathroom, into the kitchen, thinking he and Mom were the only ones home, shaking his "thing." That poor Avon Lady lost all interest in selling Mom some lotion. I've never seen a door-to-door salesperson flee the scene so fast (still wasn't as fast as Dad's exit). Dad couldn't look us in the eyes for days. Or the time Matt heard screaming in the middle of the night. He listened. No, it wasn't the Paytons. It was Mom. He bolted out of bed like Superman and rushed into their bedroom, determined to save Mom from the clutches of death, only to discover she was in Dad's clutches. Mom screamed when she saw Matt at the foot of the bed. That was the night Matt learned the difference between the two screams. Dad refused to go in and give Matt the old birds and bees lecture. I guessed Dad figured, why give the lecture when Matt saw it live in action? What more was there to say?

"Okay," I said waiting for an explanation.

"Help carry the groceries in and I'll explain everything," she said. Dad and Matt were already carrying bags in the house.

I didn't like the feel of this. It had the same feel I had felt hundreds of times before I got into serious trouble. The calm before the storm strategy. Make Mike think everything was okay. Then, boom! You're grounded for a month.

What could I have done? I wasn't even living at home. There had been so many things over the years, though nothing serious. Practical jokes on neighbors, smoking cigars when my parents weren't home. Drinking a little beer since going to college. Nothing recent. And nothing that would warrant serious trouble.

I felt beads of sweat on my forehead.

"We have somebody staying with us for a little while," she said.

"Okay," I said, relieved it had nothing to do with me. "Who?"

"Shelly Smith," Mom replied. "She'll be using your room for a little while."

"Shelly Smith?" I asked. "Why Shelly?" That didn't make any sense.

"Well, we don't know everything just yet," Mom said. "But she has been abused by her dad. It's serious. Real serious."

"He's beating her?"

Mom glanced at Dad then back at me. "No. Sexual abuse. He's been molesting her."

Ugh, I thought. Sexual abuse? The same Shelly I went to church with? The same Shelly whose dad was a teacher? The same Shelly who was only four years younger than me? It made me sick to my stomach. But it didn't explain why she was staying here.

"Why is she staying here?" I asked.

"For her own safety," Mom said. "Her mom's scared. They called the police today. Her dad's going to be arrested. We're not sure how he'll react."

"Wow," I said more to myself than anybody else. I was floored. Speechless.

"Can you go back to school and stay?" Mom asked. "Until this is resolved?"

"Yeah," I said. "Sure."

This was not the first time somebody had knocked on our front door for help. It had happened many, many times over the course of my childhood. So many times that I found it a normal part of growing up. That's the price you pay when your dad is the only cop in town other than Rosco. The people my parents opened our doors to always seemed to be women and children fleeing from men who beat them, fleeing from men who molested their children, who hurt the people they claimed to love. But it had never been someone I knew so well.

I had been privy to a lot of violence growing up. Stories about violence were common at our kitchen table. It wasn't unusual to be sitting in our kitchen at two o'clock in the morning while Mom and Dad made phone calls, trying to find a woman and her child a safe place to stay. I'd heard my dad complain that there wasn't much good he could do as a police officer if the victim was too scared to file charges. The laws had his hands tied. He couldn't make the arrest. And most of the women were too scared to file the charges (and with good reason). They just wanted a safe place to stay. A place where their husbands or boyfriends couldn't hurt them.

There was no short supply of violence in Waveland, at least if you could believe everything you heard. In a small town, everybody knows everybody else's business, dirty laundry and all. I knew which men in town beat their wives or children. I saw these men at the post office, the grocery store, baseball games, driving through town. They really didn't look any different from anyone else.

It seemed that most of these men held onto the belief that ruling the house with an iron fist was the norm. Men who rarely set foot into church (not that all men who go to church don't beat their wives or children) quickly adopted misquoted Christian beliefs such as "man is the head of the household, women submit to your husband's" or "spare the rod and spoil the child." And being the "boss" was an inherent right of being born a man.

Only once had an act of violence really shocked me: the murders down the road in Hollandsburg. Those murders were so unlike the other violence that knocked at our door. It was random, perpetrated on unknown victims. It was so abnormal, so unlike the violence I was used to (or so I thought). It was a crime that could have victimized my family. The other violence I had grown accustomed to, family violence, didn't pose a substantial risk to my family unless an abuser showed up at our doorstep, trying to find his wife. Most weren't that stupid. I had a lot to learn about domestic violence.

Dad was slamming the trunk shut on his police car as I walked across our basketball court toward my car. My mind was in a fog. A sick feeling, like I had after the Hollandsburg murders, filled my stomach.

"Where are you off to?" asked Dad.

"Back to school," I replied. I stopped at my car and leaned my back against the side door. "What drives somebody to hurt their own children? Or to hurt anybody for that matter?" I was asking myself the question out loud as much as I was asking my dad.

Dad bit at his lower lip and slowly shook his head back and forth. "It's beyond me."

I knew it wasn't.

Can violence be prevented? I thought. Few things had moved me in my nineteen years as much as looking into the faces of the victims. The women and children who sat at my kitchen table throughout my childhood. The faces of Betty Jane Spencer and her sons staring back at me from the newspaper or television after the Hollandsburg murders. The piercing eyes of the four killers in the same newspapers.

"I still haven't figured out how Drollinger, Stonebraker, Smith, and Wright walked into the Spencer's home and killed them for no reason," I said. It had been ten years since the murders. "I mean, Drollinger seemed like another Charles Manson. But I don't understand how the other three went along."

"Stonebraker and Smith were both followers," Dad said. "I don't know about Wright. Don't know him. Drollinger was the leader. Always."

I had heard enough speculation over the years from police officers who knew the four killers and they always mentioned Smith's lack of a father figure and how Drollinger had assumed that role. And that Stonebraker came from a dysfunctional home. "Very rare that a child from a good home gets arrested for a serious crime," said Dad. "Most people I arrest are just acting out what they've learned at home." He paused for a second. "Be careful driving back to school."

The drive back to school gave me time to reflect. All of this violence was starting to gnaw at me as I was growing older. I wanted to know what drove a person to hurt others, how abusers could justify their violence. I realized that violence, as long as it was behind closed doors, was quietly accepted as normal, a private family matter. It wasn't the business of people outside the family. But it was violence, call it whatever you want. Doctor it up with fancy words and makeup, but violence is violence. Period. Ugly and hurtful. It is always intended to demean, hurt, or injure, to control somebody else. I thought about all the faces that had sat at our kitchen table, tear-streaked faces, fingernails chewed until they bled, kids filled with terror, their eyes darting around the room, trusting no one (who should they trust if the person who is supposed to love them more than anyone is hurting them?). The images flooded my head and made my soul ache, made me wonder about the society I lived in. A society, a country, that prided itself on being the most advanced culture in the world. And I thought about Shelly. I tried to figure out why a man would sexually abuse his child. His own offspring. His flesh and blood. No other animal does this to its own. The image repulsed me. If we weren't safe at home, in the arms of our parents, then where could we be safe? And what happens to the thousands of children who are abused when nobody intervenes? What impact does the violence have on them? I was starting to realize that it had a huge impact on them and a huge impact on our society.

PART THREE

A SEARCH FOR TRUTH

CHAPTER TWENTY-ONE

On March 31, 1992, spring had sprung, the trees were in full blossom, the Georgia Pears as pristine white as a wedding dress. Bright yellow crocuses and deep red and purple tulips bloomed. I pulled into my apartment complex in Nashville, Tennessee, thankful to have survived my first winter in the south (a heck of a lot milder than an Indiana winter). The warmer climate and twenty-two weeks at the police academy had tested my intestinal fortitude. That was all over today. Spring was here and the academy training was over. My fifty-two classmates and I would graduate tonight, be sworn in as police officers, and go to work tomorrow. We'd spread throughout the city, combating violence. My dad, Grandma McCarty, and Aunt Tracy were making the three-hundred-mile trip for the graduation ceremony.

Dad had never been too excited about me becoming a police officer. He had dreams of his eldest son going to law school (proof he didn't look too closely at my grades), maybe becoming a teacher and a coach - anything but a police officer. Anything but a public servant working for peanuts and getting no respect, risking my life, day in and day out. He knew the dangers of the career after eighteen years patrolling West Central Indiana and serving on the Governor of Indiana's security detail. He'd entered dark houses in pursuit of felons, served warrants, made countless traffic stops on lonely country roads in the middle of the night. He'd broken up bar fights and domestics. He'd searched warehouses on a burglar alarm. He knew the danger.

I have to admit it was rather unexpected that I became a police officer. I had never once while growing up considered becoming a police officer. And believe me, it was the one question I had been asked a million times: "You gonna be a cop like your dad?" "Heck, no," was my reply every time. And I meant it.

There's no denying I admired my dad. I was proud of what he did, the risk he took each day he dressed for work. These feelings influenced me. Almost all the men in my family had been police officers - Dad, Grandpa Jim, and my cousin Kert. They were all men I respected, men I trusted.

I also knew how dangerous the job was. I had spent many nights lying awake in my bed, praying to God that nothing would happen to my dad. That he would be safe as he walked into bar fights, domestics, robberies, traffic stops, the countless opportunities officers have for being hurt or killed. I would lie stiff in my bed if the phone rang in the middle of the night, my heart beating in my chest, waiting a few seconds to see if my mom would scream out in pain. I knew the job was dangerous. I knew officers were killed.

The stories would start after a huge Thanksgiving dinner, when Grandpa Jim, Kert, and the other men were lounging in chairs, digesting the feast and watching football. Dad would talk about the calm, cold, rainy night when he overheard a robbery-in-progress call come across his police scanner. He was on the south edge of Crawfordsville. Officer Russell Baldwin from the Crawfordsville Police Department had the suspect vehicle spotted on Lafayette Road. Dad was only a few blocks away, but because of a primitive radio communications system, he was unable to communicate with Officer Baldwin. Dad called his dispatcher, told her to call Baldwin's dispatcher and have him wait for a couple minutes to stop the car, to give Dad time to get there. Dad sped across town and pulled up to Baldwin's flashing lights just as the suspect vehicle fled the scene and Russell Baldwin lay dead in the middle of the street. Shot in the chest. I remembered the morning I heard the telephone ring, then watched as tears welled up in Dad's eyes. That was the morning his best friend and fellow trooper, Dan Henley, shot and killed himself in his patrol car. Yeah, I knew how dangerous the job could be. If the bad guy didn't get you, then the stress of the job often led to divorce, alcoholism, or suicide.

But I wanted to do something to help people. I didn't apply for jobs based on the salary or the potential for making money like so many of my college classmates. Money had never been a measuring stick of success for me. Making a difference, helping people, making things better for those less fortunate, that's what I wanted. And even with all the negatives, policing was the only logical career for me. I'd seen the good things my dad had done over the years. I remembered all the times Carl Hannah had run to our home, seeking out Dad, knowing Dad would help. And all the times he could have taken somebody to jail, or written him or her a ticket, and instead, he looked deeper into the situation for the root of the problem causing the behavior. Looking for a solution to the problem. However, my decision was actually made when I was a nine-year-old boy (even though I really didn't know it at the time) as I watched as my dad, Dave Blue, Loyd Heck, Stan Kenny and countless other police officers investigated the Hollandsburg murders. It was good versus evil, and I knew then that I wanted to be a good guy.

When Dad realized that I was serious about becoming a police officer, he began harping on how low the pay was. I would be poor, I wouldn't be able to afford to do anything fun. I would have to work nights, weekends, and holidays while everybody else was going to ball games or family vacations or family dinners. I understood the commitment. And I reminded him it was his fault I chose a career in policing. I was only doing what I had been taught since childhood, helping people.

I parked in front of Building Three, grabbed the freshly laundered uniform from the backseat, and walked inside the apartment that I shared with my wife, Lori, and our golden retriever, Abby.

Lori, like Dad, was less than excited about my decision to become a police officer. The commitment was clearly dangerous. And I knew she would be at home worrying about me the same way I had worried about my dad. I would be working nights, weekends, and holidays because those darned crooks didn't keep normal business hours. But as two excited newlyweds, we packed up our 1987 Dodge Charger and migrated three hundred and fifty miles south, leaving friends, family, and everything that was familiar behind.

I felt a twinge of excitement as I walked into the apartment and hung the uniform on the back of our bedroom door. I was excited to have finished the grueling academy with all the running, early morning inspections, yelling and screaming, and tests. It was intense discipline. But I had also become comfortable at the academy over the past few months. I could do it. Now I was anxious because I wasn't sure I was ready, prepared, or able to do the "real" job. The academy was a safe and structured environment, free from the unexpected danger of real life. You always got a second chance at the academy.

Chief Griggs had given us our assignments before we were dismissed today at noon. I was assigned to the South Station, evening shift. What a relief. The South Station was only five minutes from our apartment. But the assignment was only temporary. In two months I would be rotated to another training officer, another station, another shift. Then another two months and another training officer, station and shift. I had heard countless horror stories about training officers. Rest assured, we had been told, you will be doing all of the work. And don't expect to be accepted by the veteran officers, because you won't be. You have to earn their trust.

But this was a means to an end for me, since my goal was to be a detective. Wearing a suit and tie, solving the big cases like Detective Loyd Heck solving the Hollandsburg murders. Loyd was a hero in West Central Indiana. As the lead investigator on the murders, he was responsible for bringing the four killers to justice and calming the fears of an entire community (for that matter, an entire state). I remember watching Loyd on the evening news and being impressed, but unable to articulate why. Today, I know that it was his confidence, his composure under intense pressure, and the sense of duty that he demonstrated. And I wanted to be regarded as having the same qualities.

CHAPTER TWENTY-TWO

I stood in the hallway, outside of the roll call room at the MNPD West Station, browsing through the thumb-tacked postings on the bulletin board. It was right there in the middle, flanked on all four sides by updates of trainings, stolen vehicles, and most-wanted lists. The department was looking for qualified officers to implement a Domestic Violence Unit. After three years of patrolling the near west side, with its crime-ridden and trash-filled streets, I was ready for a change. An opportunity to become a detective. An opportunity to use the skills I had developed as a patrol officer. And an opportunity to cash in on what I had learned as a child. Violence could be prevented if we focused more on children who were raised in homes filled with violence. If we didn't reach out to these young victims, we would continue to see the victims grow into young men who walked into the homes of strangers and killed for sport.

Lt. Sutton read the memo at roll call as he read every memo that came from downtown. As usual, the memo drew a myriad of comments: "No way." "Internal affairs." "Nobody would be that stupid." "We shouldn't even take domestic calls." "Good luck." I chuckled to myself. The officers, mostly men, wanted nothing to do with a full-time position that worked solely with victims of domestic violence.

Domestic violence was the crime that officers hated most. It was so unpredictable and so dangerous. And the victims always changed their minds. It was so frustrating when the victim, bleeding from her lip, didn't want her husband, the man responsible for her busted lip, to go to jail. It was frustrating because officers really wanted to do the right thing. They just didn't understand the victim of domestic violence. She was so different from other victims we dealt with. Victims of a robbery always want the robber caught and prosecuted. Victims of a burglary always want the burglar caught and prosecuted. But victims of domestic violence don't always want the man responsible to be arrested. Or, they show up in court and testify for him. The problem is not the victim. The problem is that the police department - every police department in the United States - fails to prepare officers for dealing with domestic violence. We spent more than half our time answering domestic calls, never realizing that domestic violence was the root cause of the other crimes we dealt with every day.

I had witnessed this as a kid, how dysfunctional homes produced violent criminals. How kids trapped in these homes could be easily influenced and manipulated into walking into a home, lining a mother and four children up on the floor and shooting them. It required seeing the big picture. Connecting the dots.

I removed the silver thumbtack and made a copy of the memo before heading out the door to my patrol car. The posting was an awesome opportunity. It was an opportunity to become a detective, to help women and children like those who had sat around our kitchen table, scared to death, searching for a safe place, praying for a night without persistent thoughts of being hurt or killed.

The posting couldn't have come at better time. I was already making plans to leave the department. The job was nothing like what I had thought it would be. We didn't help anybody. The slogan on our patrol cars said "to protect and serve" which was a crock of bull. I had discovered that most police departments did not protect and serve but "showed up and solved." We always got the call after somebody had been victimized.

Being a police officer did not make me feel like I thought it would. The feeling of accomplishment and satisfaction I longed for was not there. I had been convinced that police officers lived off of satisfaction and accomplishment in helping people. I saw it in my father and Dave Blue as they assisted in the investigation of the murders of Ralph, Reeve, and Raymond Spencer, and their stepbrother

Greg Brooks. I could see it in Loyd Heck and Barney Thrasher's faces on the news or in the newspapers. There was a sense of accomplishment when the four killers were brought to justice. I had yet to feel that as a police officer.

Officers, for the most part, become police officers because they want to help people. And then they get frustrated because the job doesn't allow them to help people. Police agencies were not set up to help people or prevent crime. They were organized to solve crimes after people have been robbed, burglarized, assaulted, raped, or killed. I had spent three years answering call after call, night after night, never solving a problem, only placing a Band-Aid on a problem that I knew would resurface. If I was lucky, it would not surface again until I had gone home and the next shift had checked in service.

But now I had a challenge. The Domestic Violence Unit would definitely be a challenge. It was already receiving resistance from the rank and file, as well as the command staff. This would be an opportunity to help people, which was exactly what I wanted to do. I had been assured that the unit would be proactive, not reactive. We would focus on preventing crime by intervening in violent homes and breaking the cycle of violence.

I parked my cruiser across from the fire station at Forty-Fifth and Alabama and filled out my request for a transfer to the Domestic Violence Unit. I would give it to my sergeant at nightly "mail call" when I turned in the rest of my paperwork. If the transfer came through, I would stay. If it didn't, a career change was imminent.

CHAPTER TWENTY-THREE

I was cleaning out my desk in our den when I stumbled across the dusty manila folder of newspaper articles chronicling the Hollandsburg murders. These were the articles I had clipped from newspapers as a nine-year-old boy. I grabbed the folder, which I had kept close at hand for seventeen years, and walked into our living room. I was excited.

I sat down on the couch and glanced at my watch, realizing I had two hours before Lori would be home from school. She was working on her undergraduate degree at David Lipscomb University, in addition to working full-time at a real estate office. That meant I spent a lot of time by myself on Tuesdays and Wednesdays, my much-sought-after regular days off. Frighteningly enough, I had actually adjusted to the midweek days off and enjoyed them with the same enthusiasm that most people enjoyed Saturdays and Sundays. Plus, the transfer to the Domestic Violence Division had come through, so I was enjoying my job much more.

The transfer had been granted last August, but the resistance to the new unit, five months later, was still intense. Just last night, standing outside a crime scene, waiting for the crime scene technician to arrive, a veteran officer had asked me, "Why'd you transfer to domestic violence?"

"Because it is a great opportunity for me," I replied.

"You guys are kinda like internal affairs," he said. He seemed uneasy with me.

"Why is that?" I asked nonchalantly while making some notes:

blood soaked carpet, telephone torn from the wall, furniture busted, victim transported to Vanderbilt Hospital by EMS.

"Because y'all got a hard-on for cops," he said laughingly, as if he were kidding. I knew he wasn't.

"First off," I said, "there ain't nothing about you that gives me a hard-on."

He smiled. "Man, y'all have arrested several officers, though."

"The only people I've ever arrested were criminals." I was looking at my notes, not challenging him. "Would you arrest me if I walked in that bar across the street and shot the first person I saw?"

"I don't know," he said. It wasn't easy for an officer to say he would arrest another officer. "I guess I would. I'd have to."

"Then why do the majority of officers on the department think we should let an officer off if he beats the crap out of his wife? Or beats his kids?"

The officer shrugged his shoulders.

"You're not scared of homicide detectives are you?"

"No," he replied.

"You're not scared of robbery detectives are you?"

"No."

"You're not scared of them because you're not gonna kill or rob anybody," I said. "Then you shouldn't be scared of me unless you beat your wife or girlfriend. Or both," I added for some humor.

"Makes sense," he said. But I knew it didn't make sense to him. I could tell by the look on his face.

"My dad was a cop," I added as the crime scene technician pulled up in a van. "My grandpa was a cop. I have a cousin who's a cop. There is nothing better than a good cop." I raised a hand to the technician. "But there is nothing worse than a bad cop. A cop who beats his wife or kids ain't a cop. He's a criminal."

But that was last night. Nothing to waste my time thinking about on my day off. You can't make everybody happy all the time. And I had never been one to fret over being different or not being accepted, especially when I was standing up for something that was right.

I opened the manila folder and pulled out the yellowish newspaper clippings. I looked through them, the headlines, the pictures. The memories came flooding back.

My eyes were drawn to an article from the Indianapolis Star, *"Drollinger's 'Fun' Killing Reminiscent of Manson,"*[7] written ten years after the murders, in February 1987, that I could not remember reading. I settled back on the couch and began reading:

> Inside her family's double-wide mobile home in rural Parke Country, Betty Jane Spencer was finishing some sewing at the kitchen table on an icy February evening 10 years ago.
>
> Her husband, Keith, had just left for work and her son stretched out on the couch. Two of her stepsons got ready for bed as she waited for another stepson to return from his job.
>
> It was the night before Valentine's Day and Mrs. Spencer chided one of her younger boys about how many valentine cards the girls at school would give him the next day.
>
> Lurking outside the isolated house, four young men in a rented Oldsmobile were checking their shotguns and plotting a chilling crime that would shock the nation.
>
> Before the four finished their horrible work, the four young men inside the house would be slaughtered cold bloodedly and Mrs. Spencer would be left for dead.
>
> "It was a thrill kill. They had done just about everything except kill someone. They thought it wouldn't be any different," recalled Indiana State Police Detective Loyd W. Heck, who led the investigation.
>
> The random, apparently motiveless slayings

---

[7] Dave J. Remondini, "Drollinger's 'Fun' Killing Reminiscent of Manson," Indianapolis Star, 8 February 1987.

would horrify a nation and draw worldwide attention. Mrs. Spencer would live and become a powerful catalyst for recognition of victim's rights and later would be honored by President Reagan at a White House Ceremony.

I was completely focused on the article, unaware of how long Abby had been barking at the door. She finally got my attention by pawing on the back door. It snapped me from the depths of my concentration. I walked over to the back door, let her in, grabbed a can of Coke from the refrigerator, and hurried back to the couch to finish the article.

> Despite the ten years that had passed, the Hollandsburg murders seemed permanently etched into the state's memory banks.
> Many remember the story of how the four killers pumped 11 shotgun rounds into Mrs. Spencer and her family as all five lay neatly in a row on the floor of their home.
> A number of factors have elevated the Hollandsburg slayings to an almost mystical plane: the fact that they occurred on Valentine's Day; the lack of any motive other than pleasure; and court testimony that suggested the defendants considered writing "Helter Skelter" with blood on the refrigerator in an imitation of mass murderer Charles Manson.

I laid my head on the back of the couch and stared at the beam running across the crown of the vaulted ceiling. Why did this one crime have such a profound impact on my life seventeen years later? I might go two or three years and not think about the murders, but then I would find myself sitting on the couch rereading each newspaper article, paragraph by paragraph, line by line. I still couldn't fully explain it. Was I a freak? I walked into the den, shut the desk drawer, and turned on the computer. I began a letter filled with question after question, telling the would-be-recipient what a profound impact this crime had had on me. It was time to find the answers to the questions that had been haunting me since childhood. And it was time to answer questions so I could use the information to prevent future crimes.

> Dear sir,
>
> I am originally from Waveland, Indiana, but now live in Nashville, Tennessee, where I am detective with the Nashville Metropolitan Police Department. You know my father, Tom McCarty, who is retired from the Indiana State Police. My dad said he had arrested you for some petty stuff like stealing gas and that he used to come by the Clark Station where you worked. But he couldn't believe you were involved in the murders.
>
> The murders had a profound impact on me as a nine year-old kid (and really shaped my decision to become a police officer). I remember staring at the composite pictures that first appeared in the newspapers and the bone-chilling fear I felt. Then you were indentified and your picture was splashed on the television and in the newspapers. It was the first time I had been utterly scared in my life (other than scared of the dark or the boogeyman). And it was the first time I had ever seen my mom and dad scared. That was terrifying. Whenever I had been scared of the dark in the past, I simply looked to my mom and dad for comfort. All I got from them after the murders was an affirmation of my fears.
>
> Well, the reason I am writing is because I have lots of questions surrounding the murders, many of them personal. However, I hope that I will learn something that I can use to educate other police officers so we can prevent a crime like this from hap-

pening again.

I have several questions (and I'm sure your participation will generate more):

Did Drollinger have a control over people like Charles Manson?

Do you believe that Drollinger was a lot like Charles Manson, a cult kind of leader? He seemed to have a lot of control over people in Montgomery County.

Did Drollinger want to be like Manson?

Did Drollinger plan the murders that took place on February 14, 1977?

At what point did you decide to murder? That night? Months prior?

Many people speculate that the murders were drug related, is this true? Did you know any of the boys?

What was said as you pulled into the Spencer's drive-way?

Did drugs play a role in your involvement in the murders?

I've heard that Drollinger wanted to write "Helter Skelter" on the walls with the victims' blood, why didn't he?

What was going through your mind as you stood in the Spencer home and the shots were being fired?

What was your reaction (Drollinger's, Smith's, Wright's) after you found out that Betty Spencer had survived?

Was it true that there were plans of killing more people, but that you became sick and that is why no more people were killed?

What in your life was missing that led to your getting involved with drugs and Roger Drollinger? Family?

I signed the letter and sent it to Daniel Stonebraker, Inmate#11818, at the Indiana Reformatory Prison.

CHAPTER TWENTY-FOUR

I stood just inside our back door, talking with my dad while Lori and my mom set the table for a Father's Day dinner. Mom and Dad had driven down to Nashville for the weekend. I was thankful that even though they had their differences and had divorced three years ago, they were still friends and could get together in the same house.

For the first time since joining the police department, I finally had parts of a weekend off as regular days off. No, I still didn't have Saturdays and Sundays off like normal people, but I had Sundays and Mondays off, which was pretty darned good for a cop. It beat the Tuesdays and Wednesdays off I had enjoyed for the past four years. One day off over the weekend was better than none.

My brother Matt had graduated from high school last year, the class of 1994, and found himself in quite a dilemma for an eighteen-year-old boy. He was slated to attend the University of Illinois on a baseball scholarship, but ended up being drafted by the Los Angeles Dodgers. After careful consideration, weighing all the options, and studying the contract (which included college tuition and a signing bonus larger than anything my parents or I had ever made in a year), Matt signed. And as we readied ourselves for a Father's Day dinner of chicken and noodles, mashed potatoes, green beans, and apple pie, Matt was playing shortstop in the Los Angeles Dodgers rookie league in Great Falls, Montana.

The telephone rang.

Lori grabbed it. I watched her, looking at her face, trying to figure out who it could be. She turned toward me, eyes wide. My heart sank. Something bad had happened.

"It's Dan Stonebraker," she said, tossing me the phone like it was a hot potato.

Dan Stonebraker, I thought. It didn't sink in right away.

I put the phone to my ear, ready to speak, though unsure of what I would say. A female voice, monotone, obviously a recording, was in mid-sentence: "...if you accept the charges, you cannot use three-way calls or recording devices. Please press one now to accept."

I pushed the phone from my ear and smashed button number one with a shaking index finger. Then I walked briskly through the living room and out the front door onto the porch. The Tennessee sun was scorching. I started to sit down on the white porch swing, but stood back up, too nervous to sit.

"Hello," the male voice said. "Mike?"

"Yes," I said, mouth dry. "Is this Dan?"

"Yeah," he said. "How are you doing? Happy Father's Day."

"Thanks," I replied. "How are you doing?" "Then I thought about what a stupid question that was for a man serving two life sentences.

"Fine," Dan said. "Sorry to call you collect, but that's the only way we can make phone calls."

"Oh, that's okay," I said. "I'm glad you called."

Nearly three months had passed since I had mailed out letters to each of the four men convicted of shooting Betty Jane Spencer and killing Greg Brooks and Ralph, Reeve, and Raymond Spencer. And it was a month after the letters had been sent before I received a reply from Dan Stonebraker. He was the only one of the four convicted killers who responded. I learned from Dan that David Smith was going to participate but then decided against it, and that Mike Wright said he would not participate (Stonebraker, Smith, and Wright are all incarcerated at the Pendleton Reformatory Prison). Drollinger did not respond.

After the third letter exchanged between us, I gave Dan my home telephone number and asked him to call.

"Are you having a big Father's Day get-together?" Dan asked.

"Actually, we are," I said. "My dad and mom came down for the weekend."

"How's your dad?" Dan asked. "Is he still a state policeman?"

"He's fine," I said. "He actually retired in 1988. He tore up his knee during a training course put on by the U.S. Secret Service. He was working a security detail that protected the governor of Indiana."

"Well, we only get thirty minutes to talk," Dan said. "And we probably should talk a little about what you are wanting to do."

"Okay," I said. "I think in my first letter I mentioned that I was just trying to find the answers to some of my questions about the murders. Questions that I needed answered for me. I also think understanding why you did this will help me in working with some of the suspects I encounter."

"Yes," Dan said. "And I have always been open to helping others. If someone can benefit from what I've been through, I'm always willing to share it."

"Now," I said. "I mentioned in my last letter that I have been talking with Betty Spencer. And I've decided to write a book. I wanted you to know what I intend to do with the information you give me."

"I got your letter several weeks ago," Dan said. "That's why I have waited so long to call. I have been praying about this. There's clearly no reason for me to want to help. A book will bring all this back up in the papers and in the news. And I don't want my family to go through all of that again."

My heart sank. He wasn't going to help.

"But I have always known that a book or a movie would be written about this," Dan said. "There have been lots of authors who have contacted me over the years. And many of them would come here to the prison to talk. I could see the dollar signs in their eyes. But, I believe that God had brought you into my life for a reason. I will answer your questions and help you write the book so it's accurate. And does away with some of the myths that have been out there for so long."

"Thanks," I mumbled, surprised. What a relief.

"I would hope that people could see the Dan Stonebraker of today," Dan said. "Not the Dan eighteen years ago that killed those boys."

"I know," I said. "But I can't guarantee you anything if you help. The focus of the book will be on the murders and what effect they had on me, my family, and my community."

"I understand," Dan said.

"But," I replied, "the book has to be about more than just the murders themselves. I want there to be some value to the book. I need to know how four men from my community could be led to kill four boys. To see if there is anything we can learn that could prevent something like this from happening again. Or prevent some kid from going down the wrong path, the same path you traveled. And raise awareness so family, friends, neighbors get involved with kids that are teetering on the brink of destruction. There has to be something we can learn from such a horrific tragedy."

"Well, that's why I've decided to help," Dan said. "If I can reach one kid, then dredging all of this back up will be worth it."

"I sent similar letters to Roger Drollinger, David Smith, and Mike Wright," I said. "None of them responded. I know Drollinger is in Michigan City Prison. But do you ever see Wright or Smith?"

"Yes," Dan said. "I see Mike and David every day. I'm not surprised the Roger didn't respond. They sent us to different prisons because I testified against him. We were fearful he would try to kill me."

"Did Wright or Smith get the letters I sent?" I asked.

"Yeah," Dan said. "Mike came right down to me with the first letter you sent all of us. I told him I was going to reply. I always reply. Plus, I know your dad."

"Did he say if he was going to respond?" I asked.

"He wanted me to hold up replying to you," Dan said. "He was a little uncomfortable with the directness of some of your questions. And he wanted to have someone check you out and see if you were who you said you were."

"Check me out?" I snapped. "Does he have a private investigator at his disposal?"

"I don't know," Dan chuckled. "David said he wasn't going to reply."

A female voice interrupted, "Your call will be terminated in thirty seconds."

"We better wrap up," Dan said.

"I'll be in touch," I said as the line went dead.

CHAPTER TWENTY-FIVE

She sat forward in the weathered recliner, elbow resting on the arm pad, cigarette gripped firmly between her index and middle finger, and coughed. A raspy cough from the depths of her lungs. A lifetime of smoking cough.

I glanced around the sparsely furnished apartment. The walls were bare, holding no pictures of smiling children. At her age there should have been pictures of grandchildren. And it was quiet. No television. No radio. It was an apartment haunted by bad memories.

I sat down next to Lori in a fold-up lawn chair.

"It feels good to be home," Mrs. Spencer said. "Even though my furniture won't be here for several weeks. I don't have the money for the moving truck."

I smiled. As bad as I felt about her finances, I also admired her for the same reason. She had turned down many offers from producers and publishers over the years because she could see the greed in their eyes. Principle meant more than money. And that was rare these days.

I studied her face, weighted with the grief she had carried for eighteen years. She had aged considerably since the last time I saw her, nearly ten years ago, on the front porch of our house in Waveland. "Betty Jane, this is my wife Lori."

"Nice to meet you, Lori," Betty Jane said. "It's really nice to see you, Mike."

"I was surprised at how quickly you moved back to Indiana," I said, squirming in the chair to get comfortable.

It had only been seven months since I had tracked Betty Jane Spencer down in Jonesboro, Georgia, a suburb of Atlanta. At the time, she was the Statewide Victim Assistance Coordinator for the Georgia Mothers Against Drunk Drivers. I had lost track of her as our lives had taken us in separate physical directions, but similar professional directions. Shortly after her visit with my mom ten years ago on our front porch, Betty Jane had accepted the position of Executive Director of the Florida Mothers Against Drunk Driving. If ever anybody could understand the sudden and unexpected loss of a child, it was Betty Jane Spencer. Then Hurricane Hugo devastated the Florida economy and funding for her position was cut. She migrated north to Jonesboro, Georgia.

"It just felt like the right time to come home," she said, then squinted her eyes and puffed on the cigarette. She turned her head from Lori and me and blew a cloud of white smoke in the air. "I needed to leave ten years ago. For my own well-being."

I wasn't sure why. I assumed the best place for her was near family and friends, strong support systems, pillars she could lean on. "That was a pretty big step," I said. "Moving away from your home. Your roots."

"A little," Betty Jane said. "But I had lived away from here before. Actually, Greg and I had only been back in Indiana for about a year before he was killed. We had been in Southern California for almost twenty years. It's hard to believe we fled the high crime of Southern California, the Charles Manson murders, for the safety and security of rural Indiana. And to think we would come into contact with a group equally as dangerous as Manson and his followers." She exhaled and her eyes drifted off in the distance, then snapped back as quickly as they had drifted. "But I needed to leave because everybody around here was feeling sorry for me. They meant well. And I'm glad they cared so much. But I was still feeling sorry for myself. And I had to quit feeling sorry for myself. I had to turn this horrible tragedy into something positive. The boys' deaths could not be in vain."

"So, how did you and Keith meet?" I asked.

"Well, shortly after Greg and I moved back here," Betty Jane said. "I heard that Keith was also divorced. Keith and I had been high school sweethearts."

Lori smiled. I knew she was anxious about listening to the details of this horrific crime. I had never met anyone who cared so much about people. I could tell by her smile she was moved by the hint of romance, even though she knew the tragic outcome of this love story.

"We started dating," Betty Jane said. "And I fell in love with his children. Ralph, Reeve, Raymond, and Diane. Diane was in college at the time. At Purdue University."

"Thank God for her," I said to myself. I knew very little about Diane. Not much had been written about her at the time of the murders. I remembered seeing her picture in the newspaper during the funeral for her bothers.

"The boys were such good boys," Betty Jane said, reflecting. "Such quality young boys. With such distinct personalities. Ralph was the youngest, athletic and handsome. A very charismatic boy."

"He was just a few years older than I was," I added.

Betty Jane nodded her head, then stood and walked to and bent over a box in the dining room. She fumbled around in the box, then returned and stood facing Lori and me. "Here are some pictures of the boys. You can have them."

I looked at each photograph carefully before passing them to Lori. These were the pictures nobody in the United States had ever seen. The photographs of the boys that had been splattered across newspapers and televisions were older pictures of the boys found in school yearbooks. The pictures the country had seen looked nothing like the handsome boys killed on Valentine's Day 1977.

"Reeve was the middle one," Betty Jane said while reaching for another cigarette. "He was the little mechanic of the family. Always out in the garage next to the house. Tinkering with cars. Keith had accidentally ran over Reeves's foot with the tractor when he was younger so he couldn't play sports.

"And then there was Raymond. He was a real worker. He farmed over eighty acres himself. Only a junior in high school. And worked nights down at the Hollandsburg Restaurant bussing tables and cleaning up after they closed."

Raymond had been at work the night Dan Stonebraker, Mike Wright, David Smith, and Roger Drollinger burst into their home. Unfortunately, he had walked right into the middle of everything. I could only imagine what was running through his mind as he walked in the front door, and for a split second tried to digest his brothers and Betty Jane lying on the living room floor, facedown, hands behind their backs. But he wouldn't have had much time to think because David Smith shoved a shotgun in his face and threw him to the ground.

"I think the thing that bothers me more than anything," Betty Jane said, "is the fact that everybody said the boys were killed because they were involved in drugs. That hurts so badly. Our boys were not involved in drugs."

"I know," I said. "I have talked to hundreds of people, including investigators of the case, and have scoured the state police case file. There is absolutely nothing to substantiate that rumor. And I know this was something the investigators looked at. They looked at anything that might lead them to the killers. I've even read police reports from Barstow, California, that were submitted to the Indiana State Police after they did a detailed background check on Greg. And they found nothing."

"Well, Greg looked a little different." Betty Jane smiled. "He had long hair and wore pukka beads. But remember he was raised in Southern California."

"Tends to be a little conservative around here," I said with a smile. "Greg didn't realize that flannel shirts and Levi's were the fashion around here."

Betty Jane smiled.

"Anyway," I said. "I really think that people wanted to believe the murders had something to do with drugs. Because if the murders were random, then it could have been them. Even today, people around here don't want to accept the fact that these guys could have as easily pulled into their drive that night. Hell, I still hear people today talking about how this was drug-related and that the boys owed money to Drollinger. People have a hard time with the randomness of this crime."

"I think you're right, Mike," Betty Jane said. "But it still hurts me. The boys aren't here to defend themselves."

I knew it hurt. She had lost her children, murdered in front of her eyes. And then to hear people saying bad things about them that were not true. She still had to deal with the victim blaming.

"I want to shift gears a little bit," I said. "When did you and Keith divorce?"

Betty Jane smashed the butt of her cigarette out in a clear ashtray while nodding her head. "We divorced about ten years after the boys were killed. That's when I decided to take the job with the Florida Mothers Against Drunk Drivers. Keith moved to Hawaii and started a radio station. The strain of the murders was just too much for our marriage."

"Dad told me that you and Keith moved back in the house," I said. "Where the boys were murdered."

"Yes," Betty Jane said, nodding her head. "It's true. Keith had the modular cleaned, new carpet and paint. But you couldn't carpet over or paint over what had happened in that house. I hated it. Hated everything about moving back in the house. Keith bought me a gun and taught me how to shoot it. He was still working nights in Indianapolis, so I would sit in the bathroom with the gun all night. I was so scared, I couldn't move. Still, to this day, I sleep fully dressed in case I have to get up in the middle of the night and run."

"Why did Keith want to move back into the house?" I asked, unable to imagine living in the same house where four members of my family had been slain. I don't even think I could have walked into the house again if I had been Betty Jane.

"Keith never talked much about what happened," Betty Jane said. "I think he felt guilty that a few minutes after he left for work his sons were killed and his wife left for dead. He probably felt guilty for not being there. But there wouldn't have been anything he could have done. Nothing.

"During Drollinger and Smith's trials, Keith always left the courtroom. He never wanted to hear what happened to his boys or to me. I think moving back in the house was his way of trying to convince himself that this had not happened and everything was normal. I felt so bad for him. I had people to talk to, which made me feel a little better. But Keith dealt with everything by himself."

At some level, I'm not sure I blamed him. I would not want to know the details of how my sons were slain. Maybe I understood because I was a man. And we weird creatures have always been taught to deal with things alone, quietly, "like a man" (whatever that means).

"But I'll never be able to get that night out of my head," Betty Jane said as she reached for a cigarette and her lighter. She lit the cigarette, inhaled, and sat back in her chair, then exhaled. "I was sitting in the kitchen at the breakfast nook, making a grocery list. Keith had just left for work, not ten minutes before. I heard footsteps outside and thought Keith must have forgotten something. Then the front door flew open and Mike Wright ran in with a shotgun."

"You didn't know Mike Wright at the time?" I asked, even though I was confident of the answer.

"No," Betty Jane said. "I didn't know any of them. But anyway, Greg was lying on the couch watching television. Wright yells, 'Get on the floor, buddy, now. Move.' That's when the back door flew open and Stonebraker and Smith came running in. Smith was yelling, 'Get on the floor, lady! Facedown.' I slid out of the nook onto the floor, hoping this was some kind of joke one of the boys had orchestrated. Then I realized it wasn't and I started crawling into the living room, trying to get to Greg."

As I listened, I visualized myself in Betty Jane's position, three armed intruders busting into my home and ordering my family and me onto the floor. A feeling of helplessness flushed my body.

"Smith asked me if there was anybody else in the house," Betty Jane said. "I didn't answer because I hoped they would rob us and leave without waking and frightening the younger boys."

Betty Jane's hands were trembling as she talked.

"Then I heard Smith yelling at Ralph and Reeve," she said. "I had my face buried in the floor like they had ordered me. I was wearing glasses and they were smashing into my face. Then I glanced up quickly to see Reeve. If anybody could have figured a way out, it would have been Reeve. All Reeve did was shrug his shoulders nervously and lie down on the floor, defeated. Ralphie was trembling."

I glanced at Lori; she took deep breaths and exhaled loudly, trying to control her breathing like an expectant mother during labor.

"When they had all four of us on the floor," Betty Jane said, "that's when I heard a new voice. A more authoritative voice. It was Drollinger. I turned and looked at Drollinger and said, 'You can have anything you want. We'll do anything you want us to do.' Drollinger screamed, 'Shut up, bitch, and put your head down!'"

"Then they started smashing the telephones and some equipment that Keith had stored in the dining room. Keith was getting ready to start a radio station in Parke County. It was going to be the whole family running the radio station. At this point, I still thought they were only going to rob us. Maybe tie us up and we'd all have a big laugh in the morning when Keith found us. Why else would they bust the telephones and equipment they thought we could use to communicate?"

"Were the lights on in the house or was it dark?" I asked.

"The lights were on at this point," Betty Jane said. "This was about the time Raymond came home." She shook her head as she relived the night. A night she had relived hundreds and hundreds of times. "I was hoping that Raymond would see what was going on and go get help. I heard a scuffle at the front door. But I didn't look. They kept saying they would kill us if we didn't keep our heads down. Then I heard somebody scream, which turned out to be Smith. "You stupid bastard, think you're smart don't you, coming in on us like that.' I prayed it wasn't Raymond. So I said, 'Is that you, Raymond?' There was no answer. I asked again, 'Raymond, are you home?' My heart sunk when I heard Raymond's voice, 'Yes, I'm here.'"

I couldn't fathom how terribly helpless and fearful she must have felt with her family defenseless on their living room floor. The same living room floor where they had played card games, wrestled, done homework, and watched television. And there was nothing she could do. They were at the mercy of the four armed intruders.

And the thoughts that must speed through your head when you feel like you might be killed. Sure, as a police officer, I had been in some situations where my life was in danger, where being killed was a real possibility. But it had been different. I wasn't lying on a living room floor with my family. I didn't think about the risk until after the incident was over, when I was safe and still alive.

"Then Drollinger came back in the living room," Betty Jane said, "And I knew we were going to be killed. He said, 'We need to get this cleaned up and get out of here.' He ordered Greg to go over by the couch and lie down, then kicked Greg as he was crawling over there. Then he ordered me next to Greg, then Raymond, Ralphie, and Reeve. Drollinger ordered us to put our hands behind our backs. I knew we were being lined up to be executed."

I had viewed the crime scene photographs. The boys, with the exception of Greg, were still lying face down on the floor, hands behind their backs as ordered.

"I turned to look at Raymond," Betty Jane said, "and he was shaking terribly. Just scared to death. I reached over and patted him on the back. I think I was probably saying good-bye."

Lori fanned herself with an open hand.

"Then Drollinger asked me if we had an ice pick," Betty Jane said. "I told him I didn't think so. I just prayed to God that they wouldn't stab us to death. That if they were going to kill us, they would shoot us and get it over quickly.

"I didn't hear anything from Drollinger for a while. But Smith walked down the line behind each of us, asking how old we were. Reeve said, 'Sixteen,' Ralph said, 'Fourteen.' Raymond said, 'Eighteen,' even though he wouldn't be eighteen for two more days. He asked me how old I was, then laughed and moved on to Greg before I could answer. Greg said, 'Twenty-two.'"

I sighed and rubbed my eyes. The conversation was surreal.

"The lights were off at this point," Betty Jane said. "But there was still light in the living room from an outside security light. That's when I heard these clicking noises. It was so loud. I'll never forget the sound. Metal on metal. Then a loud boom..."

Betty Jane stopped for a second to regain her composure. I thought about the irony of a security light being the light that aided the four killers in the massacre.

"It was just boom, boom, boom. I felt Raymond die next to me. Then I heard a boom and felt the buckshot splattering my back and shoulder. I turned to my right and looked at Greg. He was raised up on his knees screaming, 'Oh, God I'm flying. Oh, God I'm flying.' I knew he was dying. That's when Drollinger ran up and grabbed Greg by his ponytail and stuck the shotgun to the back of his head and fired. That was my baby. A boy I had carried in my womb for nine months. And had raised for twenty-two years. Gone that fast." She shook her head.

She paused for a moment. And I had nothing to say, couldn't think of any words to say. The words "I'm sorry" just weren't strong enough to express what I felt. My blood boiled with hatred for Roger Drollinger. He was the mastermind. It was his sick psychosexual lust to kill that cost four boys their lives and wounded a mother for life. It's not that Wright, Smith, and Stonebraker shouldn't share in the responsibility. They pulled the triggers on their shotguns. But Drollinger was the reason Ralph, Reeve, Raymond, and Greg were killed. How could somebody kill another person, especially young boys, for sport?

"I heard somebody behind me," Betty Jane continued. "And I tried so hard to go limp. Make them think I was dead. And then somebody kicked me. It was Drollinger. He went down the line kicking all of us to make sure we were dead. My ears were ringing. The noise of the shotguns was so loud.

"I kept praying to God that he would spare us. I didn't know if Ralphie and Reeve were still alive. And I knew I needed to get help for them. Then I heard Drollinger say, 'Shoot the woman again.' That's when I knew I would die. It seemed like forever, but then I heard the shotgun. And felt the buckshot hit the back of my head. It must have blown my wig off."

"Did Drollinger check to make sure you were dead after they

shot you again?" I asked.

"No," Betty Jane said. "It seemed like forever before they left. They were looking for all their spent shells. Drollinger was questioning each one of them about how many times they had shot. Making sure they had all their shells."

"It's amazing first of all that you survived," I said. "And secondly that you were still conscious." I had studied the carnage from the crime scene photos. I knew that Stonebraker and Wright were standing to the left of the Spencer family, at the entrance to the dining room, and that Drollinger and Smith were standing at their feet. There was crossfire. It was an absolute miracle that Betty Jane survived. Her boys, on either side of her, were dead. There was no other way to explain it.

"I wiggled my feet and my hands to make sure I was really alive," Betty Jane said. "Then I heard this horrible sound. Like a waterfall. Or a train. It was the blood gushing from the boys. Then I jumped up because I heard a car taking off. I saw our Thunderbird pull out of the driveway real fast. As soon as our car disappeared, I turned and asked hysterically, 'Is anybody alive?' There was no answer."

"I ran into the bathroom and grabbed a towel to wrap around my head. I wasn't sure how badly I was hurt. Then I put on boots and a coat and ran out the back door, down the hill, through the trees. It was about a mile to Mr. Escue's. I had to get up on the road and run the final half mile to his house. I was sure the killers would be hiding along the way and would kill me."

This was a strong woman sitting in front of me. Very small in stature, but enormously courageous. I wondered if I would have had the same courage in the face of such unbelievable fear - fear that would have paralyzed most people.

"I was just beating on Mr. Escue's door," Betty Jane said. "Screaming for help because I'd been shot. Poor man. I know I scared him to death. Things like this don't happen where we live. And here is this woman standing on his front porch in the middle of the night screaming for help because I've been shot. And my boys have been shot. And I have this blood soaked towel on my head."

Choking in Fear

Betty Jean stood and walked over behind us and grabbed a three-ring binder. I watched her, admiring her for being able to get out of bed each morning, to go to work, to function. Knowing that, at times, she had to think this was all a nightmare, something concocted in the depths of her mind.

"I want you to take these and make copies," said Betty Jane. "I've never given these to anybody else. These are letters I wrote to the boys."

Wow, I thought. I wanted to rip open the binder and eat the words. But I couldn't. I would have to wait. I accepted the binder, hugged Betty Jane, and waited for Lori to hug her. Then we walked out of her apartment and down the breezeway in silence. Mentally exhausted.

I had barely negotiated the turn from Betty Jane's apartment complex back onto the main road when Lori opened the binder and started reading the first letter. I studied her face, waiting for some reaction, some clue as to the power of the letters. I was, admittedly, a smidgen jealous that she would have a chance to read the letters before I did. I glanced back at the road just in time to yell, "Damn," and smash the brake pedal to the floorboard. The car in front of me was at a dead stop, obeying a stop sign. Lori lunged forward and put one hand on the dash, bracing herself for a crash, then looked at me when it was apparent we weren't going to hit the car. I shook my head as if the driver in front of me had done something stupid and I had reacted with talent to save the day.

After shaking off the effects of the near collision, which took several miles, memories of my childhood flooded my head as I drove through the countryside that had been my home for the first twenty-three years of my life. Fall was in full swing, trees crisp with colors of orange, red and yellow. Pickup trucks and grain trucks were parked in the fields as farmers mowed down the beans and corn with combines.

I turned north on State Route 59 in Bellmore, past the Big Berry Ice Cream Shop. How many ice cream cones had I consumed while sitting on that weathered picnic table out back of the shop? That was my parent's reward for no air conditioning on muggy summer evenings.

Traffic was heavy, but to be expected this time of year. A state police officer, about my age, stood in the intersection and directed traffic. This was the two-week period each year when people flooded Parke County for the Covered Bridge Festival. Parke County was noted as the covered bridge capital of the world for the expansive nineteenth century wooden tunnels that stretched over sprawling creeks. The festival brought craftsmen and artisans from all over, with their array of crafts and quilts and delectable dishes and desserts prepared over open fires. I rolled my window down and took a deep breath. This was home and the smell was autumn.

I peeked at Lori, conscious of the heavy traffic and careful this time to avoid a near rear-end collision. She had tears in her eyes, and her lip quivered while her right hand fanned her face like she was swatting gnats from her eyes. Then she slammed the binder shut.

"What's wrong?" I asked.

She shook her head several times, clearing the sorrow that gripped her tongue. "The first letter is so sad..." The tears dripped from her chin.

I slowed down then pulled our Isuzu Rodeo onto the side of a rural country road. I reached over and grabbed the closed binder from Lori's lap. I couldn't wait any longer. It was only ten miles to her mother's where we were staying for the weekend, but I couldn't wait. I had to read the letters. I had to know what Betty Jane had written to the boys.

"Here," Lori said as she sniffled while pinching her nose with her thumb and index finger, then reached for the binder. "Take the first letter. Let me have the next one. I want to read them."

"Are you sure?" I asked while taking the first letter out, laying it on my lap, and handing her the binder back. "Don't read them if it's going to ruin your day."

"It won't," she said, her voice still congested from crying. "But those were her boys. Greg was her flesh and blood. I don't know how she goes on."

I nodded my head, locked my eyes on Lori for a second to make sure she was okay, and then turned my eyes to the first letter.[8]

Dear Boys,

Today is Valentine's Day, a day for lovers, but for me this is the worst day of my life. I need to talk to you so much, so I will write a letter. Maybe this will help.

I am in a private room in Terre Haute Union Hospital. The drapes have been closed all day and an Indiana State Trooper is sitting outside my door to protect me. Everything seems so unreal.

I have been told that you are all dead. The words have no real meaning right now. Surely, you are not gone from my life forever! It must be a bad dream. I am sure I will soon awaken and everything will be as always. I will get up, fix your breakfast, Greg will go to work, the rest of you will go to school and everything will be normal. I really know that can't be. The terrible physical pain, and the horrible ache inside, is a constant reminder that this is real. You are dead. Our boys, gone from this life forever. How will we go on without you? Why did I live? How I wish, I had died with you. Why did they do this? I did not know any of them and none of you gave any indication that you knew them. Why did God let you die and save my life? You are such good boys, your lives are just beginning, you have so much to offer the world. I have contributed so little during my life and will probably never contribute much, yet I am still alive and you are dead. If only someone could tell me why!

---

[8] Betty Jane Spencer private journal, 14 February 1977 Personal papers of Betty Jane Spencer. All letters printed with the permission of Betty Jane Spencer.

After they finished shooting last night, I listened to them as they hunted spent shells. They seemed very concerned with finding them all. When they were satisfied that all were found, they turned out the lights and left the house laughing. Can you imagine? They thought we were all dead, yet they laughed. What kind of people are they? How could they do this? Why did they want us dead?

I raised up, just as they were driving away. I looked at you and asked. "Is anybody alive?" No one answered, but I still would not believe you were dead. I felt certain one of you had survived.

Although I felt no pain, I knew that shots had hit my back, arm and head. Not wanting to frighten anyone with my appearance, I wrapped a towel around my head, put on my boots and Greg's heavy coat and ran to Mr. Escue's house.

I pounded on his door, shouting, "It's Mrs. Spencer. I've been shot. Please help me!"

After entering the house, I gave Mr. Escue a brief account of what happened and then tried to call the Sheriff's Department. Having lost my glasses in the confusion, I could not see to dial the phone, so I dialed the operator for assistance. In her confusion, she connected me with Montgomery County Sheriff's Department. The dispatcher seemed not to believe my wild story. He asked to talk with someone else in the house, so Mr. Escue verified my story and gave him directions to our house.

Next, I phoned Channel 13 to speak with Keith, but he had not arrived yet. I phoned twice more to tell him what had happened, but he was still not there. It was decided that when Keith arrived, he would be told that there had been an accident and he should go directly to the hospital.

Choking in Fear

I phoned my sister, Mary Ellen. She and her husband, Charlie, agreed to meet me at the hospital.

By this time, the police and an ambulance had arrived. I was now suffering from horrible pain and I was quickly taken away in the ambulance.

I begged everyone not to tell me how many of you were dead. I knew Greg and Raymond were dead, but I could not stop hoping that either Ralph or Reeve had survived.

Keith arrived while I was in X ray, therefore, Mary Ellen had to tell him that his three wonderful sons and step-son were dead.

Soon, a man entered the room, followed by a state trooper.

"Mrs. Spencer," he said. "I am Detective Byron Thrasher with the Indiana State Police. Now, tell me what happened at your house tonight."

It was so difficult to describe what happened. I wanted to forget it all, but I knew the only way those four could be captured was for me to help all I could. For some reason, I could only describe three of the four. Maybe tomorrow I will remember more.

Keith returned to the hospital this evening. He looked so old as he stood at the end of my bed. I knew that I had to know if any of you had lived.

Looking into his sad face, I asked, "They're all gone, aren't they?"

As Keith nodded his head, I fell back into a tormented sleep.

I have been sedated most of today. I have alternated between sleep, terrible pain and the horrible realization of what has happened. Boys, I don't think I can go on living without you. I don't want to survive.

February 15, 1977[9]
Dear Boys,

I awoke this morning, unsure of where I was and then I remembered. I wanted so much just to return to sleep and forget it all. However, I could not sleep and I could not forget.

Today, I realized there will be a funeral. I had not thought of this before. It will be held Thursday afternoon and the doctor has assured me that I will be released on furlough to go to the funeral, and also the funeral home tomorrow night when our friends will pay their last respects. My brothers and sisters are concerned about me going, but I must. I am beginning to realize that you are really dead. I must be there with you.

Early this morning, an artist from Indianapolis arrived to make composites of the killers. We worked together for quite some time. It is really much harder to do than one might expect, but we were able to do two composites of which I was reasonably satisfied. When I started to describe the third person, the artist produced a composite of him. Apparently one had been involved in another crime.

It was impossible for me to describe the fourth person. It's as if I do not want to remember how he looked. I will keep trying to remember.

Detective Thrasher came again today. He is so kind and patient. He makes me feel that he really cares.

Together, we went over the killings. It is so difficult, but necessary. I am afraid he left with no new information. It is so frustrating. How can they find the-

---

[9] Betty Jane Spencer private journal, 15 February 1977, Personal papers of Betty Jane Spencer. All letters reprinted with the permission of Betty Jane Spencer.

se people we really know nothing about? It would be so much easier if they could establish a motive.

Reverend Fred Stewart and his wife Mary came today. He and Reverend Carl Huxford will take care of the funeral. I asked him to keep it as short as possible and to say God does not make mistakes. Although, right now, I really wonder. Does God make mistakes?

February 16, 1977[10]
Dear Boys,

It's really true! You're dead! I do not want to believe it, but I know you are all dead. I feel so numb. I might as well be dead. How I wish, I had died too.

Keith and I, with two state troopers, entered the funeral home. There were four beautiful hard-maple caskets in one room. On top of each closed casket was a spray of red and white carnations with each of your names on the ribbon. A picture of each of you was beside each spray. Your pictures, your names...

Hundreds of people came tonight. They were so kind. I am so glad that many people cared.

Raymond, today would have been your eighteenth birthday. What a celebration we would have had. Your favorite meal, served on china dishes, birthday cake, plus lots of fun and laughter. But instead, it was an evening of tears.

February 17, 1977[11]
My Dear Boys,

---

[10] Betty Jane Spencer private journal, 16 February 1977, Personal papers of Betty Jane Spencer. All letters reprinted with the permission of Betty Jane Spencer.
[11] Betty Jane Spencer private journal, 17 February 1977, Personal papers of Betty Jane Spencer. All letters reprinted with the permission of Betty Jane Spencer.

No words can describe the agony of today. I felt as though a giant hand had reached into my body and pulled every emotion from it. My body is an empty shell. Nothing seems important, except your death.

Nearly eight hundred people attended your funeral. Parke County schools were closed in your honor. Television and newspaper reporters were everywhere, but nothing really mattered except those four closed caskets, side by side at the church. Four caskets holding the lifeless bodies of four boys. I remember little about the service, except Reverend Stewart began with, "God does not make mistakes, man does. Oh, the evilness of man."

At that moment, I did not care who did or did not make mistakes. I only wanted to wake up and find that this was all a nightmare.

I do not know whether the temperature was warm or cold, the sun may have shone or it may have rained or snowed. I really felt nothing, except the agonizing pain.

I stood beside your caskets after the service at the cemetery, silently telling each of you good-bye. I knew that soon your bodies would be lowered into the ground.

Good-bye my son, Greg, my reason for living, my purpose in life. We have shared more than twenty-two years. I have watched you grow from a tiny baby into a young man any parent would be proud to call a son. You have been all the things I had hoped you would be. My son, my friend and my reason to live.

Good-bye Raymond. How often I have watched you work. How careful you have always been to do everything just right. Night after night we have sat across the table from each other, sharing our views. We didn't always agree, but I understood and I love you.

Good-bye Reeve, my carbon copy of Keith. How could I help but love you. I loved your dad when I was your age and you are so like he was. All the teasing, all the little tricks are just the things he once did.

Good-bye Ralph. Good-bye sunshine. That is what you are to me. Your smile had brightened my life daily. Believing is hard. Our Ralph, always smiling, never complaining, is dead. I love you so much.

You were all buried today. I feel as though my life has ended too.

Dear Boys,[12]

At last, I am out of the hospital. The little room with the drapes closed was seeming more and more like a tomb. I was extremely happy when the doctor announced Saturday that I could go home. But then I wondered, "Home? Where's that now?"

Keith told me we would be staying with his mother near Marshall. We would also have a state trooper with us at all times. At that moment it really did not seem to matter. If they thought they must protect me, then they should.

The doctor showed me some exercises to help me regain the use of my left arm. Until then, I did not realize that I could not move my arm. It hurt so much that I had not really tried to use it and it does not seem very important. The use of my arm is small compared to the loss of you boys, but I will do as he says.

---

[12] Betty Jane Spencer private journal, February 1977, Personal papers of Betty Jane Spencer. All letters reprinted with the permission of Betty Jane Spencer.

Before we left the hospital, we had another session of questioning. I am already tired of answering these same questions over and over, but I know that is the only way the killers can be caught. They must catch them. They must not have an opportunity to do this to anyone else.

I was shown a large group of pictures. I found one young man that looked somewhat like the youngest one. Maybe it will provide a lead.

When we arrived at your grandmother's house, I realized I am very much afraid. I suppose the small room did make me feel secure because now I am terrified of everything. I am afraid to enter an empty room. Keith is so understanding. He realizes how frightened I am and enters the room ahead of me. I am so glad he understands.

I have been questioned nearly every day. I suppose this will continue for quite some time, unless they catch those four men. I wish so much that you were here to help me. I'm sure you saw things that I did not see. This is such a great responsibility. I don't want to miss some important thing and yet I wish I could put that night out of my mind. Over and over I tell the detective what happened. Sometimes I remember something more, but I never know whether it is really important or not, I just keep trying to remember each tiny detail. Today, I remembered the one that entered the house first was left-handed.

I don't know how long the police will continue to guard me. I think it would be very hard if they were not here. Most every night, I awaken and go into the kitchen for a cup of coffee and find my "Blue Angel" sitting at the table. I call them that because I can never remember their names. Each eight-hour shift there is a new trooper. They are so patient with me. If I feel like talking, they listen. If I feel like crying, they do not try to stop me. If I wish to be alone, they ignore me. They are really great people, working many long hours on this case and they continue to assure me that this case will be solved.

Dear Boys,[13]

Today has been a very typical day, raining, dreary, just as my mood has been. I am beginning to become discouraged. Are they ever going to find those men who killed you? Surely God did not mean for them to go free, otherwise why am I alive, if not to help capture those four? Late this afternoon, Detective Thrasher phoned saying they had a lineup ready for me to view in Indianapolis. I felt very frightened. The responsibility is so great. I do not want the killers to go free, yet I certainly don't want to pick the wrong person.

As we drove to Indianapolis in the rain, talking about the case, repeatedly, there seemed to be nothing new. I thought maybe, tonight in the lineup, there would be a new development.

When we arrived, television reporters were outside the City County Building with their cameras pointed at me. I find myself looking at the ground instead of looking into the cameras. When I see myself on television, I see a very old looking woman, walking around with her eyes closed. You guys would enjoy that view of me. You would make fun of me because I really look terrible. Quite frankly, I feel terrible.

When I walked into the City County Building, I was greeted by State Trooper Dan Clevenger. You

---

[13] Betty Jane Spencer private journal, February 1977, Personal papers of Betty Jane Spencer. All letters reprinted with the permission of Betty Jane Spencer.

remember him. He has lived in this area for quite some time. Dan shook my hand and it made me feel so good to find someone I knew.

We entered a small office, where we were joined by several other troopers I knew. It was a tense time, but the troopers tried to make it easy for me. As easy as possible.

When we were called in to view the lineup, I was terribly frightened. So many people were in this large room, people that I did not know. Later I learned they were mostly law officers.

Six men were marched out behind one-way glass. I knew they could not see me, but the man asking questions was near me and they looked toward him, giving me the feeling that they were watching me. Turn to the left, turn right, full face, just like we have seen on television, only this time it was up to me to decide whether or not any of those six people had killed you.

After sufficient questioning, the first group left and six more entered. Disappointment overwhelmed me. None of the killers were there.

Barney Thrasher and I left Indianapolis feeling very depressed. Will we ever find them? Surely we will. Those killers cannot be allowed to go loose. They must be found...soon.

Dear Boys,[14]

I am so tired of these days. They all seem the same. I get up each morning wishing I did not have to face another day. I have my coffee, Keith changes the bandages on my wounds. I dress and by that time I

---

[14] Betty Jane Spencer private journal, February 1977, Personal papers of Betty Jane Spencer. All letters reprinted with the permission of Betty Jane Spencer.

am so tired. I must rest awhile. Barney Thrasher comes and the questioning begins. I call Detective Thrasher "Barney" now. Barney is the name all the troopers call him. He has become a very dear friend. I look at new pictures, we talk, hoping I will remember something new.

After lunch, I take a long nap. When I awaken, I talk to whichever trooper is with me that day, go through the mail with Keith when he arrives home and after we have our supper, I watch the news. Then I sit around the kitchen talking with Keith and the troops. Several times each night, I awaken and tiptoe into the kitchen and talk to the state trooper. When will life be normal again? This is not living. This is existing. Existing with an unbearable ache inside me that will never go away and an unbelievable fear of every noise, no matter how slight.

I have a recurring dream now. I dream that Keith and I are young and I have just given birth to a baby boy. It is as though I wanted to wipe the past away and start my life over. Although the pain is sometimes overwhelming, I would not wish to have missed one moment I had with you. Of all the things I have done in my life, the thing I have enjoyed the most was being a mother and now I am no longer a mother. I'm not sure what I am.

It seems that you are gone on a trip and it is time for you to return. If only that could be the truth.

March 3, 1977
Dear Boys,

Keith has decided to continue his plans for the radio station. The construction of the tower has started. It appears that he feels much the same as me. A job to be completed, not a labor of love, but something that has to be done. He is very busy, so I'm sure this is helpful to him. He discusses some of the plans with me, but I cannot seem to be interested in what he is doing. Nothing seems important to me at this time, except finding the people who killed you. His dream is coming true, yet all I can think about are my lost dreams. His plan is just as great as mine, but he is doing something constructive while I'm so weak and tired that I only exist. It seems to take all my energy just to get through the day.

How does one start their life over? Just a short time ago, we were a family. I was a mother, but right now I feel like nothing. How can I go on? Where is my place in life right now? What is my purpose now? Will I ever really smile again? Will I ever really laugh? I wonder.

Each day is much like the day before. I did not like yesterday, I do not like today, and I don't expect to like tomorrow. If only I had died with you.

March 7, 1977[15]
Dear Boys,

In yesterday's news it was said that the Indiana State Police had come up against a blank wall in the solution of the Hollandsburg massacre. I do not believe that. I still believe we will find the killers. Today, when Barney Thrasher came, he had Detective Loyd Heck and Trooper Goldner with him. They asked me to go into a room with them and they closed the door. Barney handed me a small group of pictures. I sat down and started slowly thumbing through

---

[15] Betty Jane Spencer private journal, March 1977, Personal papers of Betty Jane Spencer. All letters reprinted with the permission of Betty Jane Spencer.

the pictures. There he was, the one that stood in front of the television barking orders. I stopped, looked at the picture and felt the urge to spit on it.

I handed the last letter to Lori before exhaling a breath that I seemed to have been holding in my lungs since reading the first letter. Tears pushed hard against my eyelids, longing to break free and slide down my face.

The letters, so personal and from the heart, were never intended to be read by anyone. They were written by Betty Jane at a time when she was consumed with grief, longing for the assassins who had executed her family to be caught and brought to justice. When she was wondering if in fact they would ever be caught. It seemed less likely as the days passed into weeks and, for a time, Betty Jane did not even write a date on the letters.

It wasn't just the raw emotion of the letters, but the whole idea of her having to say good-bye to her boys in a letter. Not even allowed the decency of leaning over and kissing each of the boys, saying good-bye, I love you, before Drollinger, Smith, Wright, and Stonebraker filled them with buckshot.

"This whole thing is so sad," Lori said between sobs. It was totally beyond her comprehension.

I knew what she was thinking: Why are you dredging all this up? Why are you so consumed with these murders? I knew the questions; they had been asked before when I sat on our living room floor, re-reading the newspaper clippings or flipped a tape in the VCR of news coverage from the murders - or obsessed, as Lori had accused me of many times.

After reading the letters, I wondered myself why I didn't just let all of this go. Forget about it. Why couldn't I forget about it, like my supervisors had told me to do after investigating cases where children have been hurt or killed? Sure, I said at the time. No problem. But you never forget the look on the child's face, the last look in their eyes before they were killed. Those images were frozen in my mind for the rest of my life. And I guess these murders were no different.

The letters moved me more than anything I had ever read, but they still didn't answer the questions spinning in my head. That's what I really needed. Answers. I still had no idea why the boys were executed. I still had no idea if there was anything from this horrible crime that I could learn and use to prevent this from happening again. Anything I could use as a friend, a neighbor, a detective, to steer someone in the right direction who was teetering on the edge between productive citizen and self-destruction.

And that nearly worn-out manila folder of yellowed newspaper clippings that was lying on the backseat. I wanted answers so I could file the newspaper clippings away in a box, knowing full well that I would never forget this crime, but at least I would have something...as much understanding as you can have of a quadruple homicide.

After I cleared my head enough to drive, I suddenly realized where I was parked. We were less than a mile from where the boys had been executed. We were sitting beside the same road the killers had taken from the Spencer home the night of the murders, a road they had traveled as the blood rushed from the boys and Betty Jane ran through the night for help.

Even eighteen years later, the picture came back perfectly. The ice-covered road. The only thing stirring in the night was the Spencer's brown Thunderbird, which Drollinger had stolen and was driving with Stonebraker as copilot, and the rented orange Omega that Wright was driving, Smith riding shotgun (literally).

I stared at the pavement, chipped and dented from years of bearing the weight of heavy farm machinery and from neglect. This would have been the exact spot where the killers had learned that Betty Jane Spencer had survived their execution. Drollinger had been so prepared that night, he had equipped the Omega with a portable police scanner. And shortly after they had fled the Spencer's home, Drollinger was plotting their next stop, their next massacre, when Mike Wright almost ran over the brown Thunderbird as it stopped. At the stop sign next to where Lori and I were parked. Wright and Smith were panicky, having heard the Parke County Sheriff's Department being dispatched to the scene of a multiple homicide, mother survived. Thoughts and images swam through my head incoherently as I visualized the conversation between Wright and Drollinger, parked very near to where I sat daydreaming.

My heart beat rapidly against my chest. I pulled back onto the rural country road.

"Where are you going?" Lori asked.

"I'm going to show you where all this happened," I said. "The murders happened just up the road here. I didn't realize it when I stopped." My voice was even after a day of up and down emotion.

Out of the corner of my eye, I noticed Lori locking her door.

We drove in silence. I crested a hill and then stopped at the bottom. A trailer sat next to the road. "That's where Harold Escue used to live," I said. "He used to have a small shack right where the trailer sits. Betty Jane ran over here for help." I glanced from the trailer to the hill in the distance where the Spencer home sat. Nearly a mile, I estimated.

Lori drew her legs up against her chest. The sun was setting in the rearview mirror. A cold burst of wind, the first real snap of cold air to remind us that winter was just around the corner, came unopposed through the open window and hit me in the face. I thought of how cold it had been the night Betty Jane raced across the frozen countryside, praying with each step that Reeve and Ralph were still alive, while the shock of being shot twice and overwhelming fear of being ambushed by the killers choked her.

A lady appeared in the doorway of the trailer, staring at me, wondering who I was and why I was parked in front of her home. We were strangers. I hadn't lived around here in many years and the license plate on our Isuzu Rodeo was from Tennessee. Strangers were no longer welcomed around here with open arms.

I drove up the road, slowed as we reached the top of the hill, and pulled into the gravel driveway. "This is where it all happened." I said.

"That's the house?" Lori asked, studying it intently.

"No," I said. "The Spencer home was destroyed by a tornado a few years ago." God's way of cleansing the desecrated house, I thought. "But that's the same garage." The same garage where Reeve and Raymond spent countless hours working on their cars, swapping stories with their friends, contemplating their long lives in front of them. Having no idea that they would not even have the chance to graduate from high school.

We were sitting in the same driveway that Drollinger had pulled the Omega into, headlights off, where he gave his final order. "Seek and secure." I put the Rodeo in reverse, afraid I would frighten whomever was living there now. Shocked that anybody could even live on this plot of land, forever referred to as the Spencer place, the place those murders happened.

I had chills tingling my spine as I backed from the driveway, glancing one last time at the garage, then drove down the hill and turned north on the gravel road. The same gravel road where the killers had parked, after driving by the house twice, and plotted the murders.

"Ooh," Lori shrieked.

"Crap," I said at the same time.

A huge cornstalk slid across the road in front of us. I slammed on the brakes while reaching for the gearshift, intending to grind the transmission into reverse and retreat. The area was haunted. Then I saw the muskrat leading the parade. He was dragging the cornstalk across the road to the creek. The same creek Betty Jane had run through on her way to get help.

"Get me out of here," Lori said. "Now!"

I spun the tires. Then locked my door.

CHAPTER TWENTY-SIX

The sound of the metal door clanking shut behind me sent a chill down my spine. I had made the decision to enter and there was no turning back. I snuck a glance over my shoulder at the world I was leaving. I told myself I would be back shortly, but I wasn't convinced. The slamming of the old metal door sounded so permanent.

"Put your hand in the box," the male guard said like he had uttered this phrase a million times already today. He was sitting in a control room, surrounded by glass on three sides. All movement in and out was controlled from this glass cage. This was a cage that, by design, was meant to keep people out, not in.

I walked over and put my hand in a box of ultraviolet light as ordered. A white image appeared on my hand, which gave me permission to enter and would be my permission to leave. Who the heck is going to switch places with one of these guys? I thought.

I was in limbo, waiting for the second door to slide open and swallow me fully into the new world. Both sets of doors were never opened at the same time. These two doors were charged with the heavy responsibility of keeping the two worlds separate. They could not be opened at the same time, eliminating any chance of human error.

This was a world far removed from the one in which I lived. A totally different culture, with its own rules, language, monetary system, and morals. I had traveled through the two doors less than thirty feet apart, but I felt like I had been dropped into a foreign world. Everything that was normal had disappeared.

When the final door slammed shut behind me, I knew I was no longer in control. I would leave when they wanted me to. It was an eerie feeling, a feeling of vulnerability. It was the first time since childhood that I was completely dependent on someone else.

As I stood just inside the threshold of the door, acclimating myself to the new environment, it was hard for me to believe that the people in this world were actually not that much different from those in mine. I knew that from experience, from working hundreds of criminal investigations as a detective, from interviewing lots of suspects. But for most of my life I had believed that only animals, genetic mutants, or psychopaths could end up in this world. I was reverting to my earlier beliefs as my heart pounded and the fear of the unknown gripped my soul. I spoke silently, trying to convince myself that it was a fine line between my world and this world. Keep an open mind. Don't let your fear cloud your judgment.

I glanced around the meeting room, very plain, no pictures, drab colored walls, tile floor. The place could use a splash of paint and some wallpaper, but I knew this would never happen. There were several round tables with chairs which reminded me of a high school cafeteria, a row of private meeting rooms - as private as clear Plexiglas allowed - for visiting attorneys or police officers, and two vending machines adjacent to the security desk which sat high above the meeting room like a judge's bench. The two guards perched behind the desk talked casually while their eyes scanned the crowded room back and forth.

I felt like a fish out of water. I stood motionless, the decisive police officer, unsure of where to go or what to do. Like every other person in the room, I looked to the guard for direction. But neither one seemed interested in giving advice.

It was easy to tell the visitors from the residents. It would have been easy to pick me out - I looked like a drunk who had wandered into church by mistake. The residents were all wearing the same thing: blue jeans and white T-shirts. A black number stamped above their heart was all that distinguished them. This number was more important than their name. It was their identification.

Several people brushed past me, already familiar with this world. I was excited about my meeting, but the only picture I had of my guest was eighteen years old. The person I remembered was a young man, early twenties, shoulder-length dark brown hair parted in the middle, a bushy mustache, and piercing eyes. It was the eyes I was looking for. The eyes that I had stared at and that had stared back at me for eighteen years. Those eyes had swept me from an innocent childhood and introduced me to the real world, a world where people hurt other people. A world filled with fear and hate.

Out of the corner of my eye I noticed a middle-aged man with short salt-and-pepper hair stand up from behind a table and look directly at me. He was near a Plexiglas cubicle and alone at the table. But he looked nothing like the young man I was searching for. We made eye contact. I didn't recognize him. He could have been anybody waiting to speak with his attorney or a police officer he had never met.

"Mike?" the man asked cautiously.

"Yes," I answered softly before walking toward him. I still wasn't convinced it was the man I was to meet. "Dan?" I mumbled.

He held out his hand. I quickly brushed my hand along my khaki pants to dry the nervous perspiration. My heart was pounding in my throat. Calm down, I told myself. But the harder I tried, the stronger the pounding became. I had thought of this day for eighteen years, and was thankful we were meeting on my terms today, and not on his terms eighteen years ago.

"Have a seat," Dan said as we walked into the small cubicle, which had barely enough room for two grown men. "Glad you could make it."

"Me, too," I replied with a dry mouth. All of the water in my body had escaped through my hands. It was hot. Really hot. My eyes darted around the room. A long list of rules was posted on the far wall. Inmate must face guard at all times. No hugging. No kissing. No standing. The list went on and on.

"What do you think?" He had to sense my uneasiness.

"A lot different from what I had imagined." That was the truth.

"What were those two areas on each side of the front entrance? There were people yelling, screaming, cussing. Sounded like a riot." I had recently read Jack Henry Abbott's In the Belly of the Beast about his life as an inmate. As well as Abbot wrote about being institutionalized, it still had not prepared me for the reality of walking inside a prison.

Dan smiled warmly. A kind of jolly-ole-smile. Not the type of smile expected of a man serving two life sentences for murder. "That's the cell blocks. It's like that all the time. Horrible place to live."

"Is that where you live?" I asked. My pulse was finally under two hundred beats per minute.

"No. Not anymore. We have dormitory buildings in the back of the prison. I've been back there for several years. They keep the worst inmates and the new inmates in the cell blocks. It's incentive to behave so you can move back where I am. It's very quiet compared to the cell block. And you have more privacy. I have my own room. I can turn the lights on and off when I want to. More freedom to exercise. But I don't get any free passes to McDonald's." He smiled. "I still have a guard watching me use the bathroom, shower, sleep, and head counts every four hours." He spoke matter-of-factly, not like he was trying to draw sympathy. Just merely explaining where and how he lived.

I stared at Dan's eyes and could not believe it was the same man, the same set of eyes. Where was the rage and evil that had jumped from his picture eighteen years ago? His eyes were no different from anybody else's now.

I was finding it hard to focus with all of the noise in the visiting room. Dan had laser focus. He had adapted to the noise and chaos all around him. I was in police mode. Who wouldn't be? I was surrounded by men who had done some awful and violent things.

"How's your dad?" Dan asked. "He's a guy I think of from time to time."

"He's fine," I said. "He wanted me to tell you hi. He also wanted me to tell you that you look like an old man. He saw you a couple years ago in the newspaper. Clemency hearing or something." I smiled.

Dan laughed from deep inside his barreled chest. "Your dad use to come by the Clark Station, on the east side of town. He would come in and buy gas in his state police car."

I chuckled, having heard this story a hundred times from Dad. "He came by there because he knew you guys were selling more drugs than gas," I added, feeling more comfortable.

"That's no joke. There were times we had semis backed up around the corner. We were charging fifty cents a hit on speed. Must've been the only people in town selling it."

I thought about how much the world had changed since Dan had last seen it. The Clark Station had been gone for years and was now a vitamin store. Bell-bottom pants were gone (but coming back in vogue). Cars were smaller and sportier. The price of a house had more than doubled.

The smile faded from Dan's face. "That was the last place I saw your dad. He came in and was getting gas." His eyes drifted away, while he thought of an earlier time. "He always got out of his police car and stood next to the pump, talking to me. He told me I better get my act together, that Roger was going to get me into big trouble. Something I would regret the rest of my life."

Dan didn't have to say it, I could hear the regret in his voice. Simple advice, but so prophetic. And the fact that it came from my dad was of little surprise to me. He was always for the underdog. My dad had told me many times after the murders that Dan was really a good kid. A little rowdy, liked a good time, maybe didn't have enough direction in life, and definitely didn't have the right influences. Especially Roger Drollinger. But even after the revelation of such a horrendous crime, my dad still stuck to his belief that deep down inside, Dan was a good kid who chose the wrong path. Dad felt this way because he knew the line between the right and the wrong side of the fence was much thinner than people realized or wanted to believe. At a deeper level, I think maybe my dad saw himself in the young Dan. Two kids that had basically looked after themselves their whole life and then came to a fork in the road and had to choose a path that would lead to success or a path that would lead to destruction. What was it that led Dad to the state police and Dan to enter a home and kill four people? It had to be people who influenced their lives. For dad it was his Grandpa McCarty and his athletic coaches. They were positive role models. For Dan, unfortunately, his role model was Roger Drollinger.

"He was one of the ones that really did try to help me, talk to me, but I just seemed bent on destruction." Dan sighed. "It must have been very frustrating for the people who wanted to help me. Watching me throw my life away."

Silence lingered in the air for several seconds as we both thought about how things could have been and digested how things really were. After several seconds, Dan changed the topic.

"How about you, Mike? Did you always want to be a cop like your dad?"

There was that question again. The idea was funny and drew a laugh from me. "No way. All of my life people have asked me that. But I always said no. And I meant it. I never wanted to be a cop until my last semester of college."

"It seems like such a great job," Dan said. He was serious, no smiles, no joking.

"It can be at times," I replied honestly. It could also be as boring as hell and discouraging. It became discouraging because some of the people I worked with had less-than-desirable motivations for becoming a police officer. They were using the power of the badge to further their own interest, some legal and some not.

I assumed that if I polled the other men sitting around us that few of them would share Dan's belief that the law enforcement profession was a great job. This was prison, where everybody was serving time because of the police. It was the damn officer who made me drink a case of beer, drive my car, and kill an innocent family; it was an officer who made me kill my wife; it was an officer who made me rob the market or use drugs. But I didn't get the impression from Dan that he blamed anybody but himself, even though it would be

Choking in Fear

easy to blame it on Roger Drollinger like so many others had, my dad and some detectives included.

"You're gonna think this is crazy," Dan said. "But I would have loved to be a police officer."

"That's pretty wild," I said, considering he was serving two life sentences for murder.

"Are you a state police officer in Tennessee?"

"No, I'm a detective in Nashville. I work domestic violence cases."

Dan exhaled very slowly. "I bet that keeps you busy."

"It does," I said. "We average from forty to eighty cases per month. Generally about two murders involving husbands or ex-boyfriends. Plenty of job security."

"I know," Dan said. "I saw a lifetime of it growing up."

"What do you mean?" I asked.

Dan leaned forward on his elbows and intertwined his fingers. "My father used to hit my mom when I was younger. I hate to say that because, for the first time in my life, Dad and I have a relationship."

"How old were you?"

"I was pretty young. I can remember one time that they were going at it in the living room. I stood there trying to get the courage up to stand up to Dad. But I couldn't. I was too scared. I was scared of Dad. I felt so guilty for not helping Mom. Like a coward."

I knew there was not much he could have done as a young boy because I went to hospitals on a daily basis to interview mothers and young boys who had been beaten savagely by an abusive father. Sons beaten beyond recognition for standing up to protect their mothers. Seldom did the young boy win.

"Another time," Dan said, "I was so scared I stood right there and peed my pants."

A guard walked up to our table, said nothing, but dropped an identification card with a yellow Post-it note on the table. I watched the guard repeat this exercise a dozen times at different tables.

"What was that all about?" I asked.

"Time's up," Dan said.

The clock on the wall read 2:20 P.M. It had been nearly three hours since I had been escorted through the doors. Where had the time gone? The questions I had prepared were still mostly unanswered. And now I had hundreds more questions about the violence in Dan's life growing up. We had started to open the lid on a jar that had been closed for eighteen years. And I wanted to beg the guard to allow me to stay until I had answers to my questions. I had driven three hundred and fifty miles for the meeting. It wasn't so much that I wanted answers, but that I needed answers. I wanted to walk back through the double set of metal doors, into my world, armed with the answers to the questions that had been nagging my spirit since I was nine years old.

"Do I need to leave?" I asked while glancing around the room. Nobody else seemed to be in a hurry to leave, so I relaxed a little and turned back to Dan.

"No, we have about ten minutes before they will make you leave." He spoke quickly, a man with only a few minutes remaining and so much left to discuss. And interestingly enough, a man with all the time in the world. "I have something I want to tell you. I need to tell you this before you leave."

"Go ahead," I replied, but my mind was sorting the hundreds of questions, trying to narrow down the list to two or three since I only had a few minutes.

"On the night all of this happened..."

The words penetrated my head. He had my undivided attention.

"We drove right past your house." Dan paused for a second, like he didn't want to tell me the rest. "Roger said we should stop at your house and kill a pig and his family."

A lump developed in my throat the size of a basketball and it wouldn't go up or down. I couldn't speak. My knees became weak and I knew they would crumble if I tried to walk. He was not joking. I knew he was truthful because the only logical way to get from Crawfordsville to the Spencer home was to drive right past ours. Another four miles and you were there. I could feel myself drifting back in time. The snap of that cold St. Valentine's Day morning in 1977. The choking fear. The fear of unknown killers lurking outside my bedroom. And now I knew how close to my bedroom window they had actually been.

CHAPTER TWENTY-SEVEN

I stood on the threshold of the doorway, breathing in the warm summer night while listening for the telephone. The moon bounced off the Cumberland River below. I filled my lungs with the humid night air before walking back into the lonely reception area and sitting down at the desk. It was my turn to pull desk duty, answering the telephones and assisting victims who walked into the office. We rotated the assignment each day.

There wasn't a detective in the office who didn't hate his tour of duty at the receptionist desk. Sitting behind the desk, caged like an animal at the zoo, answering the telephone, taking messages, transferring calls to the other detectives, and chewing your fingernails off in boredom.

The television in the far corner was tuned to CNN. I left it on for the company. The office was a lonely place at night. Once our shift started, calls from officers in the field and hospitals scattered us throughout the city. If we were lucky, we'd get a break late in the evening, a chance to catch up on the mountain of paperwork each case demanded - incident report, evidence sheet, supplemental reports, affidavits, protective orders, arrest reports, safety plans. Tonight was no different. Shortly after roll call at 3:30 P.M., the other detectives scattered around the city to investigate crimes from homicide to assault.

I leaned back in the chair and watched as an officer pulled up to the gas pumps across the dead-end street and filled the tank of his patrol car. My thoughts were not on Nashville, or my job, but on my recent visit with Dan Stonebraker. "We drove right past your house that night. Roger joked about stopping and killing a pig and his family." The words had stung my ears for the entire five-hour drive from Pendleton to Nashville. It had been in my every waking thought since. I had called my dad shortly after leaving the prison to inform him of what Dan had told me. How close to death we actually had come that night eighteen years ago. He wasn't shocked or speechless as I had anticipated. This was old news to him. He'd known this for years. But as the good father and protector of his family, he'd kept it from us. He didn't want to scare us any more than we already were at the time.

I pictured the request sliding off Drollinger's lips as he imagined the headlines a slaughter of a cop and his family would generate. Whereas most men wanted to make headlines for their prowess as an athlete, or for their business ventures. Drollinger longed to be the next Charles Manson. As it was, the murders of the Spencer family made national news and thrust Drollinger into the national spotlight. It made a nobody into a somebody. But the Spencer murders wouldn't have compared to the murder of a police officer and his family. That would have been huge.

The telephone rang, startling me from my thoughts. "Domestic Violence. Detective McCarty, can I help you?" I transferred the caller to the detective working her case.

I looked down at the black binder in front of me, a case file I needed to review for an early morning court hearing. The stalking case had started as a simple phone call like the one I just transferred to one of my colleagues.

"Domestic Violence Division, may I help you?" I asked. The reception area was empty and my police radio abnormally quiet, even for a Sunday evening. That wasn't all bad, though. A quiet night now and then was a good thing since they were so few and far between.

"Uhm, yes," the female voice said evenly but with hesitation. "I'm having some problems with my boyfriend. Ex-boyfriend."

"Is he there right now?" I asked.

"No," she said. "No, he's not here."

"Do you need me to send a patrol unit by your house?"

"No. He's not here."

"Is he on his way over? Do you know?"

"No, not that I know of. And I don't think he'll come over here tonight."

"Are you sure you don't need me to send an officer over right now? It's gonna be a while before I can get out to you." I still had over an hour of office duty left.

"No," she said. "It's not an emergency. I just need to talk to someone about our problems." Her voice was calm and collected. I knew that didn't mean anything. I had worked with a victim who had talked to a dispatcher, as cool as a cucumber, while her spouse held a shotgun to her head. The constant threat of physical violence, the unending emotional abuse, made them even and unemotional. The violence was a normal part of their life, not an event that startled them.

"Okay," I said. "I'll be out in a little bit. If he calls or shows back up, call 911." I jotted down her address on a yellow Post-it -note and stuck it to my radio.

As I turned the corner onto Wimbleton Drive, my heart skipped a beat. Patrol cars lined the street. Crap? I hoped this had nothing to do with the victim I had talked to on the phone earlier. I glanced at the house numbers. Yep, the police cars were parked in front of the house I was looking for.

"The front door's gone," Steve said. Steve Huntley was my partner, a good ole country boy from North Carolina.

"Crap," I said as much to myself as to Steve.

"I hope he didn't show back up after you talked to her."

"I know," I mumbled while stepping out of the unmarked car, staring at the house for any sign that everything was okay and waiting for my shaking legs to calm enough to carry me inside.

I stopped at the front door, studying the busted door jamb. It had been kicked open, completely off the hinges. That was no easy feat. Hollywood made it look so easy in the movies, but seasoned street cops know how hard it is to kick a door open, let alone kick it off the hinges.

I didn't want to step inside. What if he had come back and killed her in the short period after I spoke with her? No, dispatch would have already called for a domestic violence investigator. Then again, maybe they called homicide. Damn, I hope I didn't screw up. It's so hard to gauge how dangerous the situation might be when talking with a victim on the telephone. Victims in survival mode might downplay the violence.

Had I missed something?

I stepped across the threshold into a small living room packed with officers, huddled in small groups talking. An officer I recognized stood from his sitting position next to a female on the couch. I hated that I couldn't remember his name, but in a department of over a thousand police officers, it was hard to remember every officer's name. The female smiled. Late thirties I guessed. I exhaled slowly, anxiously waiting, wondering what the heck was going on.

The officer stuck out his hand. I shook it as he glanced over his shoulder, gauging whether or not we were far enough away from the victim so he could speak freely. "Hey, we've been over here a hundred times. Her boyfriend shot up her van last week. He was arrested. Another time he was hiding under her bed with a fire poker when the officers found him. He bonded out last Friday morning."

"OK," I said, not a bit surprised a judge would give him bond. Heck, no cop in the city expected the courts to set a reasonable bond on a domestic violence case, even when it did involve weapons being fired. That didn't mean we didn't argue our cases until we were blue in the face, though.

"That's when it got interesting."

Doesn't it always, I thought. A young officer, standing only a few paces from the victim, let loose with a laugh. God only knows what they were talking about. I tried to make eye contact, to see if I could get them to move outside. The officers were simply there to back up the officer I was speaking with. I didn't expect them to be interested. But I expected professionalism in front of the victim.

"Well, Rebecca, the victim," he pointed over his shoulder at the woman on the couch. "She came home Friday morning. Thought her ex-boyfriend..." He glanced at his notepad. "Mark Hopper. She thought he was still in jail. Turns out he had already made bond. She comes home and finds him in her shower. She runs out and calls the police."

"Okay," I said.

"Captain was getting sick of this guy causing all kinds of problems out here," the officer continued. I glanced inconspicuously at his name tag, but the glare from the overhead light turned it black. "Captain brought in unmarked directed patrol units. Then set up a perimeter of marked units. He had Rebecca call Hopper and lure him back to the house so we could arrest him. Somehow," the officer shrugged his shoulders of the responsibility, "she walks down the street to meet Hopper. Before they can arrest him, she gets in the truck with him and he takes off. Truck was stolen."

"Okay," I said, wondering why the Domestic Violence Division hadn't been contacted before the victim was used as bait, dangled in front of the suspect like a worm in front of a fish. It seemed, at least from listening to the officer's language, that the problem was the victim. She walked down the street and got in the truck. Why would she go through the trouble of calling the police, calling me, to talk about her ex-boyfriend? If it was as simple as getting in the truck and driving off, then why was the house filled with officers? And why was the front door leaning against an interior wall? It didn't make sense. Then again, each case was always a fuzzy picture at first, until we had a chance to investigate and tune the picture.

"Do you need anything else?"

"No," I said. "Just knock out a supplemental report. Just what you told me. We'll take care of the rest. If we get warrants, I'll give you a call."

"That'll work," he said.

Steve ordered a pizza as soon as we returned to our office. Steve and I had planned to eat after I finished with desk duty, and Rebecca mentioned she hadn't eaten all day. I wasn't sure how this was going to unfold, if we would obtain warrants, and if so, when we would have time to eat. It didn't look like we would be going home at midnight when our shift ended.

We walked into the interview room (which was the day shift detectives' office while the building was being remodeled). Steve would get the pizza when the deliveryman arrived and we'd take a break from the interview.

"Okay," I said, while sitting down and turning on the tape recorder. "I'm taping this because I can't write fast enough to take good notes." I smiled. "Now, Rebecca, can you tell me what happened last Friday?"

She told me exactly the same version the officer told me, right up to the point where her ex-boyfriend, Mark, screamed up in a stolen green Ford Ranger truck. "He was holding a gun, kind of pointin' it at me. So I got in the truck." She rolled her eyes as if to say, "What else do you expect?" She talked matter-of-factly. No tears, no emotion in her voice. She even flashed a smile occasionally.

"Did you get in the truck on your own free will?" I asked, knowing the question would come up again.

"No," she said like I was stupid.

I smiled, acknowledging the question seemed stupid. "I have to ask some questions that may seem obvious. But I have to ask them. I have to meet certain statutory requirements...certain elements, so I know which warrants to obtain. That doesn't mean I don't believe you. I know you're telling me the truth. I just want you to know why I'm asking so many questions."

She nodded her head.

"Okay, then what happened? After he forced you in the truck."

"Mark took off," she said. "He was flying. He knew there were cops all over the place. We got on the interstate and drove even faster. Then down about Murfreesboro or so he stopped and made me take some money out of an ATM machine. He used the money to get a motel room. Then he brought me back this morning. He had his son drop me off at home. He knew Metro was looking for him."

Metro was the street slang for the police department. I glanced at Steve. He was thinking the same thing: why didn't we know about what happened Friday? It was Sunday. Two days later.

"This is a tough question, but I have to ask it. Did he rape you? Force you to have sex against your will?"

The buzzer on the front door sounded. Steve left to pay for the pizza.

She shook her head. "No."

I didn't say anything for a minute. I let the silence hang in the air, sure that he had probably raped her but had no way to prove it. "Okay. How'd your door get busted?"

She threw her arms up in the air. "Last Tuesday or Wednesday...I can't remember which day...he kicked it in to get in the house."

"You've been staying there all week with no front door?" I asked, admiring her bravery. "With all that he was doing?"

"Didn't have no choice," she said.

Steve walked back in the room and laid the pizza on an empty desk, then handed me a printout of Hopper's criminal history, which was lengthy and included charges of domestic violence, stalking, and aggravated assault. "He's been arrested a couple times," I said.

"Yep," Rebecca said. "He did the same exact thing to his ex-wife. He's still on parole for that. A community corrections violation."

"He's been arrested for assaulting a police officer, too," Steve said while pointing at the charges on the paper. "Assaulted a Brentwood officer. I called down there while this was printing. It turns out the officer was working. Said he arrested Hopper and when he went to get him out of the car, Hopper kicked him and ran off. Hopper's some kind of black belt. Get this, though. The officer said a few days later, he got his handcuffs back in the mail. Hopper had them cut off and mailed them back. He's got some 'nads."

"I can't let you go back home tonight," I said. "I mean, it's your choice, But it's too dangerous. We may or may not find him tonight. I still have to file the warrants in Night Court."

"He's at his dad's" she said. "Over in Lebanon."

She had told me this earlier and I ran it past my supervisor. It seemed only logical to get him picked up as soon as possible. But logic often collided with fear of making a decision when it came to supervision on the department. And that was my sergeant. Not one to make a decision. She wanted to be a sergeant because you didn't have to answer calls and it paid more, but the responsibility didn't suit her.

Steve and I went to Night Court to obtain warrants for kidnapping, stalking, and vehicle theft while another detective escorted Rebecca to a local YMCA shelter for battered women. Hopper would not be arrested tonight, and wouldn't be in police custody for almost six days.

My pager danced like a hot potato on the nightstand. I had forgotten to turn it from vibrate to audible before going to bed last night. I scooped it up, stared at the number for a second before realizing it was the Domestic Violence Office.

Rebecca had left the shelter early this mooring, having decided to go to work against the advice I had given her after assessing the potential dangerousness of Hopper trying to hurt or kill her. The lethality assessment - a tool of predicting future danger to victims by studying risk factors - rated Rebecca's potential for dangerousness as high. For some reason, she decided to go to work (probably because she couldn't afford to miss a day's work). While waiting downtown for a traffic light to turn green, Hopper jumped in her van. He had been lying in wait, stalking her like a predator. He timed it perfectly at the red light. Thankfully for Rebecca, a Homicide supervisor was behind her at the traffic light. Though unsure of what he was observing, he flipped his dash light on, spooking Hooper in the process. Off Hopper went, stealing another vehicle from a market and fleeing the city at a high rate of speed, a stunt he would repeat several times over the week - stealing cars, fleeing at high speeds, then leaving a voice mail message for Rebecca. It was his twisted way of showing his love.

I answered the telephone after one ring. It was my Captain, Shirley Davis. Hopper was being perused in Wilson County, the county hugging Nashville to the east, in a stolen Mercedes Benz. It was Friday, the sixth day of the investigation, and I was physically and mentally drained from pursuing Hopper, empathetic to the stress Rebecca had endured for years at the hands of this man.

 I took a shower, dressed quickly in a suit, and headed out the front door. Before I reached the office, Hopper flipped the Mercedes Benz negotiating a winding curve, was thrown from the car, but was able to run more than fifty yards with a punctured lung. I was glad this nightmare of a case was concluded or, at least, that the pursuit was over. I would be buried under the weight of the paperwork for weeks.

The telephone on the receptionist's desk rang once, jolting me from my daydream, then turned silent before I could pick it up. A wrong number. Or a victim working up the nerve to call for help, maybe while her husband was at work, who then lost her strength to share her story. A woman certain she was the only one in the world being mentally and physically abused by someone she loved, sure that she was to blame for most of what was happening in the relationship. Brainwashed into believing she had no merit, was worthless, and couldn't do anything on her own. Scared and feeling alone. Unaware that thousands of women in the City of Nashville were staring at their telephones, contemplating making the same phone call. She was a member of a very large sorority.

 I closed the Hopper case file and stared at the binder of Hollandsburg newspaper clippings I had brought to work. They were yellowing, turning brown around some of the edges. I had spent six days tracking Hopper-the-stalker, the mounting pressure from the police department and community weighing me down. Now I began to appreciate the pressure Loyd Heck must have felt in February, March, and April of 1977 as he searched for the killers of Greg Brooks and Raymond, Reeve, and Ralph Spencer. Seven weeks came and went for Loyd before all the killers were in custody, and another ten months before all four of the killers were tucked away in prison.

 I leaned back in the chair, folded my arms behind my head, and stared at the muted television while formulating a list of questions in my head that I needed to ask Dan Stonebraker.

CHAPTER TWENTY-EIGHT

"The movie Helter Skelter was on TV just a few weeks before the murders," Dan said. "Roger and I watched it at his mom and dad's house. That's where Roger lived with Kathy and the kids."

"Why'd he live with his mom and dad?" I asked. "He was twenty-four years old." A little old, I thought, to be living at home, especially with his kids and second wife.

"Roger had always lived with someone else as long as I'd known him," Dan said. "Mike, you had to understand that Roger's parents were his protectors. His dad always stood up for him, every time he got in trouble. I think his dad truly believed that Mike Wright and I did the murders and were framing Roger."

Dan wasn't the first person who had told me that. Police officers, school associates, former friends had all said the same thing. I knew parents like that, who could never except that their children weren't perfect. They always seemed to be the parents of the kid who was into trouble all the time. But if the parents always stand up for the kid and say he didn't do it, what can you expect from the kid?"

"Who all watched the movie?" I asked.

I scanned the busy meeting room, busting at the seams with holiday visitors, while waiting for Dan to answer. This was probably the only time of year that most of the inmates had visitors. I watched as the inmates interacted with friends and family, amazed at how some of the meanest men in Indiana - men who had killed - were moved to tears while hugging a mother or father, saying goodbye. How could a convicted killer still have the capacity for loving and caring for others?

"Just Roger and I," Dan said. "His parents were there, but they didn't watch the movie with us."

"Did Roger say much during the movie?" I asked.

"He didn't say nothing," said Dan. "He just sat there and watched the movie. I don't think he ever got out of the chair. He was mesmerized."

"Did you like the movie?"

"Sure," Dan said. "It was a good movie. But looking back, it's hard to believe I was involved in a crime so similar."

"How much of an impact do you think the movie had on Drollinger?" I asked.

I had mailed a list of questions to Dan several weeks ago to prepare him for the interview. I wanted him to have time to think about the questions, refresh his memory, and even bounce things off of Mike Wright and David Smith to make sure his recollections were accurate.

I knew he had thought long and hard about the questions, because in a recent letter he talked about what a drain on his spirit this had become. He said it felt like he was describing a crime somebody else had committed.

Dan leaned forward and placed his hand on the table. "Well," he said, "it was about this time that Roger started talking a lot about family. Like the Manson family in the movie. And he didn't refer to Manson as Manson, he called him Charlie." Dan laughed. "Like he knew him personally."

At some level, he probably understood Manson, I thought. And I wondered what it was about Manson that fascinated Drollinger. The control he had over people? The drugs? The sex? Or the fame and notoriety that the crime had brought Manson?

"Roger was remodeling a house on his dad's property that we were all going to move into. Roger's own little family. He had one room set aside as the arsenal. He wanted a stash of guns."

"What was it about Roger that you liked?" I asked. "Didn't you think he was a psycho at times?"

Dan laughed, then tilted his head back, stared at the ceiling for a second, gathering his thoughts, before looking back at me. He maintained eye contact while speaking better than anybody I had talked with in a long time. At times I had to move my eyes away from his, unable to maintain the intensity of his eye contact and focus. He'd learned the fine art of concentration. "I was fascinated by Roger. He could do just about anything. He could fly a plane. I had watched him pick a safe one time with a paper clip and a spent .32 cartridge. I've seen him climb a telephone pole, tap into the phone line, and make a phone call. I was very impressionable and he impressed me.

"Roger had me, and all the others around him, believing that the cops were stupid, that we were doing the right thing. He always had money. At the height of our drug trafficking, he was bringing in several thousand dollars a week. I was along for the thrills. The money didn't do much for me. But at some point, he started believing he had the same power as Charles Manson did."

I slid my cup of Mountain Dew to the right and leaned forward on the table, resting on my elbows. The noise of families chattering around us was making it hard to hear.

"Here's an example," Dan said. "We were at this party one time and, as we were leaving, this woman came running after Roger and he didn't see her and he closed the door. She ran her arms through the glass door. It cut her wrists pretty bad. Roger asked her why she did it and she said, 'Because I thought you would stop me.' Like Roger had some mystical connection with her." Dan rolled his eyes. "We laughed it off as too many drugs. But I could tell Roger was wondering if it was true."

Many of the boys hanging around with Drollinger did so out of fear as much as respect. I had learned, from talking to many men who used to hang out with Drollinger, that he loved to pull his pistol (which he always had) and put it to their head while telling them exactly how he was going to blow their brains out. Roger had done it to Dan, Mike, and David just minutes before they burst into the Spencer home. The day before the murders, Roger had put the pistol to the head of David Smith's stepbrother and threatened to kill him for no reason.

I had talked with many of Drollinger's former associates, boys who had grown to respectable family men without Drollinger's influences, and asked them what would have happened had they been with the group on the night of the murders. Wayne said, "I like to think I would not have participated." Several times, there was silence on the phone as they thought about a question that had surely crossed their minds before. What if...

"Mike," Dan said, "people don't realize that Roger wanted to pattern the murders after the Manson murders. The Tate-LaBianca murders. After we killed them, Roger had wanted us to write 'pigs' and 'Helter Skelter' on the refrigerator and walls in the victims' blood."

"So, the murders were purely random?" I asked. "I mean, you could have stopped anywhere that night?"

"Yep," Dan said. "Everybody thinks the murders were somehow drug-related. But they weren't. Roger just picked the house because it had a lot of nice cars in the driveway. It had nothing to do with those boys."

"There was also a big discussion right after the murders," I said, "about a book that was found in Drollinger's jail cell at the Montgomery County Jail, right before he was released on bond for the drug charges. They said he had the book In Cold Blood by Truman Capote, and that there were passages underlined."

"I've heard that," Dan said. "But I don't know if it's true."

"The crimes are very similar," I said. "The Clutter family was killed in their rural country home. The real motive in that crime was robbery, then murder. But it was a very brutal murder. Like yours."

It was the randomness of the crime that people didn't want to accept - or couldn't accept. As a detective, I had learned over the years that random crime was rare. A homicide generally always had something we could grasp, like a robbery gone bad, a drug deal gone bad, or an estranged husband tracking his wife down and killing her for leaving him. To walk into a house and kill for sport was rare.

Dan leaned forward. The noise was getting louder as people filled the tables around us and a small line snaked its way around our table: friends and family waiting for the metal doors to slide open and let them back into the free world.

"Driving around the countryside, smoking pot, is what we did every night," Dan said. "But those few days before the murders, we started getting bolder. Needed an extra kick. So we broke into a house over at Kingman. Me, David, and Mike broke in the house. Roger stayed outside to cut the phone lines just like at the Spencer's."

"But he didn't," I interjected. "He never cut the phone lines at either place. It was falsely reported in the newspapers that the phone lines were cut. But they weren't. That's why Roger busted the phones from the wall when he finally came inside. If he had cut the lines, why would he destroy the phones inside?"

Dan smiled. "I understand that now. But that's what he said he was doing." He rolled his eyes, an expression I interpreted to mean that he had learned a lot about Drollinger over the years. "Anyway, we break into this house and put this guy and his wife on the floor in the living room. Then we just tore the house up. Stole a shotgun."

"Why didn't you kill them?" I asked.

Dan exhaled and leaned back in his chair; the free world had swallowed the line of people that had been surrounding us. "I don't know. I don't know." Dan paused while he thought. "Roger hit the guy in the face with the butt of the shotgun. Threatened to kill them if they got up. But we left without killing anybody. I don't know why two nights later it was different."

"Did Drollinger talk a lot about killing people?" I asked.

"Believe me, Mike I've thought a lot about all of this over the past eighteen years," Dan said. "I think it was a gradual progression with Roger. At first we were selling drugs. Now, Roger always had a gun and talked about using it if he needed to. I never doubted him. And I've seen him stick a gun to the head of almost everybody I know." Dan pointed a finger in the air, alerting me to the importance of what he was about to say. "But when he got out of jail, the January before the murders, he was different. The way he talked was different. Talk of killing came up every night."

Dan sipped the plastic cup of Diet Coke I had purchased for

him.

"I think Roger always had a desire to kill somebody," Dan continued. "And I think when they let him out of jail, he knew he didn't have much time to do it. I mean, they had a lot of evidence on us. We had been selling drugs to undercover state police officers for months. So, I think he felt like his opportunity to actually kill somebody, or leave his mark, was running out.

"The day before the murders, we pulled up next to a dog running down the road and Roger shot and killed it. Just to show us how easy it was to kill."

Why? Why would someone just want to kill for the sport of killing? As hard as I tried to get into Roger's head and understand him, I just couldn't do it. I couldn't understand his motivations, his desires, his fears. What made him tick?

"There were many times in the month leading up to the murders that we went to the point of killing somebody, and then didn't do it," Dan said. "We were driving down the interstate one time and we pulled up next to this young girl in a Volkswagen. Real pretty girl. Roger said to kill her. I was hanging out the window of his Blazer, pointing the shotgun at her. Roger, David, and Mike were screaming 'Shoot her! Shoot her!' Her eyes were filled with fear. Then Roger yelled. 'Shoot the tires and we'll rape her.' But I couldn't shoot her. I don't know why." Dan sighed. "I don't know why I couldn't shoot her and a month later I walked into the Spencer home and shot them."

I cleared my throat while wiping beads of sweat from my forehead. The meeting room was hot. The temperature was always too hot or too cold. I guessed they didn't want people to get too comfortable. I'm not sure I could ever get comfortable inside the secured walls of the prison, even knowing I could leave at any time.

"I just can't understand why Roger didn't order you to kill the family in Kingman. If that's what he wanted to do."

"I think it was all a warm-up for us," Dan said. "I think Roger saw how easy it was to break in, and line everybody up on the floor."

"No," I said. "Drollinger saw how easy it was for you, Mike, and

David to break in the house and line people up on the floor. That made it real easy for him. Something goes wrong, he runs off like he had in the past, leaving you guys to fend for yourselves. Roger Drollinger loves Roger Drollinger. Period. That's it."

Dan pressed his lips together while nodding his head slowly in agreement. There was little doubt that Dan understood how Drollinger had used him over the years. Used him like he had used everybody else in his life.

"There were some real differences between the home invasion over at Kingman and the murders," Dan said.

A guard walked toward our table and I held my breath, saying a quick prayer that our time was not up. The guard walked past. Thank God. We were finally breaking through the myths that had surrounded this crime for eighteen years, getting to the motivations of the participants, moving toward some understanding of how a tragic and horrible crime could happen in such a quiet, crime-free community.

"We wore masks in the first home invasion," Dan said. "We didn't want them to see us." Dan paused for a second. "Things were different down at Hollandsburg. When we were sitting down on the gravel road, behind the Spencer's house, I pulled a handkerchief from my back pocket and was tying it around my face. Roger said, 'No, we don't need masks. Nobody will be alive to identify us.' Then he handed each of us a pair of gloves. Those old Handy Hank farmer gloves."

"So that's where you planned the murders?" I asked. "From the gravel road?" I assumed that Drollinger had been planning the murders in his mind for years.

Dan nodded his head. "We drove past their house twice. Roger had been asking me all night, 'What about this house or what about that house?' I kept saying, 'No, I don't like it.' But when we drove past the Spencer home, he didn't ask me if I liked the house. He simply said, 'That's the house.' Then we pulled down the gravel road, shut the lights off on the car, and he told us what to do."

I didn't get the impression that he blamed Drollinger for everything bad in his life, or that he was shifting all of the blame to

Choking in Fear

Drollinger. Dan talked matter-of-factly, explaining how things worked, who made the decisions. But he was also quick to accept responsibility for pulling the trigger of one of the shotguns that killed four boys. He didn't blame Drollinger for that. It was a decision ultimately he made.

"Why was he so confident of this house?" I asked.

"Well, Mike, as you know there were four boys living at home, so there were a lot of nice cars in the driveway," Dan said. "He thought they were having a poker game or something. Said we go in, kill everybody, and then rob them. We stopped to kill them first, robbery was only secondary."

"What was the conversation like in the car?" I asked. "As you plotted the murders."

"Roger turned the car around and parked it on the gravel road," Dan said. "I remember staring at the house, wondering if there were any kids inside. Then Mike and I got out and peed next to the road. When we got back in the car, Roger pointed his pistol at us and said, 'Everybody kills or gets killed.'"

"I said, 'I don't think I can kill kids, if there are kids inside,'" Dan continued. "Mike said he couldn't either. David was in the backseat and he said, 'That's too bad, you just have to do it.' Roger pointed the pistol at me and said, 'We have to kill the kids because if we don't, they will hunt us down someday and kill us.' He said something like, 'If my kids saw somebody kill me, they would hunt the killers down when they were older. We don't want no kids hunting us down later.'"

"Did everybody agree?" I asked.

"In a roundabout way," Dan said. "I never said okay. But I didn't jump out of the car and run. I just felt like maybe we would just do another home invasion. That we really wouldn't kill anybody once we got inside. But at the same level, I knew we were going to kill. This time was different. I took off the sweater I was wearing, a white sweater, so I wouldn't get blood on it."

I glanced at the clock. I had about an hour left to visit, if the guards didn't renege on the promise of extra visiting time because of the holidays and the fact that I had driven three hundred and fifty miles. But I could see through the bars of the two secure metal doors and people were lining up to check in with the guard at the front desk. It was just like a restaurant; if it got too busy, I knew they would push me out the door.

"So, you were wearing a T-shirt?" I asked.

Dan shook his head. "No, I didn't wear any shirt." His voice low and even.

"It was below zero that night," I said. "Wind chill was like twenty below."

"I was in a zone," Dan said. "Kind of like playing football. That's not a good way of describing it, but that's the best way I know how. I never felt the cold air."

"What was going through your head as you ran toward the house?" I asked. I tried to put myself in his shoes, to feel the cold air against my exposed flesh, understand the thinking of a man before he breaks into someone's home and takes them captive. I knew the fear of serving arrest warrants on violent offenders: the slow, deliberate, well-orchestrated approach of the house. Always knowing the layout of the house, who was possibly inside, and what kind of criminal history they might have.

"My only thought was not getting shot busting in the house," Dan said. He lifted his plastic cup of Diet Coke, arranged the napkin, and then sat the cup back down. "David slipped a couple times on the back porch. The steps were ice covered. We'd had an ice storm earlier in the week."

I sat completely still, didn't nod or shake my head, eyes focused squarely on Dan, absorbing the words he spoke and trying to transfer them into a moving picture in my head.

"Then we ran in the back door," Dan said. "Mrs. Spencer was sitting in the kitchen. I just remembered staring at her. Then David hollered for her to get on the ground."

"Whose idea was it to get everybody on the floor?" I asked, confident of the answer, but needing to hear it from a participant.

"Roger's," Dan said. "He told us to 'Seek and secure. Get everybody in a central location on the floor.' When he came in, he and Mike went through the house looking for valuables and guns. I was standing over in the dining room, next to the family on the floor."

I leaned back in the chair, arms folded across my chest, eyes and ears focused squarely on Dan.

"Then Roger went back outside," Dan said. "He was getting the cars ready. We were going to steal one of the Spencer's cars and leave it at the next house we stopped at. I started getting nervous because we had been in the house a long time. Mike had walked into the kitchen. I followed him. Mike was holding a T-shirt and a calculator, a couple things he was taking for himself. Then he grabbed an apple and took a bite out of it."

How could he calmly eat an apple while waiting to kill four boys and their mother? I thought. The half-eaten red apple was found in the toilet. The investigators had retrieved it as evidence, preserving the impression marks.

"Then Roger came back in the house," Dan continued, "I said, 'Let's get out of here.' Roger said, 'Let's get this cleaned up,' and walked back in the living room. He started lining them up, shoulder to shoulder, execution style." Dan used his finger to draw a diagram on the table.

"At what point did you decide to murder?" I asked. "I mean, you said that you were still thinking of how to keep this from happening before you got inside. When did you finally decide to pull the trigger?"

"The point at which I decided to murder was the point at which I realized I didn't have what it took to stop it," Dan said. "I knew Roger would kill me if I backed out. And I was afraid that Mike and David would turn on me if I shot Roger. It was a sinking, helpless, pitiful feeling. There was a moment just before the first shot was fired when I looked down the barrel of my shotgun and it seemed like something ran up the gun and jumped in my left eye. If there was a point I became demon possessed, this was it. I dismissed it at the time, but have never forgotten it. Matter of fact, I wear these glasses because of my left eye." Dan removed the glasses from his face as we both looked at them. "My right eye is fine. It would be easy to just say I was on drugs or trippin'. But to me, that was the point of no return. Then Mike fired."

I sat silently, letting the words sink in.

"Did you know Mike was getting ready to shoot?" I asked, then looked closely at Dan's left eye as he put the clear-framed, prison-issued glasses back on. His eyes looked normal. But I remembered how scary his eyes had looked in the composite picture that was in the newspaper for weeks, and how one eye had looked different, maybe lower than the other, or smaller. Something had been different.

I felt a chill go down my spine.

Dan nodded his head. "Just before he shot," Dan said, "Roger looked over at Mike and nodded his head. Then the shooting started. Mike was shooting, David was shooting, I shot once and my gun jammed. Then I looked up as the oldest boy, next to the couch, who I now know was Greg Brooks, raised up on his hands and knees and yelled, 'Oh God, I'm dying. Oh God, I'm dying.' Roger grabbed the sawed-off shotgun from David and walked up and grabbed him by his ponytail and rammed the shotgun to the back of his head and fired. I watched his brain fly across the room and land on the coffee table. It looked like his whole face came off in one piece and flew across the room." Dan's eyes drifted away as he paused for a second. "I think he pissed Roger off because he didn't lie there and die quietly like he was supposed to. Then Roger went down the line kicking each of the bodies."

I thought about how loud it must have been inside that home. The deafening sound of three shotguns being fired rapidly. The flashes of light from the muzzle in the otherwise dark house. The paralyzing fear that accompanies such evil. The shrieks and screams of children being murdered with shotguns. The overwhelming helplessness Betty Jane Spencer felt, the protector, unable to protect her boys. Unable to do anything but witness the slaughter of her family and pray to God to spare them.

"After Roger kicked each of the bodies," Dan said, "he walked up to me and told me to shoot the woman again. He said it like I hadn't shot anybody. Like if I didn't shoot her, he was going to shoot me. I said my shotgun was jammed and threw it to him. He cleared the jam and gave me the gun back. I pointed the shotgun at her, then raised it a little and aimed at the couch. I didn't want to shoot her again. I don't know why, because I really thought she was dead. Evidently, it blew her wig off. I had my eyes closed. Roger must have thought it was her head. He made us gather up all of our shells and then we left. That's when I got sick."

"You must have freaked out when you heard on the scanner that the mother had lived?" I asked.

"It really heightened my fears," Dan said, "I had committed an act against not only the Spencer family, but God and nature. And I was certain I would be killed for this. Expected it. Deserved it."

"Did it really sink in?" I asked. "What you had done?"

"Not until the next morning," Dan said. "I turned on the television and they had breaking news about the murders. Photos from the crime scene showing the blood splatter on the ceiling. I mean, I knew there had to be a lot of blood and stuff. But it was pretty dark inside the home, so you couldn't really see what a mess it made. The pictures on TV floored me. They showed blood all over the ceiling, walls, furniture. Then they said that they had a couple guys in custody."

"Yeah," I said. "After you guys heard the broadcast on the scanner, every cop in the area started toward Hollandsburg. A trooper stopped a car about ten miles from the scene. There were a couple of guys from Indianapolis in it. They kind of matched the description, so they were taken to the Parke County Jail and interviewed. Turned out they picked a crappy night to drink and drive around Hollandsburg."

"I was freaking out," Dan said. "I thought the cops were going to arrest the wrong people."

"What did you do the rest of the day?" I asked. "The day after the murders? Or, actually, the day of the murders. Valentine's Day."

"I went to the courthouse," Dan said. "Roger was on trial. We had both been arrested for dealing drugs and were facing some serious time. Anyway, David and Mike were there also. At one of the breaks, Roger told Mike and me to get out of there, that we shouldn't be seen together. There were too many cops at the courthouse and he thought they might figure out we were involved with the murders."

"That's what blows my mind," I said while shaking my head. "That Roger was sitting on the witness stand, in his own defense, only hours after killing four boys and shooting their mother. I've read the transcripts from the trial. His responses were well thought-out and coherent. How could a normal person concentrate after doing that? Especially knowing that one of the victims had lived and the police were looking for the killers. That tells me a lot about Roger Drollinger."

"That's Roger," Dan said. "Like I said earlier, he was really wanting to kill somebody. Maybe now he felt satisfied. He'd accomplished his goal, so to speak."

"So, you didn't talk much with Roger after this?" I asked.

"Not much," Dan said. "We still met, mostly at the Captain's Table for lunch. His trial lasted most of that week after the murders. When the jury was out, we met for lunch. People don't realize it, but David was sitting in the courtroom every day with a .357 pistol inside his jacket. When the jury came back, if Roger was convicted and taken into custody, David was supposed to shoot their way out. We were out of control. We had even stolen a bunch of dynamite and thought about blowing the courthouse up."

I exhaled, patting my face gently with both hands. This was surreal. More like a movie script, not a true story from my childhood. Dan smiled. He knew this was all a little overwhelming.

"It's hard for me to believe I was one of the men who participated in the murders," Dan said. "It's like I am talking about somebody else, not me."

"All four of you - you, Roger, David, and Mike - met at the Captain's Table?" I asked.

"Uh-huh," Dan said. "We had lunch one day, about three days

after the murders. When I sat down, David and Roger were talking about finding pieces of flesh and brain on their clothes after they got home the night of the murders. I think it was Mike who asked Roger what he had done with the brain matter. Roger smiled, swiped a French fry through the ketchup, then said, 'Fed it to the cat,' and ate the French fry."

I wrinkled my nose and lips in disgust.

"Mike and I were both really high-strung," Dan said. "The composite pictures had just come out all over the TV and newspapers, and one looked just like me. Roger finally ordered Mike to get out of town. Mike wanted me to go with him. He bought a bus ticket to California. It was only fifty dollars, but I wasn't going to run."

"Why didn't you just confess when Dave Blue interviewed you?" I asked. "The first time. A couple days after the murders."

"I was all prepared to confess," Dan said. "I couldn't live with myself. And for the first time in my life, I couldn't get high enough or drunk enough to numb the pain. My dad had tracked me down that day and said Dave Blue wanted to talk with me. He said he and my cousin Bill Stonebraker were looking for me. Bill was a police officer in Lafayette. Anyway, my parents took me down to the Crawfordsville Police Department and we were sitting there in a little room waiting on Dave. I was going to walk in and confess. Then Dave walked in, said he needed to talk with me, then asked me and my parents to come back to another room."

"Okay," I said, feeling like I needed to offer some feedback, more than a simple nod of the head, but having nothing to add.

"This is going to sound crazy at this point," Dan said. He was serious. No smiles.

Nothing could sound crazy at this point, I thought.

"There was no way I could confess to killing anybody in front of my parents," Dan said. "As crazy as that may sound, I just couldn't do it with my mom sitting there."

I thought about it and it didn't sound crazy. It made perfect sense to me. I remembered getting suspended from school my junior year for throwing a snap rock during typing class. The suspension, embarrassing as it was, did not compare in the least to the guilt I felt for letting my parents down. That was nothing compared to what Dan struggled with. But at some level I understood what he was saying. No matter how bad a person was, they still, at some level, wanted to please their parents.

Then Dan smiled. "You know," he said, "the funny thing about the whole interview was at one point when Dave Blue asked me if I had been using drugs. I said I had smoked a little pot. My dad went crazy, yelling at me. Saying I had promised I was going to quit. And I sat there numb, thinking about how crazy this was when I knew that smoking pot was nothing. I had been involved in the murder of four boys.

"I wish Dave would have pulled my shirt back and looked at my shoulder," Dan continued. "It was all bruised up from the shotgun. And every time he asked me a question, I had to get him to repeat it. My ears were still ringing from all the shotgun blasts. That was like three days later."

Dave Blue was a great police officer, but even a great police officer could have his judgment clouded by a belief that someone he knew was not capable of participating in a crime of this magnitude. Dave wasn't alone. My father couldn't believe that Dan Stonebraker was involved even after Dan confessed several weeks later. He found it hard to believe that the killers were residents of our community. I had talked to Dave several time over the years, and he readily admitted that he didn't think Dan Stonebraker was capable of murder. Nobody thought Dan Stonebraker was capable of murder. But he was.

"Why didn't you call Dave up later and confess?" I asked.

Dan nodded his head. "I wanted to," he said. "I really did. I used to walk up and down the street in front of the sheriff's department, trying to get the nerve up to walk inside and confess. But I just couldn't do it. I wanted to get caught. I felt like I had let people down all my life. I just couldn't walk in there and tell them I was one of the killers."

"I guess that's why you didn't run away with either Mike or Roger and David," I said.

"Yeah," Dan said. "I wasn't going to run from what I did. I knew they would catch me sooner or later." He shook his head and smiled. "I was beginning to wonder there for a while if they would actually catch us. I started to get scared that they wouldn't figure out it was us. I knew I couldn't live with this the rest of my life if I wasn't caught."

I looked over Dan's head at the clock on the wall. It read 2:10 P.M. We had about twenty minutes before I would have to leave.

"Has Smith ever told you what he and Drollinger did while they were on the run?" I asked.

"Well," Dan said, "Roger wanted me to go with them. He said they were going to Detroit."

"Detroit?" I said. I knew they went south, not north.

Dan nodded his head like he would get to that in a minute.

"Roger was messing around with this girl Linda," Dan said. "He had her come into Crawfordsville and get me one day. This would have been early March. Anyway, Linda came by and said that Roger needed to see me and to bring some money and a gun. He said to get the gun from Scott Hamilton."

"Why didn't Roger come into Crawfordsville himself?" I asked.

"He was due in court," Dan said. "His parole had been violated because of the drug conviction. All the cops knew Roger."

"Okay," I said, then took a sip of the Mountain Dew that had been setting untouched in front of me for nearly two hours. It was flat from the melted ice.

"After I got the money and the gun from Scott," Dan said, "we went out in the country to pick up Roger and David. They were hiding in a hog barn. Then we went to Terre Haute to pick up some marijuana. Roger owed somebody some pot. After we picked up the pot, Roger was ready to get out of Indiana. He tried to get me to go with them. I kinda thought he might force me to go, but he didn't. I guess that's why he said they were going to Detroit. He didn't want me to know where they were going. Roger dropped me off at the Midtown Motel in Terre Haute with the dope and some money and they left. I just figured they were going to Detroit."

"How'd you get back to Crawfordsville?" I asked.

"I had a weird feeling about Roger," Dan said. "When he left...I felt like he was up to something. Then about an hour later, somebody knocked on the door of the room. I jumped. I was scared Roger had come back and decided to shoot me. It seemed liked he didn't trust me. But it was my sister Cheryl. She had been looking for me, and Scott Hamilton told her I was in Terre Haute and that we usually stayed at the Midtown."

"When did you find out that they actually went to Florida?" I asked.

"After they were arrested," Dan said. "David and I didn't talk for several years after he was sent to Pendleton. He was upset because I had testified against him and Roger. He was still thinking like Roger, thinking that the reason we were in prison was because Mrs. Spencer had lived and because I had testified against him. That's just how Roger would think, not accepting responsibility for the fact that we broke into a home and killed four boys.

"Anyway, David and I finally sat down one day and talked," Dan continued. "He said they went to Florida with Linda and stayed with some of her relatives near Daytona Beach. Roger got them new social security numbers so they could work. Then one day, they were at a laundromat and Linda called back to Crawfordsville to check on her older daughter. She called over to the Captain's Table where she used to work. David's stepbrother got on the phone and told her that Roger and David were wanted for the murders down at Hollandsburg. He told her I had confessed and was in jail."

"Well, I guess you were dropped from Drollinger's Christmas card list at that point," I said with a smile.

"Oh, yeah," Dan laughed. "David said when he got off the phone, Roger slammed his fist on a washing machine and said 'I knew I should have killed that fuckin' Stonebraker.' They grabbed their guns out of Linda's car and ran off."

"Linda was arrested by the FBI when she got back to her relative's house." I said. "I don't think she knew that Drollinger and Smith were actually wanted for murder when she drove them to Florida."

"No, I don't think so," Dan said. "She knew Roger was wanted for the parole violation, but not for murder."

"There was a time," I said, reflecting in my mind while I talked, "shortly after they fled the laundromat, that the Florida Highway Patrol had them surrounded in a swamp. Somewhere near Daytona Beach. But Roger and David got away."

"I don't know a whole lot about that," Dan said. "But David told me that he was hiding inside some kind of bush and a police officer walked right up to him. Within a couple feet. David said he had the gun pointed right at the officer, and he swore the officer saw him because he was looking right at him. Then the officer left. Roger and David started jumping trains and heading back north."

"They ended up getting separated around Lexington, Kentucky," I said. "Did he tell you how that happened?"

"I think David got off the train and tried to get something to eat," Dan said. "A couple of railroad workers picked him up. They thought he was a runaway. He was only seventeen, and looked younger than that. And I guess his clothes and boots were in really bad shape. David called his mom. Mrs. Smith called Loyd Heck with the state police and said she would tell them where David was if they took her along. They agreed and all of them flew to Lexington, Kentucky."

"Yeah," I said. "Then it was a couple weeks before David came back to Indiana. His attorney wouldn't let him waive extradition."

"Then Roger turned himself into the FBI a couple of weeks later, or so," Dan said. "He made sure there was plenty of news and television coverage."

"Heck," I said emphatically. "Roger's attorney put him up over the Easter weekend in a hotel in Indianapolis so Roger could spend time with his family. He was also later quoted in the Indianapolis star newspaper as saying Drollinger was the only client he ever feared. And he represented some bad dudes."

"I remember reading in the newspaper that Roger said he turned himself in to the FBI because he was afraid the state police would shoot him on sight," Dan said. "They kept him in jail in Indianapolis. Roger said he was afraid for his life in Parke County."

"I would have thought that all four of you would be scared to step back into Parke County," I said. "People were scared to death for months. Then they were mad as hell."

"I know," Dan said while nodding his head. "The day after I confessed, Loyd Heck and Barney Thrasher escorted me into the Parke County Courthouse for a hearing to issue warrants against all of us. People were lined up on the sidewalks, saying things. Everybody inside the courthouse was standing in the hallway staring at me."

"First time any of them had ever seen a killer," I said. "Probably be the only opportunity in their life. I hope."

"I know," Dan said, embarrassed. "And so Roger stayed in Indianapolis. I saw him on the news after his arrest saying how scared he was of me and Mike Wright. That we were setting him up for something we did."

"A true sociopath," I added just as the corrections officer dropped Dan's ID on the table with a yellow Post-it-note indicating the time, our signal that visiting hours were over. "People use that label too frequently these days, but Drollinger, in my opinion, is a true sociopath."

"I know he is," Dan said. He paused for a moment. We looked at each other, digesting the information shared during the visit. Then we shook hands.

I made my way out of the prison, through the two security doors and the ultraviolet hand box to make sure the right person was leaving, retrieved my personal belongings from a locked box, and went out the front door. The crisp air bit at my neck as I walked across the large employee parking lot to the rear parking area reserved for visitors. The conversation from the last two hours clogged my head like a nasty head cold.

Dan didn't look and act like Hannibal Lector, nor did he scare me like his photo had when I was a child. He acted and looked like most men I knew. He had feelings. And when we discussed the grisly details of the murders, he had genuine remorse on his face and in his voice. The pieces of the puzzle were coming together for me. Drollinger was the key. Without him, Greg, Raymond, Reeve, and Ralph would still be alive. The question I needed to answer was how did guys like Dan Stonebraker, Mike Wright and David Smith - who, without the influence of Roger Drollinger, were no more likely to kill than the man in the moon - become stone-cold killers with his guidance? I needed to know if I were ever going to prevent something like this from happening again. Every night, I looked into the faces of Dan Stonebrakers, young boys trapped in homes filled with domestic violence. Young boys eager to follow a sociopath like Roger Drollinger at the drop of a hat if someone didn't intercede. Not necessarily interested in murder but in desperate need of a father figure. Somebody who cared for them. Not a sociopath like Drollinger who acted the part to further his sadistic desires.

CHAPTER TWENTY-NINE

"Tell me about his eyes," Betty Jane said. "I'll never forget his eyes. He had the most evil eyes. If you look at the composite pictures, Stonebraker's was the best. And look at his eyes in the composite." Her eyes drifted off in the distance, then she shook her head. "His eyes were evil."

She was right. Dan's eyes had always looked evil. I had always been amazed at how accurate the composite pictures were. "How did you remember so much about them? I mean, they had you face down on the floor - there was a lot happening real fast."

Betty Jane smiled. Clearly, this wasn't the first time she had been asked this question. "Well, Mike, Stonebraker and Smith came in the back door...right into the kitchen. I just remember staring at Stonebraker. Smith looked so young and was so small. I just assumed that Stonebraker was the one in charge."

"Makes perfect sense," I said. I could picture her looking over the smaller Smith at Stonebraker. "Stonebraker's composite picture was by far the most accurate. Not that the others weren't. They were all amazingly accurate...considering the circumstances."

"Anytime they asked a question, I tried to glance up and look at them," she said. "And they were asking all kinds of questions: 'Do you have any guns? Any money in the house?'" She mimicked his voice mockingly, laced with anger. "I would glance up at them and concentrate on their eyes. I knew they might change their hair, or moustache, or whatever, but their eyes wouldn't change. I was figuring they were going to rob us, and catching them would depend on how good I remembered their faces."

Intelligent thinking under such stressful circumstances, I thought. "Why were there only three composite pictures?"

"Because Drollinger didn't come into the house until later," Betty Jane said. "I saw Wright. He was the first one to bust in. He came in the front door. He kind of had his hand over his face, though." She wrapped her right arm around her face, demonstrating Wright's attempt at disguise. "I saw Stonebraker and Smith the best. They were the two who stood over us most of the time...barking orders."

"So you helped the detective put together the three composites?" I asked. "Just a few days after the murders?"

"I only did two of them," she said. "I did Smith and Stonebraker. Then, as I described the third one, the detective pulled out a composite. It was Wright. He had done it earlier in the day. They had broken into a house a couple days before. But I'll never forget Stonebraker's eyes for as long as I live. Never."

"That's understandable," I said. "But his eyes don't look like they did back then. I was shocked. I figured they would still look all evil. His composite scared the hell out of me as a kid. It was the anger in his eyes."

And I did understand Betty Jane's perspective. The only reason my memory of Dan Stonebraker's eyes had changed was because I had seen him today. I had looked into his eyes, searching for the evil that had stared back at me from the composite pictures in the newspapers and from the television as a child. But the evil wasn't there. And there was no chance in the world that I had missed it because I had stared long and hard into Dan's eyes, searching for a hint of that evil I remembered.

"Did you ask Stonebraker about our dog?" Betty Jane asked. "He was a German Shepherd. Very protective. Not the kind of dog that let strangers around the house without a warning bark."

"I did," I said. "Dan said the dog ran up and growled at him and he just growled back and the dog ran off." I shrugged my shoulders.

"I've never been able to figure out why he didn't bark," Betty Jane said, more to herself than to me. "He was always snipping at people when they came by the house. And after the boys were killed, he stayed in his doghouse. He was real gun shy. He acted like he knew what happened and he hadn't done anything to protect us."

Dogs have such keen senses, I thought. And the evil pouring from the killers that night surely frightened the otherwise brave guard dog. "He sensed what he was up against," I said.

"Anyway," Betty Jane said. "Tell me how your interview went." She lit a cigarette, held the smoke in her lungs for a few seconds, then sent a cloud of smoke sailing skyward.

"It went really well," I said. "It's hard to believe he's the same guy that busted in your house and shot you and the boys."

"That's what I hear over and over," Betty Jane said. "Stonebraker's a Christian. He's a good person today." Her voice was sharp. "I don't care who he is today. He's still the man that killed my boys."

"I totally understand," I said defensively, though I knew her anger wasn't directed at me. I was well aware that many people had tried to convince her over the years that Dan Stonebraker was a good person. A Christian. I bore witness to the new Dan Stonebraker, having left the Pendleton Reformatory less than three hours ago. But what right did anybody have telling her to forgive and forget when it was her boys who died helplessly next to her that night? I surely wasn't going to try and convince her of what I witnessed in Dan Stonebraker. Yet I would also be honest in answering any questions she had, hoping that in some way what I shared might alleviate some of the fears that had consumed her for so long.

"I respect what you say, Mike," Betty Jane said, her eyes boring holes through me. "I've known your mom and dad a long time. I know you wouldn't do anything to hurt me."

I exhaled, emptying my lungs of the weight of what I was learning. The tightrope I was walking, on the one side respecting Betty Jane as a survivor, and on the other my thirst to know and understand why the murders happened. Hell, I was a victim advocate. Every day, I went to work, aiding victims of domestic violence, feeling their pain, their helplessness, their hopelessness. And at some level I was starting to feel that I was betraying everything I stood for, that I was in some way betraying my community by having a dialogue with one of the killers. That I might even be betraying my own family, who were so intimately tied to this case. After all, my father was a police officer involved in the investigation and my mother a friend and colleague of Betty Jane Spencer's. I felt like I was betraying my family because I was having conversations with one of the killers, someone who could just as easily have walked through my back door that Valentine's Day in 1977.

I realized that, no matter what conclusions I came to, or what I learned about the killers and the factors that may have contributed to their involvement, that the brutality of this crime could never be erased. Nor should it be forgotten.

"Stonebraker sent me a letter once," Betty Jane said. "Right after he was sentenced. Right before Christmas of 1977. The first Christmas after the boys were killed."

I raised my eyebrows. "I didn't know that," I said while thinking about how quiet their home must have been that morning without the ruckus of four boys ripping open wrapped packages, the blaring of Christmas music, and the bantering back and forth that goes with boys.

She nodded her head. "He sent me a letter," Betty Jane said. "Apologizing for his part in the murders. He said he hoped one day I could forgive him for what he did." She shook her head fiercely. "It scared me so much when I got the letter. I called the Department of Corrections and complained. They assured me I wouldn't get any more correspondence from any of them. And I haven't."

It had never been clearer than as I sat in Betty Jane's living room, thinking about how incredibly strong and determined this small, frail woman was, that we were talking about two different Dan Stonebrakers. Betty Jane was talking about Dan Stonebraker the cold-blooded and ruthless killer who, on a thrill-seeking mission, ended the lives of her four boys and wounded her physically and emotionally. She didn't know the Dan Stonebraker I had met, the Dan Stonebraker who was not a killer. As I sat there staring at her, I thanked God again that I had not met the Dan Stonebraker she knew. It would have been on his terms. In 1977.

"Are Stonebraker, Smith, and Wright still good friends?" Betty Jane asked.

"No," I said before pursing my lips together, trying to decide for myself how to label the relationship between the three men. "Not close friends...I mean, I don't think they are hanging out together. They've all kind of done their own thing, have their own groups of friends. But I think there is a bond." I hated my choice in words the minute it slipped from the end of my tongue. "I don't mean a bond because of what they did to you and the boys, though that has certainly tied them together. I mean a bond because they have known each other for so long."

Betty Jane nodded her head slowly as I spoke, eyes squinted and face wrinkled with concentration.

Knowing that Stonebraker, Wright, and Smith were not close friends had to be of some relief to her. I knew she still feared that they wanted to see her dead and that they might still be plotting her death from prison. These fears were real for her. And I'm not so certain that the killers hadn't, at one time or another, thought about how this all would have unfolded had Betty Jane died on her living room floor with her boys like Drollinger had planned. I'm confident that it would have all ended the same way because Stonebraker's conscience was getting the best of him. As for the other three, I'm not so sure they couldn't just wipe the slate clean and go on, especially Drollinger. He has never accepted any responsibility for his involvement in the murders.

"They've all been talking a lot more since I started sending letters and visiting Dan," I said. "Wright and Smith are concerned with what I am doing."

"What do you think of Dan Stonebraker?" Betty Jane asked.

She caught me off guard. The question was leveled and hit me hard with surprise, like having the wind knocked from your body. I paused to make sure I answered honestly, careful not to sugarcoat it for her protection, but at the same time making sure I did not hurt her with the directness of what I had to say. I knew she didn't want to hear what I was going to say.

"Uhm, I think the best way to explain it," I said, looking directly at Betty Jane now, "is that the Dan Stonebraker I met is totally different from the Dan Stonebraker that busted into your house on February 14, 1977."

Betty Jane studied me carefully, her eyes focused, no expression on her face, arms folded across her chest.

"That doesn't mean he wasn't a cold-blooded killer," I said. "And it in no way erases what he did to you and your family. But, honestly, I couldn't sit here and tell you he was the same monster who killed your boys."

"I think he may have you snowed," Betty Jane said politely, as politely as you could say it.

I smiled. We had an honest and trusting relationship, and thank God she felt comfortable in saying exactly what she felt, because I wanted to tell her how I felt and what I thought about Dan Stonebraker. I didn't want to hurt her. And I didn't want her to think that by understanding Dan Stonebraker today that it would soften my view of what happened to her boys. It hadn't. Heck, it could have been my family that night.

I tried to understand where she was coming from, her unique perspective. And I felt like I did understand. Yet I knew I could never fully understand without lying on a living room floor and witnessing the slaughter of my family.

"Stonebraker's a liar," Betty Jane said. "He said that he didn't shoot me the second time that he shot into Greg." Her jaw tightened. "Is that supposed to make me feel good? To think he shot into my son again instead of me?"

I shrugged my shoulders, respecting Betty Jane's pain, a pain that intensified when she heard that Dan Stonebraker was a good guy today, a Christian. I knew it angered her, hurt her, ate at her intestines that her sons would never be referred to as "good guys" as adults because the opportunity to live a long life was stolen from them. Stolen by four men, one of whom had changed.

I knew Betty Jane needed to vent, that realizing her anger toward

Dan and the other three killers was good, even therapeutic. And I didn't know how Dan's statement that he raised the shotgun and shot Greg instead of Betty Jane was supposed to make her feel, or how it would make me feel under the same circumstances. But I was convinced that Dan Stonebraker did not try to kill her the second time. I was convinced more by my own understanding of the crime and studying the crime scene than by anything Dan had told me. Having been raised with shotguns, I knew that double aught buckshot spreads outward from the shotgun after being fired, killing anything in its path. I knew from hunting as a child that buckshot allowed me to be a proficient hunter, even though I wasn't a proficient marksman.

At the same time, I don't think it was Dan Stonebraker, standing in her living room that night, who saved her life. Absolutely not. I didn't want anyone to draw that conclusion. Because Raymond and Greg, on either side of her, had been shot multiple times, with their heads nearly blown off, I don't think it would be fair to label Dan's decision to raise the shotgun and fire into Greg or the couch as a moment of compassion. There was no compassion granted that night. It was a guiding hand from above that raised the level of the shotgun and spared Betty Jane's life.

"I don't want you to think that I'm siding with Dan," I said. "I'm taking all of this in, have been taking this in for the past eighteen years and trying to process it, to find the truth. I'm simply searching for the truth. My goal has never been to find out all the gory details. That's too Hollywood." I forced a smile. "I want to know what leads a person to kill another person. A person like Dan Stonebraker who everybody says isn't capable of murder, but who did kill. What variables in his life made him capable of killing?"

I leaned back in the chair and exhaled loudly, discouraged. Maybe I was searching too deeply for the answers to this horrible crime that had nearly choked the life from my community for many months in 1977, and shocked the nation. Maybe it was nothing more than a savage and brutal homicide that could never have been prevented. But something deep inside my gut said there was more to this, that maybe it could have been prevented. That I should keep looking, even though I was scared of hurting Betty Jane. Because if I found the answer, I might save families from experiencing what Betty Jane had been experiencing since Valentine's Day 1977, and will continue to experience until she dies. Maybe I could help save young boys from throwing their lives away, from feeling their lives are so out of control, so useless, so inconsequential that they follow a Roger Drollinger into a home and slaughter a family.

I began to wonder if something so simple as love and a loving family could have prevented this tragedy.

"The only way I can figure all this out is to find out as much as I can about the killers," I said. "I'm not going to offer excuses on their behalf. Whatever I find out, whatever conclusions I come to, will be used to educate people so we can prevent it from happening again. I'm not trying to erase the consequences for their actions. Do the crime, do the time. But if there is something I can put my finger on that could prevent such tragedies, then I have an obligation to find it."

I paused, trying to read Betty Jean's mind, her body language. She was quiet, watching me intently, not moving, arms still folded across her chest.

"And believe me," I said, "I know all about jailhouse religion."

She smiled.

"I'm a cop," I said. "We don't trust anybody. Just ask my wife. She says I'm a pessimist. I think I'm a realist. I'm not saying I couldn't be fooled, but I walked into the prison very skeptically. Jailhouse religion usually fades about the time the final appeal is up. I think Dan is sincere. I've been wrong before. But I've always been a good judge of people."

The room was silent for a few moments while both of us fully absorbed what I had said.

"Somebody told me once that I needed to forgive him," Betty Jane said. "God can forgive him. Only God can forgive him. I can't. It's not for me to forgive him."

"Nobody has a right to tell you to forgive him," I said. And they don't. I would surely never have a right to tell, or even hint, that she needed to forgive. That wasn't my intent. I had no idea how I would react if my son was slaughtered on the living room floor. My brain tells me I would do the right thing, and let the criminal justice system work. But my heart says, if that were my son, I would dedicate my life to tracking down those responsible and killing them slowly, careful to inflict a tremendous amount of pain and suffering. That's human nature, and I prayed I would never be in a situation to make the decision. So nobody should say, "She has to forgive. The Bible says so." The Bible also says we shouldn't commit adultery, take the Lord's name in vain, lust in our hearts, and many other things we do on a daily basis. And none of us know what we would do if we were in Betty Jane's shoes.

"Don't get me wrong," Betty Jane said. "I consider myself a Christian."

"How did your faith in God see you through this tragedy?" I asked.

She shook her head. "Shortly after the murders," Betty Jane said, "I actually said, out loud, 'I hate God!' It shocked me that I said it. It scared me. But I hated God for letting my boys die. I laid on the living room floor praying that God would spare Reeve and Ralph, since I knew Greg and Raymond were dead. But He didn't. I was so angry at God."

I tilted my head toward the ceiling while holding a deep breath in my lungs for as long as I could, then let the air out slowly through my pursed lips.

"It took me a long time to get over that," Betty Jane said. "I think that was my lowest point, blaming God."

I sat back in the chair and snapped my knuckles nervously.

"Thanks for coming by to share what you learned from Dan," Betty Jane said. "Whether or not you ever publish a book about this, you've answered a lot of questions I've had about the killers and the investigation."

Dan? She called him Dan. Not Stonebraker. That was odd.

"Well, I told you when I started this that you would be involved," I said. "I gave you my word. And I have to be honest about what I find. It's too late to save Dan, Mike, and David. But if I can put my finger on one thing that could have prevented this, then I have to pursue it.

"It has affected so many people. You and Keith, and your boys. Keith's daughter Diane. Ralph, Reeve, and Raymond's biological mother. Grandparents. The four killers. The families of the killers. The names of Stonebraker, Drollinger, Smith, and Wright will forever be linked to this crime. Especially Stonebraker and Drollinger, Smith and Wright are names that are a little more common. And it has affected me and many others who lived around here. That is what people don't understand about crime, it effects so many more people than the victims and suspects. I think the greatest thing that could come from this horrible tragedy would be to prevent something like this from happening again. Prevent it because we understand the signs in young boys teetering on the edge. Prevent it because we all take responsibility for raising children who need help. And prevent it by locking sociopaths like Roger Drollinger away long before they have a chance to kill."

CHAPTER THIRTY

"Well, how was Stonebraker?" Dad asked as he held open the door to his apartment for me. He spoke nonchalantly, as if he didn't care. That was a front. He cared what I had learned and was eager to hear it. Excitement to him was a sign of weakness.

"Good," I said as I brushed past him and started up the stairs. "He wants you to come with me next time."

He turned to shut the door before any more cold air sneaked inside. He didn't answer right away.

I walked into his living room, took my jacket off, and plopped down on his sofa with a black binder of psychological reports and trial transcripts from the murders tucked under my arm. Dad walked in and sat down in a brown high back chair, near the window.

"When are you coming up again?" Dad asked. "To the prison?"

"I'm not sure." I said. "Pretty soon. I've got a few things I need to ask Dan. And I want to do it in person. It's too hard to answer questions by letter."

"What's it take for me to get in?" Dad asked. He chewed nervously on his lower lip, pondering a trip to the prison.

"Dan will put you on his visiting list," I said. "Takes about a month."

Dad raised his eyebrows and turned his head upward, palms toward the ceiling. "If he can get me on the list. I'll go next time."

"I'll send him a letter when I get back to Nashville."

"O-kay." He said it slowly like it was two words. "What'd he have to say?"

"We talked a lot about Drollinger," I said. "A lot about

Drollinger and things they did before the murders. About how they planned the murders that night. What Drollinger said before they broke in the Spencer home. What was said afterward. Then, we talked a little bit about Smith and Wright. I don't know much about them."

"Me, neither," Dad said. "I never arrested either one of them. I've known Stonebraker and Drollinger for years. I arrested Drollinger several times."

I stood and walked into the kitchen and grabbed a can of Coke from the refrigerator, then wiped the top of the can clean with a napkin. "Drollinger is exactly like a Charles Manson," I said while walking back into the living room. "It's like he has some kind of psychosexual thing with hurting people. Like he gets off by killing people."

"Probably did," Dad said. "We all knew how conniving Drollinger was. How dangerous he was. He didn't fool anybody." He crossed his legs. "As a matter of fact, I'm convinced he killed that hitchhiker over in Fountain County. They found his body in the stone quarry. That's just what I think." He shrugged his shoulders.

I tilted my head sideways, staring out the window at the passing traffic, thinking. "Wouldn't surprise me. Dan said after they left the Spencer's that night that Drollinger was already plotting the next stop. Dan told him he didn't want to. That he was sick. He said Drollinger turned on the dome light and it looked like he was 'licking his chops,' like it was the most awesome thing in the world. Can you imagine getting off on killing four kids?"

"No, not really," Dad said. "But, hell, Drollinger never had remorse for anything. Other than getting caught. He'd betray his own family to get away."

"Was he a jerk when you guys arrested him?"

"Nah," Dad said. "He was always, 'Yes, sir,' 'No sir.' But you always knew that was a front. That he was always looking for an opportunity to run. Or to blow your head off."

I took a sip of the Coke and placed the can on the glass end table. "Drollinger had some kind of magnetism. Something that attracted Dan Stonebraker, Mike, Wright, and David Smith. And a lot of other people who just didn't happen to be there that night."

"Look at Jerry Turner," Dad said. "You want to see the kind of followers Drollinger had."

"That's right," I said. I had forgotten about Jerry Turner.

"Turner was pissed off because he wasn't with Drollinger that night," Dad said, "so he goes over and kills Russell Foxworthy, a farmer he used to work for. Kills him just so he can go to prison with Drollinger. That was a crazy year. Never seen anything like it before. Hope I never do again."

"Me, neither," I said while resting my head against the back of the couch and staring at the square patterns on the ceiling. It was hard to believe all of this had happened right here. In my community. "Me, neither."

"Is Lori coming here?" Dad asked.

"After bit," I said. "I think her mom or dad is dropping her off."

"I'm gonna take a bath and get cleaned up," he said. "Where we going to eat at?" He walked off toward the bathroom.

"I don't know," I said. "Doesn't really matter to me." I heard the water come on and splash against the bottom of the porcelain tub.

"I don't care, either," he said. "You guys figure it out."

I reached over and grabbed the binder and started to read a lengthy letter from Loyd Heck, the state police investigator, now retired, who had headed up the Hollandsburg investigation. I was drawn to a question I had asked about Stonebraker's confession. Heck had written:

> Stonebraker was a follower. I didn't believe he could handle on his own what had happened. He tried to put up a good front but just minutes after the interview started, tears begin to show in his eyes - he began to get nervous. He knew we could prove burglary, thefts, etc., but he didn't know how much we knew about the murders. He then began to ask us questions, "How much time could a guy get that did those murders? What will happen to those guys that

did them murders?" He began to weep and ask those kinds of questions.

He soon after confessed and gave us a nine-page statement. Stonebraker was never hostile or mad acting at us. He was more timid and laid back. He needed Drollinger at this point for support. My opinion only, Stonebraker could not operate alone, he needed a leader.[16]

I flipped through the pages to a section of questions about Mike Wright. Heck and Thrasher had flown to San Jose, California, shortly after Wright had been arrested by the FBI to interview him and bring him back to Indiana.

Heck wrote: "Wright was a lot like Stonebraker in that he is a follower. Wright met us in jail irons and a jail jumpsuit with a smile on his face. Wright never, in my opinion, seemed remorseful. He confessed and gave us a written statement in a brief interview after he learned from us that Stonebraker had already confessed. His confession was for his own survival."

I flipped back and forth between Loyd's answers to my original questions in the front of the binder. Straightforward answers. No bull or fluffy words. Just like I pictured the seasoned investigator.

I laughed to myself as Dad stepped from the bathroom wrapped in a towel. "What's so funny?" He asked.

I pointed to the binder.

"What's that?"

"Loyd Heck wrote me a couple letters, explaining his thoughts on the murders and the investigation, and I put them in his binder with some of the psychological reports." I held up the binder so he could see it better. "I've never met him, but I get the impression from reading his letters that he speaks his mind."

"Yeah," said Dad. "I've met him, but I don't really know him. Everybody around the department always said he was the best investigator we ever had." Dad shrugged his shoulders as if to say, "Who

---

[16] Loyd Heck, letter to author, 21 August 1995.

knows?"

"I asked him a question about how smart Drollinger was and this is what he wrote: 'Roger was average intelligence. He was streetwise. Roger was given about all he ever wanted from his parents.'" I smiled again before reading on. "'Roger was the leader of a group of stupid followers.' Couldn't be any clearer than that," I added.

Heck continued in his letter, "Roger liked to be looked up to and to give orders, so he needed someone with less intelligence than his. Roger also had money and could always buy the drinks or drugs needed to keep on being the leader."[17]

"That's true," Dad said. "Drollinger was a master manipulator."

I scanned though several more of my questions that Loyd had taken great care and time in answering. At the time of the murders, he was a twenty-four-year veteran of the Indiana State Police and had been a detective in West Central Indiana for nearly eleven years. He had seen his share of the gruesome and grotesque products of human nature. That's why his next answer struck me. I had asked Loyd, "What was your initial reaction when you walked inside the Spencer home that morning?"

Loyd had written, "Here you may interject what one might think in seeing four bodies with their heads or faces blown away. I was horrified. It was the worst situation I had ever seen. And I couldn't believe what I was seeing."[18]

That from a seasoned police investigator.

I grabbed the television remote control from the end of the table and hit the mute button. The basketball game played on without sound.

What did the psychological reports say? That's what I wanted to know. I had spent a great deal of time trying to get into the heads of each of the four killers. I felt confident that I knew the type of people they were, based on everything I had compiled through reports, interviews with friends, acquaintances, and investigators. But now I needed to see what the professionals had said about them, to see how

---

[17] Loyd Heck, letter to author, 21 August 1995.
[18] Loyd Heck, letter to author, 21 August 1995.

close I was to truly understanding these four men.

The first report in the binder, under the section I had marked "Psychological Reports" was a pre-sentence investigation report on Roger Drollinger. I scanned the multi-page document until I got to the section titled: "Mental Health: Mr. Drollinger was found to be sane by two psychiatrists prior to the trial."

> The defendant says he has been wrongfully accused of practically all the charges ever filed against him, and he is an unfortunate victim of circumstance.
>
> He did tell this probation officer he's beginning to feel something is wrong with his mind, that maybe he does things he is not aware of.
>
> He told Dr. Gohil he had weird dreams and blackouts during his drug trial, which was immediately after the murders. Dr. Gohil was of opinion these blackouts were "self-serving" and "exaggerated."[19]

This was the first time I had heard that he claimed to have blackouts. He hadn't had any blackouts the morning after the murders while testifying in his own defense during his drug trial. His answers were well thought-out and laced with resentment at the prosecutor. The report found behavior typical of what the FBI reports as being common traits and characteristics of violent offenders: blaming others and experiencing what the FBI calls altered consciousness ("It's like it wasn't me," "I can't believe I did that").

I flipped through the rest of the pre-sentence report and located the Psychiatric Examination Report filed with the Blackford County Court by Dr. Gohil. What did it say about Drollinger's mental health?

> Dr. Gohil writes about Roger Dillinger:
> 1. The defendant does not suffer from mental illness.

---

[19] Dolan, Nancy, Blackford County Probation Department, Hartford City, IN, Roger C. Drollinger Pre-Sentence Investigation Report, 11 October 1997.

2. The defendant had the mental capacity to understand the charges against him and has the capacity to assist his attorney to help him in his defense. He is competent to stand trial.
3. His conduct and thought process did not indicate that he suffered from mental disease or defect and he did not lack substantial capacity either to appreciate the wrongfulness of his conduct to the requirement of the Law (ALI-Model Penal Code).
4. The defendant does not require any further treatments.[20]

Just a cold-blooded and calculating killer, I thought to myself. Always blaming others for his problems, never taking responsibility for any of his behaviors. Not a bit surprising.

David Smith's pre-sentence report submitted to the court was quite different, as expected, from Drollinger's. I adjusted myself on the couch and focused on DeLila Byrd's report. I knew little about David.

David attempts to get away from discussing the actual shootings. He says that he remembers things in snatches but at one point drew a diagram showing the positioning of the victims, some of the furniture and the general layout of the Spencer residence. David became very upset during this discussion, he talked very rapidly and his whole body trembled quite noticeably. David says that he went along with the others in the robberies prior to the shootings because Roger owed him $250.00 and he thought he would get it back. David said that at first the whole thing was "fun,

---

[20] Gohil, Jivanlal P., M.D., Roger C. Drollinger Psychiatric Examination Report, Blackford County Court. Hartford City, IN, 30 August 1977.

something like a joke, something to do."

When asked what would have happened to any money they got, David said Roger would have gotten it. I asked if he would ever have gotten his $250.00 and David stated "probably not."

David says, "Roger was kind of Satan or something." Roger wanted to be a big man, he liked power. Roger talked about buying a big piece of land in Texas or Mexico and starting his own town. Roger would be the judge and everything.

David says he does not remember talking of killing people at any time prior to the night of the actual event. He says that they (Drollinger, Wright, Stonebraker, and David) talked about it for a couple hours while riding around. He can't remember much about what was said as he was not paying much attention. David says he didn't think it would really happen and still couldn't believe it would happen when they entered the Spencer residence. However, David did admit that he knew there was the possibility that the killing would happen.

David does not feel that he should have been convicted of four 1st degree murder charges. He admits that he may have killed the oldest boy, Gregory Brooks, and he knows he shot Mrs. Spencer in the back but he says he did not shoot anyone else.

While awaiting trial, David overheard this interviewer visiting a twelve-year-old through the wall and at our first meeting David expressed great concern about the boy. David was reminded of his part in the killing of a boy two years older and at that time David denied killing any children saying he "couldn't kill a little kid."

I asked him what he would have done if Roger had ordered him to shoot the little kid. He didn't know what he would have done - "It was the worst thing watching him die."

After the shooting, David says he didn't feel human, felt dirty, his long hair felt like wire. He had a "really bad, dirty feeling, like the devil had took me over - devil made me do something he wanted me to do."

David found a piece of flesh on his trousers while in the car after the shootings but he didn't think about it being human. Roger found a piece of flesh on the back of his jacket the next morning, they laughed about it.

David says he didn't sleep well the night after the shootings, Roger let him stay on a mattress in the same room that Roger and his wife slept in. David says he still can't sleep on his stomach because that's the way those people died, he has nightmares.

David seems to enjoy telling of his adventures while on the run. He becomes excited and laughs about the dumb things he did, saying he could have been caught several times. He compares events to something on television.

David continued breaking in and stealing on Roger's orders while they were "on the run."

David says that Roger got mad at him several times because he cried and wanted to give himself up. Roger told him he would "fry" if he gave himself up. Roger said several times that they should have "wasted" Stoney and Mike the night of the shootings because they talked. David was afraid to sleep while they were running. He was afraid that Roger would kill him to prevent him from talking.

David says he feels like this whole thing couldn't have happened - he "could open a door and step out" - like waking up from a bad dream.

Choking in Fear

At our first meeting, David said he didn't want to say Roger's name but discussion indicates that David's whole world revolved around Roger. David says his mother tried to tell him about Roger but David wouldn't listen. Roger always told David he "loved me like a son."[21]

There it was. He "loved me like a son." David had thought. That missing piece of his life that made him gravitate toward Roger. David had no positive male figure in his life, just like Dan Stonebraker. That lack of a positive male role model made him vulnerable to a sociopath such as Drollinger. Somebody who could say the right things, the things David needed to hear. That's no excuse for David's involvement in the killing of four boys - many other men without fathers don't kill - but there was no denying it made him vulnerable to Drollinger and his manipulations. Drollinger was a master manipulator, and manipulating three young men into killing four boys was his greatest accomplishment. What a sad epitaph.

David Smith and Dan Stonebraker fit a general profile: they were young and came from dysfunctional homes where they had no positive male influence in their life and little self-worth. This profile seemed to fit most of the boys with whom Drollinger surrounded himself.

The final page in Byrd's report summed everything up:

> It is this interviewer's opinion that this same dependence led David into his present predicament. His dependence on Roger Drollinger to take care of him is evident before the killings and also while they are on the run. Even now he is only living one day at a time, not thinking about what might happen to him and relying on God to take care of him. Relying on God entirely is sometimes not easy but David is quite

---

[21] Byrd, DeLila M., Jasper Circuit Court, Rensselaer, IN, David Smith Pre-Sentence Investigation Report, 26 October 1977.

comfortable doing this and I believe that his reliance on Roger Drollinger came about in the same way as Roger took on God-like proportions to David.

I believe that David was aware that his part in the killings was wrong but that he was not strong enough to oppose Roger's will due to his complete dependence on Roger.

I would concur in the Jury's recommendation that life sentences be imposed by the court. However, I believe that David is a good candidate for rehabilitation through prison programs and feel that if David gains in maturity he should be considered for parole at some time in the future.[22]

Lori walked into the living room and sat down on the couch next to me. She startled me. I hadn't heard the door open or close. I know knew more about David Smith, recognizing that of the three followers who entered the Spencer home, David was probably the most dependent on Roger Drollinger. He was so mesmerized by Drollinger that he ultimately refused to testify against him and openly hated Stonebraker and Wright, who both had pled guilty, so there were no trials for them.

I closed the binder and leaned my head on the back of the couch. I realized I would be making another trip to Indiana in the near future.

---

[22] Byrd, DeLila M., Jasper Circuit Court, Rensselaer, IN, David Smith Pre-Sentence Investigation Report, 26 October 1977.

CHAPTER THIRTY-ONE

I leaned back in my chair, hands resting behind my head, elbows pointing out. I stared at the small television sitting on the filing cabinet and exhaled loudly. CNN carried on without interruption. The building was empty except for me.

The two detectives assigned to the graveyard shift had slipped out just before midnight to get a bite to eat before most of the restaurants closed. The only places open were Waffle House, Denny's, and Krystal's. Not many choices on midnights: greasy eggs, greasy sandwiches, or greasy bite-sized hamburgers.

Hurry up and wait. That was the name of the game. "Police work has to be so exciting," countless of people had said to me over the years. Sure, it looked as exciting as a roller coaster when you watched shows like NYPD Blue on television. Detectives worked three or four homicides each one-hour episode. The truth is, policing is comprised mostly of hours and hours of boredom, riding around alone in a patrol car, maybe chatting on a CB to other officers in your area, answering calls from neighbors who are mad because a stray dog is crapping in their yard. Or, sitting at a desk doing the ton of paperwork a call like a dog crapping in a neighbor's yard generates. Then there was that one minute. In a split second, the dispatcher calls your car number, the adrenaline pumps, and you are screaming toward a robbery in progress, or a man-with-a-gun call, or a shots-fired call. Those are the kinds of calls that keep you in police work. As a detective, the tedium of paperwork is often interrupted by a stabbing, a shooting, or what we called a "sixty-four." The code "ten sixty-four" stood for a death - usually a homicide.

I was literally sitting at my desk, alone in the office, waiting for my latest victim to die. I didn't want him to die. As a matter of fact, I had said a prayer for him as I walked out of the Vanderbilt Hospital Emergency Room. But I sure the hell wasn't crying, either. I was in police mode.

I had long since learned to detach myself from the daily dose of violence and destruction, the evil side of humanity, the sudden and unexpected deaths. Victims killed for no reason. Killed because they gave the finger to somebody who cut them off in traffic. Things that might have gotten your butt kicked a few years back now cost you your life.

Detachment was the key to surviving as a police officer. We all cared. Don't let a police officer convince you he or she doesn't care. We do. We just learn to detach ourselves from all the violence.

I remember the night Lori had called and I tried to teach her the art of detachment. What a mistake.

I was standing in the narrow hallway, shooting the bull with a couple of my friends. Talking about the latest thing the department was doing to try and stick it to us (policing also makes you paranoid). Then my pager vibrated against my waist. I glanced down, noticing our home telephone number with a 911.

"I'll be right back," I said calmly to my buddies, though my insides were churning. I walked to my desk and dialed our number with shaking hands.

"Hello," Lori said, her voice filled with sobs and sniffles. Oh my God, somebody had died. One of our parents. Or one of our brothers or sisters. "What's wrong?" I said, scared of the answer.

"I..." sob "just..." sob "saw...." sob "a little..."

I was on the edge of my seat, hanging on every sob-filled word.

"Girl..." sob "get killed." She cried uncontrollably. I was afraid she would hyperventilate.

"It's okay," I said, trying to think of something soothing to say. "Are you okay? You're not hurt are you?"

"I'm okay," she strung together before sniffling.

"You just saw a girl get killed?" I asked. "Where?" I was confused.

"Do you have your radio on?" Lori asked. "Is she dead?"

"Tell me what you're talking about," I said. "I'll try to find out."

Then I heard what she was talking about. My handheld radio, sitting on my desk, blasted three beats, alerting all officers that the message to follow was extremely important. The female dispatcher said, "Attention all cars, Twenty South has set up command on a ten forty-six, possible ten sixty-four on Old Hickory Boulevard, near Nolensville Road. Car twenty is command."

"I saw a little girl get hit by a car," Lori said, still crying, but able to speak. "I pulled out of Mapco. Then I heard a car slam on their brakes. I looked in the rearview mirror..." She broke down again.

"Okay," I said.

"All I saw was her locks of hair. Two blond locks of hair go up in the air as the car hit her. And her little friend grabbing her and holding her. She was dead. I know it."

"I'm not sure," I said. "They just said it was serious on the radio. They didn't say she was dead, though." But they wouldn't, and I knew that. There were too many media vultures listening to scanners.

"I know she's dead," Lori said. "I know it."

I clicked from caring, sensitive husband mode to police mode. "Look, Lori, just block it out of your head. Look at it like it was a doll you saw lying in the road, like it wasn't a real person." I was advising her to do exactly what I would do, what I had done hundreds of times when I showed up on a crime scene, particularly when children were involved. If you looked at the dead children as children, then it would eat you up inside. Then you were the officer turning to alcohol to numb the pain. Or an officer who finally bites the end of his gun. Oh, the times I had walked around a crime scene, notebook in hand, seemingly in control like people expected, but dying inside. Fighting back tears. Fighting off the desire to scream and cuss at the heavens.

"Oh my God?" she screamed. "You're so mean!"

"What? I meant..."

"You're an idiot!" she screamed and hung up the phone.

I dialed our number. It rang three times. The answering machine came on and I pleaded with Lori to pick the phone up. Nope. I had done it this time. I had done it trying to protect her like I protected myself, but she didn't understand me.

Detachment worked for policing, but was not a healthy technique for dealing with crisis. I had learned the hard way. Thank God Lori didn't pack up her things and move back to Indiana. I fully expected to pull in the driveway that night and find her car gone and a seething letter on the kitchen table. But she was still there.

Death was always around us. If it wasn't the case I was working, then it was the conversation at dinner with my friends. There were discussions with horrid and graphic details as we huddled around our radios, eating at one of the many greasy spoon meat-and-threes around the city (detectives always know the good places to eat). And deep down inside, in the depths of my soul, I was rotting from the violence I worked with.

I walked over to the television and flipped the channel to ESPN, then sat back down at my desk. I couldn't write the report on the incident yet, because I didn't know if it was going to be an attempted homicide or a homicide. I couldn't go home, that would prove futile. Bad luck for the victim. He would surely die if I traveled home and crawled into bed, that's just how it worked. It was no use going home anyway. I would just lie there, staring at the ceiling in the dark room, listening to Lori sleep and waiting for my pager to go off. The head nurse would page me as soon as my victim came out of surgery.

This night had started and ended like so many. My eight-hour shift had consisted of seven and a half hours of paperwork and thoughts of going home and getting a good night's sleep (no court in the morning). Maybe I would get up early and get in a three-mile run before it got too hot, then mow the yard. But it was all shattered thirty minutes before my shift ended.

The dispatcher called the office, and I answered. She said Central Patrol Units were out on a stabbing, on the near north side, a possible homicide. Victim transported to Vanderbilt Hospital. Officers on the scene have a suspect in custody. No more details. I knew that possible homicide usually meant eventual homicide.

"Okay," I said. Pissed. There went my night. If this guy died, I would be lucky to be home before noon tomorrow. The reports, the interviews, evidence reports, autopsy, on and on. But that's the nature of violent crime. It takes no holidays. It takes no days off. It respects nothing.

The crime scene was a Kroger's parking lot on the near north side of the city. I parked my car at the edge of the crime scene, nudging the yellow crime scene tape, and walked toward the officer I guessed to be in charge.

The heat from the day steamed from the asphalt pavement and the Southern air was thick with humidity. Thick enough to cut with a knife. My shirt stuck to my back like a piece of cellophane. My tie was loosened and my jacket was slung across my passenger seat.

A cameraman from Channel 4 News walked up to me. "What do you know?"

"Not much," I said. "Probably not as much as you." I smiled, then turned to the officer holding a clipboard. "What do we have?"

The officer glanced at the cameraman, who had mounted his camera on his shoulder and was taping us talking. "Victim was stabbed in the chest -"

"Stabbed in the heart," I interjected.

"No, shit?," the officer said. "Is he dead?"

As soon as the call had come in, my partner on the call, Jeff Wiser, a classmate from the academy, went directly to the hospital. I talked to him by cell phone before I got to the scene. The victim was rushed to emergency surgery. Jeff had said. "They cracked his rib cage open. Just like on ER. They're massaging his heart." One minute the victim was dead. The next he was alive. Jeff would stay at the hospital until I arrived or they pronounced the victim dead.

"Not yet," I said. "He's died twice. They've revived him. Guess he's got nine lives like a cat."

The officer turned his attention back to his notepad. "Uhm, we got a couple witnesses," he said. "This girl," he pointed to a name on his notepad. "She said she pulled into the parking lot and saw the suspect on top of the victim. Looked like she was choking him out."

I looked at the black woman sitting in the back of his patrol car. The suspect. I opened the door and motioned for her to step outside. I shined my flashlight on her hands, could see blood on her shirt and hands. She was hyped. Nervous. Jumpy. Could be drugs, I thought. Or could be the aftershock of plunging a six-inch steak knife into her boyfriend's heart.

"She's been Mirandized," the young officer said proudly. "Refused to speak."

"Why?" I asked. It was beyond me why police officers show up on the scene of a crime, and like on television, whip out their academy issued Miranda card from their breast pockets and read them to suspects. The only time Miranda is required is when the person is in custody and the police are asking incriminating questions. This officer had not asked her anything more than her name. Strike one. No suspect interview.

"And this guy saw the whole thing," the officer said pointing to another name on his notepad. "Name's John Smith. Lives over here on Buchanan."

"Where's he at?" I asked, looking around the crime scene. Nothing but officers.

"He's - " the officer said, while his head spun a complete three hundred and sixty degrees on his neck. "He must've left."

"Didya take a look at his ID?" I asked. "Get a good address? Phone number?"

"Yeah, well..." the officer said. "Got an address." He gave me the address. It was not a valid address. I had worked the neighborhood before transferring to Domestic Violence.

Choking in Fear

Strike two, I thought. Then again, I wasn't surprised. This was the same officer who had tackled an innocent man carrying groceries into his house because he matched the description of a robbery suspect. Only thing that matched was the fact that they were both black.

I walked over to the secured area, lifted the tape with one hand, and carefully walked inside the taped-off area, careful not to step on any evidence. There was a small pool of blood on the sidewalk. The victim had been stabbed in the heart and was found lying on his back, so there wouldn't have to be a lot of blood on the ground. The knife rested against the curb. I made notes, but didn't touch any of the evidence. A crime scene technician would arrive shortly to photograph the crime scene and collect all the evidence, including drawing a scaled diagram of the crime scene.

As I stepped back from the immediate area where the assault had taken place, a sign directly above where the victim had lain caught my attention. It was fastened to the Kroger wall about eye level and read, "This Parking Lot Protected by Metro Police." I chuckled. Kind of twisted humor. But how ironic that a man's life might come to an end under a sign designed to prevent crime. I laughed because I needed the release. I had to find some humor in a job that was stealing my soul, my compassion for people, my trust in people, my outlook on life. The slow erosion of my soul started the morning Officer Paul Scurry was killed and, like a mudslide, continued to erode, gaining momentum over time.

I walked from the kitchen, fresh cup of coffee in hand, heading back into the den to write, when the muted television caught my attention. "Breaking News" was plastered like a banner across the bottom of the screen. I turned, looking furiously for the remote control, to turn the mute off.

The newscaster recapped what he knew: a police officer had been shot and killed. Another officer had been shot, but injuries were not believed to be life threatening. The suspect was killed by police. Then they splashed Paul's picture and the picture of the suspect.

My knees turned to jelly. They couldn't hold my weight. I

plopped down on the footstool behind me, shocked. The suspect was Jeffrey Swafford. He was my case. I had arrested Swafford not two months before. How did he get out of jail?

My breathing was heavy. Each breath took great concentration and energy.

The telephone rang.

I stood from the footstool and walked across the living room to the telephone hanging in the kitchen. My legs felt like butter, like they felt after running to exhaustion.

It was my partner and good friend Steve Huntley. He was at home watching the unfolding events on his television. I stared at the television, as I knew Steve was. There was very little talking between us. There was some comfort in just being on the phone together. Since we both knew the officer and the killer.

The case against Jeffery Swafford had started like so many other cases of domestic violence. The victim had walked into my office, sat down across from me at my desk, and told me her ex-boyfriend was threatening to blow her car up. Like so many other cases, the original complaint paled in comparison to what had happened in the past.

The messages had come through her pager, so the only charge was harassing communication. I checked Swafford's criminal history. It was very lengthy for a man in his early twenties. He was on parole for robbery. Bingo. An arrest for harassing communication should send his butt back to the pokey, I thought.

I obtained the warrant but didn't press the victim to file the charges. The state has an obligation to victims of domestic violence to shoulder the responsibility of prosecuting to reduce the pressure on them.

My gut instinct told me to take several officers with me to serve the warrant. And I had, Steve included. Three officers went to the back door as Steve, Clarence Thompson, and I went to the front door. We knew he sublet a room in the house. The landlord answered, invited us in, and told us where to find Swafford.

We found him in his bedroom, cutting marijuana for resale with a buddy. He jumped as we screamed at him but didn't throw his hands in the air, or stand still. He dove toward the bed, which had a nine-millimeter pistol and a sawed-off shotgun lying on it. The three of us jumped on his back, dragging him from the bed and away from the guns. Then we rode him into the front room like a horse. But he wouldn't go down. As Steve and Clarence wrestled him, I stomped on his hands with my hard-soled shoes while pointing my pistol at the men in the house, a drug house, ordering them to the ground, hands in the air. We didn't need a crack-head to get jumpy and shoot one of us. Eventually, Swafford was handcuffed and went to the hospital, and so did three officers.

"So, how in the hell did he get out of jail?" I asked Steve, eyes still on the television.

"Don't know," Steve mumbled.

The charges against Swafford were serious: three counts of aggravated assault against police; possession for resale of a controlled substance (a felony); parole violation; and weapons charges. He was also charged with kidnapping a former girlfriend (not the same victim I worked with) and for shooting a friend in the face. If this dude wasn't a good candidate for no bond, then who was? Then again, the only people he hurt were ex-girlfriends and police. If he'd done the same thing to a stranger, he'd still be in jail. And Paul Scurry would still be alive. Unfortunately, a judge saw it differently, and lowered Swafford's bond. He didn't show up for court, a warrant was issued, Paul went to serve it and was killed.

I had stared at Paul's daughter at the funeral, which was attended by hundreds of officers from throughout the United States. Paul was a good man. A good father. A good police officer for twenty years. Then bam, in an instant, he was gone, remembered forever by his family. But forgotten by the community he served within weeks of his death. I began to wonder if it was all worth it. Worth the possibility of widowing my wife, causing my family heartache.

The telephone mounted on the wall, next to my ear, rang loudly. I jumped. It was the nurse from the hospital. Please don't be strike three, I thought. The stabbing victim had come through surgery, critical but stable, no guarantees. There never were.

CHAPTER THIRTY-TWO

I rubbed the sleep from my eyes and made my way through the house and into the kitchen where I found a fresh brewed pot of coffee. I had finally gotten to bed this morning at three. Since I was off the next two days, I had to write all of the reports (though there would be several more follow-up reports), and make three copies of the packet for my captain, lieutenant, and sergeant before coming home. Otherwise, my pager would have blasted first thing this morning when the captain arrived at the office.

The clock in the kitchen read 10:00 A.M. I grabbed a coffee mug from the cabinet, poured the coffee, and added some sugar. Lori walked in the back door as I turned to walk back in the living room. Her hands were covered in dirt.

"Good morning," she said.

"Morning," I grunted. I hated mornings, had always hated mornings, even when I got a full night's sleep. "What are you doing?" I asked this more for my protection than out of interest. I hoped it wasn't a home improvement project that required my assistance.

"Planting some flowers," she said. "What time did you get in? I didn't hear you come to bed." She walked into the kitchen and I could hear the water splatter against the stainless steel sink.

"Around three," I said.

"What happened?" she asked, coming out to the kitchen and sitting down on the footstool near me, still wiping the water from her hands with a dishtowel.

I shook my head. "Lady got pissed because her boyfriend was leaving," I said. "So she chases after him and plunges a streak knife in his heart."

"Did he die?" she asked, eyebrows raised.

We rarely discussed what I did at work. She knew the dangers and I didn't want to compound her fears. "No," I said. "At least he hadn't at three. They would have paged me if he died this morning. I'd have to go in and change the warrants to criminal homicide. I'm gonna call the hospital here in a minute."

"Isn't that kinda weird for a woman to stab her husband?" Lori asked.

"Boyfriend," I said. "Yeah. And this guy who was stabbed had assaulted her in the past so I had to make sure this wasn't self-defense." It hadn't been. There was no denying that the suspect had been a victim in the past, probably more than I knew. But this time, she had pursued him over three city blocks, then plunged a steak knife in his chest. There was no possibility of self-defense.

"I'm gonna hop in the shower," she said.

"Okey dokey," I said as I stood to walk into the kitchen and get my notepad with the number to the Vanderbilt ER. I dialed the number and asked for the charge nurse in critical care, knowing that the victim was in no position to speak and knowing the ER would not tell a stranger on the telephone the room number of a victim of a violent crime. The victim was in critical, but stable, condition. Not likely to die. Thank God, I thought as I thanked the nurse. What I didn't know at the time was how quickly the victim would be released, since he didn't have insurance. Three days later he was resting at home.

I was sitting at our desk, writing a letter to Dan Stonebraker, planning another visit to the prison. It had been nearly six months since our last visit. This time, Dad was coming along. I just had to make sure Dan had gotten Dad's name on the visiting list, and then I included a few more questions for him to think about.

Lori smiled from ear to ear as she walked into the den, telephone up to her ear. I was so focused on the letter, I hadn't heard the phone ring. I said a quick prayer that it wasn't the hospital calling to tell me the victim had died. "He's right here, Carl," she said while handing me the phone.

"Carl?" I asked, while cupping my hand over the receiver. "Carl Hannah?" Three hundred and fifty miles from Waveland and six years later and the name Carl still meant Carl Hannah.

She grinned and nodded her head.

"Hello, Carl," I said while leaning back in my chair and resting my feet on the cluttered desk. Stacks of police reports, transcribed interviews, and transcripts from Drollinger and Smith's trials covered the desk. What the heck would Carl want with me?

"Hi, Mike," that familiar kidlike voice from my childhood said. "Whatcha doing?"

"Not a whole heck of a lot," I said, "What's new with you?"

"Bought me a cell phone, " he said. "Needed to test it out. Can you hear me okay?"

"Plain as day," I said, wondering why Carl would ever need a cell phone. He drove too dang fast to use the phone in his car. Then again, when did Carl need anything he bought? "Did you get it so all your girlfriends could keep up with you? I still hear stories about you. Quite the stud, I hear."

Carl laughed. Then he shifted gears and said, "Here's your dad."

My dad? I thought.

Dad laughed as his voice came on the line. He knew what I was thinking: What in the hell are you doing? "You there?" he asked.

"Where are you?"

"I stopped over at Mom's and Carl came by to show me his new phone."

"You guys will be the talk of the town," I said. "Sitting on Grandma's porch talking on a cell phone."

Dad laughed, "We're sitting in Carl's car."

"Even better."

"Been sitting here for a half hour trying to figure out how to use this damn thing," Dad said. He laughed harder.

"Technology hits the streets of Waveland. Glad I'm the first person you guys thought of."

"Actually, thought of calling Hessy first," Dad said. "But when I left out there, he was loading walnuts. Didn't think he would answer."

"That makes me feel good," I said. "Hess ranks higher than me."

Since Vance's Cafe' had closed ten years ago, Keith Hess's pole barn had become the social center in town for any man who was somebody. Hess sold hunting and fishing licenses and equipment, dog food, tobacco, walnuts, and odds and ends from his gravel-floored pole barn. He'd even made it into the twenty-first century recently by adding condoms to his stock. I couldn't quite figure that one out. The men doing business at the barn were usually on their way to the solitude of the woods or riverbank. Then again, some things are better left unknown. Hess may have thought they were party balloons.

There was always a hodgepodge of men sitting around Hess's. Old men and young, retired men, and men sneaking in after work before going home. Men with graduate degrees and men who had never finished high school. The conversation was always stimulating. For instance, someone would throw out a name and Hess would give their birthday. And the gossip would sizzle like grease in a hot skillet. "I heard it at Hessy's," would be the ending phrase uttered throughout town at the post office or on the street corner when the juicy tidbits were passed along. If it was heard at Hessy's, then it was true, and everybody in town knew it.

"It's not all that bad to be second to Hessy," Dad said. "He's got big shoes to fill."

"Whatever," I said. "Hey, you better get off that phone. This first call will cost Carl a million dollars. We'll be up this weekend, anyway."

"When you getting in?"

"Friday night. It'll be late. I have to work a half shift."

"Are you going down to the prison?" Dad asked. "To see Dan?"

"Oh, yeah," I said. "I forgot to tell you in all the excitement of talking to you and Carl. I got a letter from Dan. You're on his list. We'll go up early Saturday. Try to get there by eight."

"All righty," Dad said. "Have a safe trip."

Choking in Fear

"We will," I said. "See ya." We never said "I love you." It was understood. The only time I had said "I love you" to Dad as an adult was five years ago, shortly after we moved to Nashville, when he was in a car accident. A young boy had crossed the center line and hit him head on. The phone call from my mom had jolted my world. The doctors didn't expect him to live. They were flying him to Indianapolis by Lifeline helicopter. Get home fast, she had said, he's probably not going to make it. It took two weeks in the hospital and a month in rehabilitation to learn to speak again and to walk again. I'd been in some scary situations involving men with guns, but nothing had scared me as much as sitting in that waiting room at Methodist Hospital while the surgeon operated on Dad's brain, trying to relieve the swelling.

I clicked the cordless phone off and stared out the window at the street in front of our home. The sun was shining, and it was hot. I missed Waveland. I missed those great times growing up, the carefree summer days, the warmth of our home in the winter, the security of family and friends. Family and friends so close you couldn't differentiate between the two.

"What did Carl want?" Lori asked as she walked back in the den and plopped down on the daybed.

"Testing his new cell phone." I shook my head.

"He talked for a long time. A long time for Carl."

"It wasn't just Carl," I said. "Dad was there. Sitting in Carl's car, trying to figure out the phone."

Lori threw her hands up in the air. "Oh my God," she said. "That's not Waveland. That's Weirdland."

"Oh, you're just jealous," I said. "Jealous cause you weren't raised there. You had to marry into it."

"Not hardly." She smiled. She loved these people as much as I did.

I printed the letter, proofed it quickly for mistakes, then slid it into an envelope and walked it out to the mailbox. This would be the last set of questions I would have to mail. I knew I would never forget the murders. You can't forget an event that shaped your life. But I knew I was close to being able to file it away, to understanding it. To have closure with it. Or, then again, maybe everything I learned would take me in a different direction.

CHAPTER THIRTY-THREE

I reached for the door handle, but stopped short of opening the door when a typewritten sign in bold letters caught my eye. It was taped to the inside of the door, about eye level, and read: "Inmates in G-Cell Block Locked Down. No Visitors." What's that mean?" I thought. My heart skipped a beat as I traced in my head where Dan lived. No, he was in A-Building.

I walked hesitantly through the door and toward the guard desk, afraid when I reached the desk the guard would tell me we couldn't visit, that I had wasted my time driving up from Nashville.

A young woman, maybe twenty-three years old, stood in front of me, showing her identification to the female guard and waiting as she checked it against the visitors' roster. Her two young boys ran in circles around her as she said, "Settle down." "Quit." "Be good." "We're gonna see Daddy."

What a way for a child to visit his dad, I thought. And I wondered what he was serving time for. A part of me wanted to lean forward and ask her. Homicide? Beating the crap out of her or the kids? Robbery? Drugs? Or was he a child molester? Had he hurt one of these innocent young boys playing in front of me?

"What did that sign mean?" Dad asked as he looked back over his shoulder at the door we had just walked through.

I shook my head. "I'm not sure. I don't think it had anything to do with us." At least I hoped. I watched the guard and the women in front of me closely, searching for a signal that our visit would be cancelled. The small waiting room to my right was nearly filled to capacity, a good sign that visits were being allowed.

I might have been a little paranoid considering an earlier visit had been cancelled by the Indiana Department of Corrections after Mike Wright stirred up resistance for the visit. The prison officials denied my request for that visit and referred me to their spokesperson in Indianapolis. Instead of fighting the system, Dan simply placed me on his personal visiting list. So now, Mike Wright could not prevent my visiting. But this lockdown was a different animal altogether.

"Dan lives in Building A," I added, as much to convince myself that our visit would be allowed as to convince Dad.

"Is this where we go in?" Dad asked.

I pointed to the guard. "She'll check our driver's licenses against Dan's visitor list. Then she'll stamp our hands and we go over there," I pointed to the waiting room, "and wait for them to call us."

"It's been a long time since I've been over here," Dad said. "At least fifteen years. Maybe longer."

"Visiting one of your old boyfriends?" I asked, then smiled.

The woman in front of us and her children got their hands stamped, and moved off to the waiting room.

"Can I help you?" the female guard asked politely. She was dark complected, her hair so black it shined, and attractive, looking like she belonged on the cover of a magazine, not working as a guard at the Pendleton Reformatory Prison. I figured it had to be dangerous for such an attractive woman to work in a facility filled with violent men. Men who had not been intimate with a woman in years, except in their dreams. Men who had been abusive to their intimate partners and children, who had no respect for women, or for the life of another.

"Hi," I said. "Here to visit Stonebraker. Number 11818."

The attractive guard turned and went to a file folder, searched against the names on the list. She stamped our hands and sent us off to the waiting room. Depending on where Dan was, it could take fifteen to twenty minutes for him to be notified of the visit, be given permission, walk to the front of the prison, submit to a strip search (a requirement before and after an inmate has contact with people from outside the facility), and be seated in the visitors' meeting room.

"Why were you over here?" I asked. "Fifteen years ago." My body was flushed with relief as we waited for Dan.

"I was interviewing a suspect in some burglaries," Dad said. "He'd been convicted of a couple burglaries. We felt like he had done several more in the area."

"So you've been in the meeting room before?"

"Yeah, but I don't remember much about it," Dad said. "All I remember was sitting there in uniform. No gun. And all these inmates staring at me. Sizing me up."

"These guys don't tend to be big fans of police," I said. "I doubt it's changed much over the past fifteen years."

One of the young boys stood up on a plastic chair in front of me and turned to face me. He smiled. I smiled back. He was not more than five years old, I figured, coming to prison to visit his dad. I wondered how long he had been doing that. How many Saturdays he'd spent driving to Pendleton, Indiana, to visit his father, instead of playing with trucks, tractors, and basketballs at home. He seemed at home in the waiting room, familiar with the prison. And I wondered if he even wanted to see his dad, especially if his dad was serving time for hurting him or his brother or his mother.

I felt an overwhelming sadness for the young child and his slightly older brother, who walked past each of the vending machines, placing his little fingers inside the coin return, hoping for a forgotten quarter. I felt sad for them because life was stacked against them. They had been dealt a bad hand. They would have to overcome tremendous obstacles to rise above their father's botched life. These are the types of lessons, learned early in life, that define our existence. It was obvious to me that with a father incarcerated, these two young boys had been taught some things that could and would affect their lives if somebody didn't wipe their slate clean and influence them in the right direction. I watched the young boys sitting in front of my father and me, two generations of police officers, knowing full well that had my father been a bank robber, I would have probably been a bank robber too.

I felt sadness in the depths of my heart that this young boy with a happy toothless smile, standing on the chair in front of me, might someday be on the other side of these walls, waiting for his bimonthly visit from his children. Leading his life the only way he knew how.

And I was frustrated with a society that didn't seem to care for children. Frustrated that I lived in the most civilized country in the world, but it was still a society that did not protect its children.

The toothless smile of the little boy also gave me hope that we could break the intergenerational cycle of violence in families and shatter the curse these young children inherit involuntarily.

"Visitors for Stonebraker," the female voice crackled over the loudspeaker.

"That's us," I said, standing.

Dad patted the young boy on the head as he walked past, and I did the same, hoping that the simple pat of his head would transfer the positive things I had learned from my parents when I was his age. Hoping that a small pat would give him a fair chance at a successful, crime-free, and happy life. That it would ignite a light in his head that would guide him down a different path than the one his father had traveled. That it would say that, even in the tough world we live in, people cared for him, that I cared for him, even thought I didn't know him.

I handed my shoes to the female guard and walked through the metal detector. She placed my shoes in a black plastic tub and then onto a conveyor belt, through an X-ray machine. A male guard approached me, very professionally, and asked me to raise my hands above my head and worked his hands around my collar, down my sides, around my waist and down my legs while at the same time asking me if I was carrying any drugs or contraband.

I felt violated as his hands searched me like he didn't trust me or believe me. It was nothing personal for him. I knew that. He had probably done this a hundred times already today. But it made me feel dirty. Guilty. I knew what a search meant because I had done them hundreds of times to people I had arrested, ensuring my safety and the safety of fellow officers. Nonetheless, the search was humiliating.

Dan stood as we made our way through the final set of secured doors and waited for us to make our way to the table. Dan smiled from ear to ear.

He extended his hand to Dad. "Hi, Tom," Dan said. "Thanks for coming down. How are you?"

"Dan Stonebraker," Dad said as they shook hands. "I'm good. You've aged a little since the last time I saw you. Gettin' a little gray up there." Dad smiled and pointed to Dan's hair.

Dan laughed, a laugh from deep inside his barreled chest. "I've put on a little weight, too." He rubbed his belly.

"Let's not talk about hair," I said while reaching out and shaking Dan's hand. "I wish I had a chance for gray hair."

We sat down at the circular table, Dan in the middle.

"I was thinking the other day," Dad said. "Trying to remember the last time I saw you. Before you were arrested for the murders."

"Had to be at the Clark Station," Dan said. "You weren't there when Dave Blue arrested me."

Dad shook his head and I could tell he was trying to remember the night. "I was off that night."

"I'll never forget that night," Dan said. "I was over at some friends', smoking a little pot. And then somebody knocked on the door. It was Dave Blue. I looked out the window and saw a bunch of police cars. Unmarked cars up and down the street. I dropped the pot and walked over to the door."

"That charge of simple possession would have really tacked some serious time onto your sentence," I added with a smile.

"No kidding," Dan said. "So Dave puts me in his car and drives me across town to the jail. We were sitting in front of the jail, waiting for the garage door to open, and I said, 'I'm not leaving, am I?' Dave said, 'No, I don't think so, Dan.' As we drove inside the garage it was like being swallowed."

"I didn't know you'd been arrested until the next day," Dad said.

"Loyd Heck brought that gun into the interview room," Dan said. "Dave Blue had been asking me some questions. Then Dave told me to turn to the door and identify the shotgun. Loyd was holding the shotgun I had used in the murders. It felt like somebody had punched me in the gut. I couldn't breathe. I was literally gasping for air. I fell out of the chair. And all the cops in the room tackled me. I guess they thought I was going for a gun or something. A real football pile-on." He smiled. "We took a break so I could catch my breath, then I told them everything. That night, in the county jail, was the first night I had slept since the murders. Even knowing I might never get out of prison."

"Well, Dan, I tried to tell you about Drollinger," Dad said. He didn't say it like I told you so, but more like I wish you would have listened. "That must've been the last time I saw you. Before your drug arrest and the murders. I remember standing out at the gas pumps at the Clark Station telling you that Drollinger was going to get you into some serious trouble."

"Serious shit is the way I think you put it," Dan said.

Dad laughed. "Probably so."

"Dave Blue used to tell me the same thing," Dan said. "He used to come in and get gas."

"We were keeping an eye on you," Dad said. "Keep you guys on your toes. We knew what you were doing."

There was more to it for Dad and Dave Blue than simply buying gas to keep an eye on Dan Stonebraker and his buddies. They were trying to reach Dan, to steer him in the right direction, to keep him from throwing his life away. To save him from Roger Drollinger.

"I wouldn't listen to anybody," Dan said. "I just wouldn't listen to anybody."

The smiles disappeared. The mood turned somber.

The two young boys and their mother sat down at a table behind Dan. I watched the two boys jump up and down on their father, fighting to get closer and closer to him. Hugging, kissing, laughing, breaking every rule posted on the wall behind them. Those rules were developed for the adult visitors, not the children, I assumed.

I studied the boys' father. Tattoos covered his arms and extended out of his T-shirt on the back of his neck. A part of me felt so un-

Choking in Fear

believably sorry for him. Unable to see his boys to bed each night, to read them a bedtime story, to play catch with them out in the backyard. But the other part of me objected, saying this was a man who had committed a crime against the State of Indiana. He had made choices. Not just choices, but bad choices. He might have hurt people. He might be a rapist. Or a killer. And he was paying his debt to society. And good God, I told myself, the criminal justice system never punishes somebody the first time they get into trouble. This man had probably committed several crimes before he was sent to prison, had probably hurt many people. My heart still ached for the young boys. The father was absent from their lives - which was probably a good thing - but he was still their dad and I could tell they loved him. Hopefully they had a grandpa or an uncle, a positive male role model in their lives.

"Drollinger was one of the most dangerous people I've ever met," Dad said. "He didn't respect nobody. I mean nobody. He thought we were always picking on him. Everybody's always picking on poor Roger." Dad said it mockingly. "I mean what's he expect? He's screwing a fourteen-year-old girl. Not a woman, a girl. Dropping cement blocks off of overpasses at passing motorcycles. Selling drugs. Weapons violations. You name it."

"I know Drollinger was no good, Tom," Dan said as he leaned closer, elbows resting on the table. "But I can't blame Roger. I mean, I could blame it on Roger. Or I could blame it on the drugs. But I made the decisions. You know, there's no doubt those things influenced me. But I was a coward, too scared to stand up to Roger. Scared of getting shot or killed if I didn't go along that night at the Spencer's house. Hey, I could have refused. But I didn't. I pulled the trigger. I was a coward. It was safer..It was easier for me to go along...to kill...easier than standing up to him."

"It's still hard for me to picture you as a killer," Dad said. "Especially the brutality of the crime. You know, I can't deny that you were cocky. But, man, that was one of the most brutal crimes ever in this state. The whole country."

"I know," Dan said.

"The selling drugs. The vandalism. The thefts. Those things didn't surprise me. The murders did." Dad paused for a moment. "I guess anything is possible when Drollinger is involved."

I sat back in the plastic chair, arms folded across my chest, recording the conversation between Dan and Dad in my head.

"Psychologists have told me if there would have been one solid male role model in my life when I needed it, I wouldn't be here," Dan said. He threw his arms up in the air as if to say, "Who knows?"

I surveyed the meeting room. It seemed a happy and joyous place until I glanced at the guard desk and remembered where I was.

"We have to deal with the cards we're dealt," Dan continued. "And we're expected to be normal. Or somewhere near normal. There are no excuses for what I did. I was just weak enough for someone like Roger to prey on."

"I don't think any of us are 'normal'," I said while raising both hands like the peace symbol and snapping my fingers up and down to signal quotation marks. "Tell me a little about your upbringing."

Dan exhaled. "I don't want to say anything that will hurt my dad," he said. "For the first time in my life - and I'm forty-two years old - my dad and I have a good relationship. We talk on the phone. He sends me the local newspaper. We talk."

I nodded my head. "I wouldn't want to hurt anybody," I said. "But I think it's important for me to understand a little about your family. How you were raised."

"My family life was horrible," Dan said. He said it with some embarrassment.

I was aware that being abused as a child came up as an excuse with convicted criminals. But I was starting to see the connection between family life, violence in the home, and criminality.

"I wasn't an angel," Dan continued. "But goodness gracious, I got no demonstration of love. None verbally. None demonstratively. None emotionally. No encouragement. Would you believe the most encouraging words I ever heard as a kid was, 'Boy, can that kid eat.' They seemed to say it with pride, so I ate until my guts nearly busted, just to gain their favor and make them proud of me."

I looked at Dan and thought about how lucky I had been growing up. There had been no violence in our home. No drugs. No emotional abuse. My home has always been a security blanket, a refuge from the world, not a place of fear and hopelessness.

"My mom is so remorseful of their child-rearing," Dan said. "Mostly, she just went along with Dad. Dad still doesn't get it." Dan paused for a moment, then shook his head slightly. "He must have had a terrible childhood himself."

"How old were you when you started using drugs?" I asked.

"About eighteen," Dan answered. "The drugs took all the pain of my family situation away. Numbed the violence. I don't think I was ever straight a day after that. Not until after my wheels had come off."

I had met hundreds of Dan Stonebrakers since I had become a police officer. More than I could ever remember. As a detective, investigating violence within families, I met these young Dan Stonebrakers every night. I held young boys in my arms, felt them trembling, hostages in their own home, while their mothers cleaned the blood from their mouths and noses. The fear, the hopelessness, the helplessness chiseled in their faces. I had many tools and resources available as an investigator, but I also knew I couldn't guarantee their protection. It broke my heart. Day after day the weight of the heartbreak compounded.

"There wasn't enough dope out there for me after the murders," Dan said. "Nothing could numb that pain. The guilt."

Dad cleared his throat and asked, "What about Mike Wright and David Smith. What are they up to?"

"They're both here at Pendleton," Dan said. "David lives in the next building over from me. Mike just got moved back to one of the cell blocks. I see them about every day. I usually put the newspaper, the Journal Review, in my window and David comes over and gets it in the evening."

"You guys don't hang out then?" Dad asked.

"We have our own circle of friends," Dan said. "We talk. We talk a lot more these days since Mike started coming up for visits and writing letters to us." Dan smiled at me.

"David and Mike never changed their mind about coming up to meet me on a visit?" I asked.

"Mike has no interest," Dan said. "I thought David was going to at least come up and meet you." Dan rolled his eyes and shrugged his shoulders. "The whole book thing scares them. If you write a book, they're afraid it will bring back a lot of publicity to the case. Mike particularly didn't want to see you write a book. I told them that murder is not something that society will let us forget."

He was right. Mike Wright claimed that he wasn't getting involved because he had moved on with his life, and needed to put his past to rest, to forget about it. That was crazy. When you take the lives of four boys, for the pure thrill of the kill, and leave their mother for dead in a pool of her boy's blood, then you forfeit the right to forget the past. Forgiveness? Maybe. Forgetting? Never. Mike Wright was being selfish. Betty Jane Spencer has not forgotten the past. Keith Spencer has not forgotten the past. I haven't forgotten the past. My community has not forgotten that night or the months of terror afterward. So what gives Mike the right to forget?

"I feel real guilty about Mike, though," Dan said. "He wouldn't have been involved in this if it weren't for me. He hung around us because of me. Drollinger didn't like Mike too much. Mike kinda did his own thing. Didn't always clear everything with Roger."

"But he was still capable of murder," I added.

Dan shrugged his shoulders while nodding his head. "I always knew a day would come when a book would be written," Dan said. "I have turned down several authors over the years. You could see the money in their eyes. But I knew God would bring along the right person. And I think that's you, Mike."

"I don't know, Dan," I sighed. "I don't know. I didn't start out to write a book. I just had so many questions about this crime. I've spent a lot of time and money researching the murders. Talking with you and Betty Jane Spencer. Investigators. People who used to hang out with you guys. Reading all of the trial transcripts. Trying to find that one thing that makes it all click for me."

"I don't even understand it all," Dan said. "How I could have done this?" He shook his head. "Anyway, how did your meeting with Mrs. Spencer go?"

"Good," I said. "We've met a couple times. We've been talking for a couple of years now."

"Okay," Dan said. His eyes and attention focused directly on me.

"I think she's learned a lot about this crime," I said. "I never thought there was anything I could help her understand. I've relayed a lot of our conversations. And, uh, I think it has made her less fearful. Not that she won't ever be scared again. You can't survive what she did without being scared. But it has given her some peace of mind. I think. I hope."

"I hope someday she can forgive me for what I did," Dan said. "That doesn't mean I want her support to get out of prison. Just forgiveness for what I did." Dan looked up at the ceiling, then at Dad, then back at me. "I don't think I could forgive somebody if they did this to my family. Forgiveness is not an easy thing. I know that."

What a powerful statement. Dan Stonebraker, convicted of killing Greg, Ralph, Raymond, and Reeve, saying he's not sure he could forgive a person if they had committed the same crime against his family. The tables turned. It pleased me that he at least thought of Betty Jane's perspective, had tried to understand not only what he had done to her and the boys eighteen years ago, but also the long-term psychological damage. I don't think the other three killers ever pondered that.

"People don't know how hard forgiveness is," I said. "Hell, I don't know. I have no idea what Betty Jane's been through."

"My prayer," Dan said, "is that God takes every fear out of her heart. So she can live like she once did, with screen doors, no locks, and no fears. I've taken her family and I can't get them back. But I can help Mrs. Spencer. So far, I've been able to help her most by leaving her alone. I sent her a letter once. I didn't realize how much the letter might scare her. I no longer go to clemency hearings. Maybe someday I can help her more by sharing my life, my faith, even my family with her. I didn't just mess me and Mrs. Spencer's life up. I've messed a lot of lives up along the way. Can you imagine how stunned I was when God turned the lights on in my brain-dead world of drugs and woke me up to what I'd done?"

Dad and I nodded our heads, transfixed.

"I know God has forgiven me. Dan said. "I wrestled with that for years. But I know he has forgiven me. The one thing that has always bothered me, though, was the boys. The boys we killed. I've had a hard time forgiving myself because I don't know if the boys were saved, if they went to heaven. I don't think I could forgive myself if they weren't saved, if I sent somebody to Hell."

That had never crossed my mind. The possibility of killing someone that was not saved, that did not know God, and not only taking their life here on earth, but damning them to the eternal fire of Hell. It took a couple seconds for the power of his statement to sink in and for me to be able to think clearly again.

"They were all saved," I said. "They were good boys. They had been to church the morning you guys broke in and shot them."

"I'm glad to hear that," Dan said. I could hear the relief in his voice. "I've thought about that for eighteen years."

I glanced at the clock on the wall. Our visit would end soon. "It's almost time for us to go," I said. "I've been thinking a lot about all of this. I want to do something with all this that helps others. I want to be able to help kids, to prevent them from throwing their lives away. Betty Jane's done some remarkable things for victims. But more good can come from this I know it can."

"I've done some videos," Dan said. "Public Service Announcements. Those kinds of things. I want to help kids. I don't want some kid to throw away his life like I have. Just because they're afraid to stand up for what is right."

A guard walked by and laid Dan's ID and a yellow Post-it note indicating the time on the table. He repeated the exercise several more times at other tables.

Dad watched the guard. "What's he doing?"

"That's my ID," Dan said while turning the plastic photo card toward Dad. "I give it to them after I'm strip-searched. Then they give it back after the visit with a Post-it note and the time. I have to give that to the guard back at my dorm. Account for every waking minute."

We all stood and shook hands.

"Thanks for all of your help," I said.

"You're welcome," Dan said. "Anything I can do to make sense of this tragedy."

I turned toward the door, weaving my way in and out of several tables, to the end of a long line of people, waiting for the door to slide open. I was eager to get back into the free world.

The two young boys from the waiting room and their mother were standing in front of me. The young boys kept turning back to look at their dad. I stepped to the side to give them an unobstructed view. They waved. Their dad waved back. And they continued to wave. Back and forth. They would take a few steps forward as the line moved and their mother tugged at their shirttails, but they never made more than a few steps without turning back to their father and waving.

I looked over my shoulder at the father. The rough and tough looking man had tears in his eyes. He whispered, "Be good."

Be good, I thought. Was that something he just said, because we all said it? Because it was the right thing to say to kids? Or, be good so you don't end up in here, like your dad. I could see the regret in his eyes and the way the words lingered on his lips.

The first metal door slid shut and both of the young boys bounced out of line for one last wave to their father, one last wave before entering the free world. I thought of all the regret sitting in the room behind me. The men, sitting there, watching their families leave, regretting the decisions they had made in their lives. The regret had to eat at their minds and souls day and night.

I was stunned at my own sympathy for the men, until I realized my sympathy was really for the young children, not them. There was nothing I could do to change the behavior of a grown man, no way to turn back the clock and change the way things had happened. But I still had time to alter the course of a young child's life. And that became my mission.

As I watched the two young boys walk across the parking lot toward their car, I thought about everything I had learned over the past eighteen years. I'd always known that violent homes were a breeding ground for future criminals. Common sense said that much. It's passed on as learned behavior, not genetically.

The solution, then, was to free these children from the cycle of violence before they become the next generation of armed robbers, rapists, drug dealers, or killers. Before they became the next Dan Stonebraker.

Dad and I walked across the parking lot in silence. Lost in thought. As I reached my Rodeo, I pulled the keys from my pocket and unlocked the doors. The two young boys were climbing into a beat-up old car with their mother. I stared at them for a second, wondering if I might be staring at a future doctor, a future Nobel Peace Prize recipient, a scientist who finds the cure for cancer or HIV. Or, was I staring at a young boy who would grow into the next generation of men in his family to call prison their home?

AFTERWORD

I can honestly say that after spending over fifteen years on this project, I have been able to answer many of the questions that have gnawed at me since I was a young child choking in fear. I can, with one hundred percent confidence, tell you that this was a totally random crime where mass murder was the only motive.

I am not sure that makes me sleep better these days. How could it? This means we live in a world where killing for sport is still possible. It also raises more questions about how guys like Roger Drollinger are created. Is it genetics or society that shapes these monsters?

As a former police officer and lifelong researcher of criminology, I believe that family and society creates these sociopaths. Family and society also contributed to the development of young men like Dan Stonebraker, Mike Wright and David Smith and made them vulnerable to a blood thirsty killer like Drollinger.

Sleeping better at night would come much easier if we had a logical reason for a murder of this magnitude. If I knew it was a robbery or drug related then I could wrap my head around it and it would spare me from having to accept that it could have been me and my family.

There is such irony in this tragedy. Maybe this should be expected because this is a small community and thus there is much greater opportunity for contact between the offenders, victims and residents. I mentioned Dr. Millis being my personal seamstress as a young child. He was also married to Roger Drollinger's sister.

Or Bill Stonebraker looking at the composite photos and knowing in his gut that his cousin Dan was one of the killers. And I later learned that one of Bill's younger brothers, a cousin to Dan, had spent the night at the Spencer's right before the murders.

I have also spent much time contemplating how this night would have ended had Betty Jane not survived or had been unable to run next door and call for help. Could the rented Orange Omega and stolen Spencer Thunderbird have pulled into my driveway? That was the plan and it was right on track until Smith and Wright heard cops being dispatched on the scanner they had brought along to monitor the police.

Without argument, Roger Drollinger is the central character in this story. Remove him from the story and there is no tragedy. Drollinger longed to be infamous and mass murder became his vehicle to attain it.

I generally am reserved about making assertions about people I have never met but I am completely confident that Roger Clay Drollinger was a sociopath. Understand that I do not make this claim lightly. And even with all of the human destruction and carnage I witnessed as a former violent crime detective, I don't think I ever encountered a true sociopath.

Sociopaths are rare creatures. I've read estimates that place it at two to three percent of society. Thankfully, most of us will never bump into a sociopath.

So I am not flippantly ascribing sociopathic status to Roger Drollinger. This was a man who had no conscience, no remorse and no feelings for other human beings. Dan Stonebraker told me that after they pulled out of the Spencer's driveway, Drollinger began talking about stopping at another home and killing the family. He wanted to leave the Spencer's stolen Thunderbird in their driveway as a signature. Dan kept saying he could not do that. He was sick from what he had just done. Then Drollinger turned on the interior dome light and Dan said he was literally glowing. The excitement was pouring out of his eyes.

Not only did Roger Drollinger not feel any remorse for the sadistic murders he planned and orchestrated, he actually derived a psycho-sexual elation from the murders. Drollinger even laughed later in the week as he met Smith, Stonebraker and Wright for lunch while the jury deliberated his future and he described finding brain matter on his collar and feeding it to his cat while he dipped a french fry in ketchup and ate it with a smile.

Loyd Heck, lead investigator, said that Drollinger's name came up early in the investigation as a potential suspect but he was pushed down the list because he was on trial in Montgomery County during the murders. Drollinger was facing forty years in prison if convicted. For most people, even the majority of criminals, that would be enough to keep them focused and out of trouble.

Not Drollinger. They spent the two weeks of his drug trial terrorizing West Central Indiana by conducting home invasions, trying to run vehicles off the road, shooting dogs and ultimately mass murder. I would argue that not only did the trial not slow him down, but that it was quite the opposite, it became his catalyst for murder. It propelled his sadistic plans into high gear as his freedom was coming to an end.

I think it is worth repeating that Drollinger had taken the witness stand in his own defense on Friday, February 11, 1977. It was a move he and his attorney, Nile Stanton, had to make. The risk was great because it exposed him to the prosecutor on cross examination. It opened the door to discuss his lengthy criminal history that included convictions for statutory rape and firearms violations.

However, they had decided that their only hope was for Drollinger to weave his bizarre fantasy of how he was being forced to sell drugs by the local police. Remember, as odd as this defense seems, it only takes one juror to have a little doubt and the defense wins.

Years later, Drollinger's own attorney claimed that Drollinger was the only client he was ever scared of. He also said that his own law partners would refer to Drollinger as his personal annuity.

Look at the timeline. Drollinger and his gang enter the Spencer's home shortly after midnight, lined them up and murdered them on their living room floor then left to commit another murder. However, Betty Jane cut the evening short by surviving. They made it back to the Lew Wallace Inn in Crawfordsville around 2:00 AM, split up and headed home.

Think about that. Drollinger arrived home somewhere between 2:30-3:00 AM and was back on the witness chair six hours later facing Deputy Prosecutor Donald Hopper. Does that provide a glimpse inside the head of a sociopath?

The irony doesn't stop there. Drollinger had actually been in the Montgomery County Jail all fall and winter awaiting his drug trial. Exactly one month before the murders, on January 14, 1977, Special Judge Earl Dowd from Parke County (where the murders would take place) allowed Drollinger to post bond using his father's farm as collateral.

The drug trial was scheduled to start the week of February 7, 1977. So I think it is fair to ask the question why would he be allowed to post bond only a few weeks before his drug trial after having spent months in jail? I understand that bond is not punishment but is to ensure you will show up in court. But the fact that Drollinger was on parole and had a lengthy criminal history should have factored heavily into the bond decision.

Is it permissible to wonder if things would have turned out differently for Greg Brooks, Ralph, Reeve and Raymond Spencer if Drollinger would not have been allowed to post bond? Maybe that is an unfair question or a bit of Monday morning quarterbacking. I accept that. I realize defendants are presumed innocent until proven guilty. But what if?

What is absolutely clear is after Drollinger was released on bond, he escalated his criminal behavior. Stonebraker said, looking back, that it was like Drollinger knew he was about to go to prison for a long time so if he was going to become a notorious mass murderer, then he had to speed things up. His window of opportunity was closing. Talk of murder became more common. Shotguns and pistols were always in the car. Driving aimlessly and smoking pot turned to home invasions and running vehicles off the road at gunpoint.

I want you to slip into the mind of Drollinger for a minute and question how a person could orchestrate a massacre of young boys. Literally, covering the floor, walls and ceiling of the Spencer home with boys blood and tissue. Then go home, feed part of one of the boy's brains to a cat, go to sleep and get up and go to court and take the witness stand later that morning. How could a person do that? Prosecutors and law enforcement officers have even said that Drollinger was alert, focused and his testimony, though not believable, was well-thought-out. He was not easily rattled or nervous.

Drollinger had no conscience. No remorse. He had a grandiose sense of himself and had been described as manipulative and conning. These are the key ingredients of a sociopath.

I also want to point out what might appear to be a contradiction in the book. Betty Jane Spencer said that her step-son Greg raised up on his hands after being shot and screamed, "I'm flying, I'm flying." Later in the book Dan Stonebraker said that Greg raised up on his arms and screamed, "I'm dying, I'm dying." I talked about this with both Betty Jane and Dan and each felt strongly that they heard Greg correctly. So that is why you see it two different ways in the book.

If there is a lesson in this tragedy, it is that Dan Stonebraker, Mike Wright and David Smith would have never murdered without the influence of Roger Drollinger. This is an important lesson for us. There are lots of young boys teetering on the fence between right and wrong and all it takes is the influence of a sociopath like Drollinger to make them capable of walking into a home and murdering a family. The line between someone who commits a crime like this and someone who does not is not as far apart as one might think.

If I have one unfulfilled wish it would be an opportunity to interview Roger Drollinger. Talk with him one-on-one. However, he never responded to any of my requests. I have watched countless hours of media interviews of Drollinger over the years. But the central theme is the same. Drollinger denies everything and claims that Stonebraker and Wright framed him. But he grants those interviews because he lavishes the attention.

Sound familiar? Has anyone ever heard Charles Manson take responsibility for the Tate-Labianca murders after all these years?

The opportunity to interview Drollinger ended on January 29, 2014, right after I had undertaken a rewrite and republishing of this book. He died unexpectedly of a heart attack in his cell at the Wabash Valley Correctional Facility. I have combed through numerous articles and uncovered that he had been placed in isolation a year earlier because he had tried to escape.

Dan Stonebraker has been incarcerated at the Pendleton Correctional Facility for thirty-seven years where he is serving two life sentences. I continue to visit and write him periodically as we have developed a friendship. Dan is a committed Christian who has volunteered for many projects to help steer kids away from prison.

Mike Wright and David Smith have also been incarcerated at the Pendleton Correction Facility for thirty-seven years. Wright is serving two life sentences and Smith four life sentences. Neither Smith or Wright answered any questions. We had one meeting scheduled but it was cancelled by the Indiana Department of Corrections after they both stirred up controversy with my visit. I did have a chance meeting with Wright during a visit with Dan Stonebraker. Wright came by our table and we shook hands and spoke for a couple minutes. Just small talk.

Betty Jane Spencer passed away in 2004 after moving back to her home in Parke County. Her legacy lives on as the Mother of the Victim Rights Movement. I am still amazed at how tough this little woman was. And how she turned a horrific tragedy into a movement to protect victims across the United States.

I am no longer a violent crime detective. I left policing to start Safe Hiring Solutions, which is a global background screening firm. So I am still focused on safety and security and helping thousands of organizations protect themselves from violence.

Several times in the book I speak of my wife Lori. She passed away in 2008 after we had our third child.

I am happily remarried. My wife Trish was a police officer for twenty years near Chicago. We have so many shared interests and experiences and a mission to help protect people from evil. She has also taught me that you can be extremely feminine and tough at the same time. And with five kids, we never have a dull (or quiet) moment.

ABOUT THE AUTHOR

Mike McCarty lives outside Indianapolis where he is the CEO of Safe Hiring Solutions and an internationally recognized speaker and consultant on issues of violence prevention. He has consulted to and presented seminars for the U.S. Department of Justice, U.S. Department of Defense, U.S. Homeland Security- Federal Law Enforcement Training Center, and numerous state attorney general offices, domestic violence and sexual assault coalitions, colleges and universities, and corporations.